ABOUT THIS PUBLICATION

FOR SERVICE ASSISTANCE

Customer Service Department
1.704.898.0770

North Carolina General Statues is published by The Muliti-Media Group of Greater Charlotte in Charlotte, North Carolina. Copyright 2015 by the Multi-Media Group of Greater Charlotte. This book or parts thereof may not be reproduced in any form, stored in a retrieval system, or transmitted in any form by any means—electronic, mechanical, photocopy, recording or otherwise—without prior written permission of the publisher, except as provided by United States of America copyright law.

The records required by U.S. Code 2257(a) through (c) and the pertinent regulations 28 C.F.R. Cli. 1, Part 75 with respect to this publication and all materials associated with such records are maintained by The Multi-Media Group of Greater Charlotte, Publisher and available for review by Attorney General.

www.visionbooks.org

Copyright © 2015 by MMGGC
All rights reserved!

TID: 5061387
ISBN (10) digit: 1502912856
ISBN (13) digit: 978-1502912855

123-4-56789-01239-Paperback
123-4-56789-01239-Hardback

First Edition

090520140547

Printed in the United States of America

2015 EDITION

North Carolina Criminal Law And Procedure-Pamphlet # 29

Printed In conjunction with the Administration of the Courts

North Carolina Criminal Law and Procedure
Pamphlet Reference Guide

Chapters	Pamphlet
Chapter 1 Civil Procedure	1
Chapter 1 Civil Procedure (Continue)	2
Chapter 1A Rules of Civil Procedure	2
Chapter 1B Contribution.	2
Chapter 1C Enforcement of Judgments.	2
Chapter 1D Punitive Damages.	2
Chapter 1E Eastern Band of Cherokee Indians.	2
Chapter 1F North Carolina Uniform Interstate Depositions and Discovery Act.	2
Chapter 2 - Clerk of Superior Court [Repealed and Transferred.]	3
Chapter 3 - Commissioners of Affidavits and Deeds [Repealed.]	3
Chapter 4 - Common Law	3
Chapter 5 - Contempt [Repealed.]	3
Chapter 5A - Contempt	3
Chapter 6 - Liability for Court Costs	3
Chapter 7 - Courts [Repealed and Transferred.]	3
Chapter 7A – Judicial Department	3
Chapter 7A – Continuation (Judicial Department)	4
Chapter 7A – Continuation (Judicial Department)	5
Chapter 7B - Juvenile Code	5
Chapter 8 - Evidence	6
Chapter 8A - Interpreters for Deaf Persons [Recodified.]	6
Chapter 8B - Interpreters for Deaf Persons	6
Chapter 8C - Evidence Code	6
Chapter 9 - Jurors	6
Chapter 10 - Notaries [Repealed.]	6
Chapter 10A - Notaries [Recodified.]	6
Chapter 10B - Notaries	6
Chapter 11 - Oaths	6
Chapter 12 - Statutory Construction	6
Chapter 13 - Citizenship Restored	6
Chapter 14 - Criminal Law	7
Chapter 14 –Criminal Law (Continuation)	8
Chapter 15 - Criminal Procedure	9
Chapter 15A - Criminal Procedure Act (Continuation)	10
Chapter 15A - Criminal Procedure Act (Continuation)	11
Chapter 15B - Victims Compensation	11
Chapter 15C - Address Confidentiality Program	11
Chapter 16 - Gaming Contracts and Futures	11
Chapter 17 - Habeas Corpus	11

Chapter 17A - Law-Enforcement Officers [Recodified.]	11
Chapter 17B - North Carolina Criminal Justice Education and Training System [Recodified.]	11
Chapter 17C - North Carolina Criminal Justice Education and Training Standards Commission	11
Chapter 17D - North Carolina Justice Academy	11
Chapter 17E - North Carolina Sheriffs' Education and Training Standards Commission	11
Chapter 18 - Regulation of Intoxicating Liquors [Repealed.]	12
Chapter 18A - Regulation of Intoxicating Liquors [Repealed.]	12
Chapter 18B - Regulation of Alcoholic Beverages	12
Chapter 18C - North Carolina State Lottery	12
Chapter 19 - Offenses against Public Morals	12
Chapter 19A - Protection of Animals	12
Chapter 20 - Motor Vehicles	13
Chapter 20 - Motor Vehicles (Continuation)	14
Chapter 20 - Motor Vehicles (Continuation)	15
Chapter 20 - Motor Vehicles (Continuation)	16
Chapter 21 - Bills of Lading	17
Chapter 22 - Contracts Requiring Writing	17
Chapter 22A - Signatures	17
Chapter 22B - Contracts Against Public Policy	17
Chapter 22C - Payments to Subcontractors	17
Chapter 23 - Debtor and Creditor	17
Chapter 24 – Interest	17
Chapter 25 – Uniform Commercial Code	18
Chapter 25 – Uniform Commercial Code (Continuation)	19
Chapter 25A – Retail Installment Sales Act	20
Chapter 25B - Credit	20
Chapter 25C - Sales of Artwork	20
Chapter 26 - Suretyship	20
Chapter 27 - Warehouse Receipts [Repealed.]	20
Chapter 28 - Administration [Repealed.]	20
Chapter 28A - Administration of Decedents' Estates	20
Chapter 28B - Estates of Absentees in Military Service	20
Chapter 28C - Estates of Missing Persons	20
Chapter 29 - Intestate Succession	21
Chapter 30 - Surviving Spouses	21
Chapter 31 - Wills	21
Chapter 31A - Acts Barring Property Rights	21
Chapter 31B - Renunciation of Property and Renunciation of Fiduciary Powers Act	21
Chapter 31C - Uniform Disposition of Community Property Rights at Death Act	21
Chapter 32 - Fiduciaries	21
Chapter 32A - Powers of Attorney	21
Chapter 33 - Guardian and Ward [Repealed and Recodified.]	21

Chapter 33A - North Carolina Uniform Transfers to Minors Act	21
Chapter 33B - North Carolina Uniform Custodial Trust Act	21
Chapter 34 - Veterans' Guardianship Act	22
Chapter 35 - Sterilization Procedures	22
Chapter 35A - Incompetency and Guardianship	22
Chapter 36 - Trusts and Trustees [Repealed.]	22
Chapter 36A - Trusts and Trustees	22
Chapter 36B - Uniform Management of Institutional Funds Act [Repealed.]	22
Chapter 36C - North Carolina Uniform Trust Code	22
Chapter 36D - North Carolina Community Third Party Trusts, Pooled Trusts	23
Chapter 36E - Uniform Prudent Management of Institutional Funds Act	23
Chapter 37 - Allocation of Principal and Income [Repealed.]	23
Chapter 37A - Uniform Principal and Income Act	23
Chapter 38 - Boundaries	23
Chapter 38A - Landowner Liability	23
Chapter 38B - Trespasser Responsibility	23
Chapter 39 - Conveyances	23
Chapter 39A - Transfer Fee Covenants Prohibited	23
Chapter 40 - Eminent Domain [Repealed.]	23
Chapter 40A - Eminent Domain	23
Chapter 41 - Estates	23
Chapter 41A - State Fair Housing Act	23
Chapter 42 - Landlord and Tenant	23
Chapter 42A - Vacation Rental Act	23
Chapter 43 - Land Registration	23
Chapter 44 - Liens	24
Chapter 44A - Statutory Liens and Charges	24
Chapter 45 - Mortgages and Deeds of Trust	24
Chapter 45A - Good Funds Settlement Act	24
Chapter 46 - Partition	24
Chapter 47 - Probate and Registration	25
Chapter 47A - Unit Ownership	25
Chapter 47B - Real Property Marketable Title Act	25
Chapter 47C - North Carolina Condominium Act	25
Chapter 47D - Notice of Settlement Act [Expired.]	25
Chapter 47E - Residential Property Disclosure Act	25
Chapter 47F - North Carolina Planned Community Act	25
Chapter 47G - Option to Purchase Contracts	25
Chapter 47H - Contracts for Deed	25
Chapter 48 - Adoptions +	26
Chapter 48A - Minors	26
Chapter 49 - Bastardy	26
Chapter 49A - Rights of Children	26
Chapter 50 - Divorce and Alimony	26

Chapter 50A Uniform Child-Custody Jurisdiction and Enforcement Act	26
	26
Chapter 50B - Domestic Violence	26
Chapter 50C - Civil No-Contact Orders	26
Chapter 51 - Marriage	26
Chapter 52 - Powers and Liabilities of Married Persons	27
Chapter 52A - Uniform Reciprocal Enforcement of Support Act [Repealed.]	27
Chapter 52B - Uniform Premarital Agreement Act	27
Chapter 52C - Uniform Interstate Family Support Act	27
Chapter 53 - Banks	27
Chapter 53A - Business Development Corporations and North Carolina Capital Resource Corporations	28
Chapter 53B - Financial Privacy Act	28
Chapter 54 - Cooperative Organizations	28
Chapter 54A - Capital Stock Savings and Loan Associations [Repealed.]	28
Chapter 54B - Savings and Loan Associations	29
Chapter 54C - Savings Banks	29
Chapter 55 - North Carolina Business Corporation Act	30
Chapter 55A - North Carolina Nonprofit Corporation Act	31
Chapter 55B - Professional Corporation Act	31
Chapter 55C - Foreign Trade Zones	31
Chapter 55D - Filings, Names, and Registered Agents for Corporations, Nonprofit Corporations, and Partnerships	31
Chapter 56 - Electric, Telegraph and Power Companies [Repealed.]	31
Chapter 57 - Hospital, Medical and Dental Service Corporations [Recodified.]	31
Chapter 57A - Health Maintenance Organization Act [Recodified.]	31
Chapter 57B - Health Maintenance Organization Act [Recodified.]	31
Chapter 57C - North Carolina Limited Liability Company Act.	31
Chapter 58 - Insurance.	32
Chapter 58 - Insurance (Continuation)	33
Chapter 58 - Insurance (Continuation)	34
Chapter 58 - Insurance (Continuation)	35
Chapter 58 - Insurance (Continuation)	36
Chapter 58 - Insurance (Continuation)	37
Chapter 58 - Insurance (Continuation)	38
Chapter 58A - North Carolina Health Insurance Trust Commission [Recodified.]	38
Chapter 59 - Partnership.	39
Chapter 59B - Uniform Unincorporated Nonprofit Association Act.	39
Chapter 60 - Railroads and Other Carriers [Repealed and Transferred.]	39
Chapter 61 - Religious Societies	39
Chapter 62 - Public Utilities	39

Chapter 62 - Public Utilities (Continuation)	40
Chapter 62A - Public Safety Telephone Service And Wireless Telephone Service	40
Chapter 63 - Aeronautics	40
Chapter 63A - North Carolina Global TransPark Authority	40
Chapter 64 - Aliens	40
Chapter 65 – Cemeteries	40
Chapter 66 - Commerce and Business	41
Chapter 67 - Dogs	41
Chapter 68 - Fences and Stock Law	41
Chapter 69 - Fire Protection	41
Chapter 70 - Indian Antiquities, Archaeological Resources and Unmarked Human Skeletal Remains Protection	42
Chapter 71 - Indians [Repealed.]	42
Chapter 71A - Indians	42
Chapter 72 - Inns, Hotels and Restaurants	42
Chapter 73 - Mills	42
Chapter 74 - Mines and Quarries	42
Chapter 74A - Company Police [Repealed.]	42
Chapter 74B - Private Protective Services Act [Repealed.]	42
Chapter 74C - Private Protective Services	42
Chapter 74D - Alarm Systems	42
Chapter 74E - Company Police Act	42
Chapter 74F - Locksmith Licensing Act	42
Chapter 74G - Campus Police Act	42
Chapter 75 - Monopolies, Trusts and Consumer Protection	42
Chapter 75A - Boating and Water Safety	43
Chapter 75B - Discrimination in Business	43
Chapter 75C - Motion Picture Fair Competition Act	43
Chapter 75D - Racketeer Influenced and Corrupt Organizations	43
Chapter 75E - Unlawful Activities in Connection With Certain Corporate Transactions	43
Chapter 76 - Navigation	43
Chapter 76A - Navigation and Pilotage Commissions	43
Chapter 77 - Rivers, Creeks, and Coastal Waters	43
Chapter 78 - Securities Law [Repealed.]	43
Chapter 78A - North Carolina Securities Act	43
Chapter 78B - Tender Offer Disclosure Act [Repealed.]	43
Chapter 78C - Investment Advisers	43
Chapter 78D - Commodities Act	43
Chapter 79 - Strays [Repealed.]	43
Chapter 80 - Trademarks, Brands, etc.	44
Chapter 81 - Weights and Measures [Recodified.]	44
Chapter 81A - Weights and Measures Act of 1975.	44
Chapter 82 - Wrecks [Repealed.]	44
Chapter 83 - Architects [Recodified.]	44

Chapter 83A - Architects	44
Chapter 84 - Attorneys-at-Law	44
Chapter 84A - Foreign Legal Consultants	44
Chapter 85 - Auctions and Auctioneers [Repealed.]	44
Chapter 85A - Bail Bondsmen and Runners [Recodified.]	44
Chapter 85B - Auctions and Auctioneers	44
Chapter 85C - Bail Bondsmen and Runners [Recodified.]	44
Chapter 86 - Barbers [Recodified.]	44
Chapter 86A - Barbers	44
Chapter 87 - Contractors	44
Chapter 88 - Cosmetic Art [Repealed.]	44
Chapter 88A - Electrolysis Practice Act	44
Chapter 88B - Cosmetic Art	45
Chapter 89 - Engineering and Land Surveying [Recodified.]	45
Chapter 89A - Landscape Architects	45
Chapter 89B - Foresters	45
Chapter 89C - Engineering and Land Surveying	45
Chapter 89D - Landscape Contractors	45
Chapter 89E - Geologists Licensing Act	45
Chapter 89F - North Carolina Soil Scientist Licensing Act	45
Chapter 89G - Irrigation Contractors	45
Chapter 90 - Medicine and Allied Occupations	45
Chapter 90 - Medicine and Allied Occupations (Continuation)	46
Chapter 90 - Medicine and Allied Occupations (Continuation)	47
Chapter 90 - Medicine and Allied Occupations (Continuation)	48
Chapter 90A - Sanitarians and Water and Wastewater Treatment Facility Operators	48
Chapter 90B - Social Worker Certification and Licensure Act	48
Chapter 90C - North Carolina Recreational Therapy Licensure Act	48
Chapter 90D - Interpreters and Transliterators	48
Chapter 91 - Pawnbrokers [Repealed.]	48
Chapter 91A - Pawnbrokers Modernization Act of 1989	48
Chapter 92 - Photographers [Deleted.]	48
Chapter 93 - Certified Public Accountants	48
Chapter 93A - Real Estate License Law	49
Chapter 93B - Occupational Licensing Boards	49
Chapter 93C - Watchmakers [Repealed.]	49
Chapter 93D - North Carolina State Hearing Aid Dealers and Fitters Board.	49
Chapter 93E - North Carolina Appraisers Act	49
Chapter 94 - Apprenticeship	49
Chapter 95 - Department of Labor and Labor Regulations	49
Chapter 95 - Department of Labor and Labor Regulations (Continuation)	50
Chapter 96 - Employment Security	50
Chapter 97 - Workers' Compensation Act	50
Chapter 97 - Workers' Compensation Act (Continuation)	51

Chapter 98 - Burnt and Lost Records	51
Chapter 99 - Libel and Slander	51
Chapter 99A - Civil Remedies for Criminal Actions	51
Chapter 99B - Products Liability	51
Chapter 99C - Actions Relating to Winter Sports Safety and Accidents	51
Chapter 99D - Civil Rights	51
Chapter 99E - Special Liability Provisions	51
Chapter 100 - Monuments, Memorials and Parks	51
Chapter 101 - Names of Persons	51
Chapter 102 - Official Survey Base	51
Chapter 103 - Sundays, Holidays and Special Days	51
Chapter 104 - United States Lands	51
Chapter 104A - Degrees of Kinship	51
Chapter 104B - Hurricanes or Other Acts of Nature	51
Chapter 104C - Atomic Energy, Radioactivity and Ionizing Radiation [Repealed and Recodified.]	51
Chapter 104D - Southern States Energy Compact	51
Chapter 104E - North Carolina Radiation Protection Act	51
Chapter 104F - Southeast Interstate Low-Level Radioactive Waste Management Compact [Repealed]	51
Chapter 104G - North Carolina Low-Level Radioactive Waste Management Authority Act of 1987 [Repealed]	51
Chapter 105 - Taxation	51
Chapter 105 - Taxation (Continuation)	52
Chapter 105 - Taxation (Continuation)	53
Chapter 105 - Taxation (Continuation)	54
Chapter 105A - Setoff Debt Collection Act	55
Chapter 105B - Defaulted Student Loan Recovery Act	55
Chapter 106 - Agriculture	55
Chapter 106 - Agriculture (Continue)	56
Chapter 106 - Agriculture (Continue)	57
Chapter 107 - Agricultural Development Districts [Repealed.]	57
Chapter 108 - Social Services [Repealed and Recodified.]	57
Chapter 108A - Social Services	57
Chapter 108B - Community Action Programs	58
Chapter 108C Medicaid and Health Choice Provider Requirements.	58
Chapter 108D Medicaid Managed Care for Behavioral Health Services.	58
Chapter 109 - Bonds [Recodified.]	58
Chapter 110 - Child Welfare	58
Chapter 111 - Aid to the Blind	58
Chapter 112 - Confederate Homes and Pensions [Repealed.]	58
Chapter 113 - Conservation and Development	58
Chapter 113 - Conservation and Development (Continuation)	59

Chapter 113A - Pollution Control and Environment	59
Chapter 113A - Pollution Control and Environment (Continuation)	60
Chapter 113B - North Carolina Energy Policy Act of 1975	60
Chapter 114 - Department of Justice	60
Chapter 115 - Elementary and Secondary Education [Repealed.]	60
Chapter 115A - Community Colleges, Technical Institutes, and Industrial Education Centers [Repealed.]	60
Chapter 115B - Tuition and Fee Waivers	60
Chapter 115C - Elementary and Secondary Education	60
Chapter 115C - Elementary and Secondary Education (Continuation)	61
Chapter 115C - Elementary and Secondary Education (Continuation)	62
Chapter 115C - Elementary and Secondary Education (Continuation)	63
Chapter 115D - Community Colleges	63
Chapter 115E - Private Educational Facilities Finance Act [Recodified]	63
Chapter 116 - Higher Education	63
Chapter 116 - Higher Education (Continuation)	63
Chapter 116A - Escheats and Abandoned Property [Repealed.]	64
Chapter 116B - Escheats and Abandoned Property	64
Chapter 116C - Continuum of Education Programs	64
Chapter 116D - Higher Education Bonds	64
Chapter 117 - Electrification	64
Chapter 118 - Firemen's and Rescue Squad Workers' Relief and Pension Funds [Recodified.]	64
Chapter 118A - Firemen's Death Benefit Act [Repealed.]	64
Chapter 118B - Members of a Rescue Squad Death Benefit Act [Repealed.]	64
Chapter 119 - Gasoline and Oil Inspection and Regulation	64
Chapter 120 - General Assembly	65
Chapter 120 - General Assembly (Continuation)	66
Chapter 120 - General Assembly (Continuation)	67
Chapter 120C - Lobbying	67
Chapter 121 - Archives and History	67
Chapter 122 - Hospitals for the Mentally Disordered [Repealed.]	67
Chapter 122A - North Carolina Housing Finance Agency	67
Chapter 122B - North Carolina Agricultural Facilities Finance Act [Repealed.]	67
Chapter 122C - Mental Health, Developmental Disabilities, and Substance Abuse Act of 1985	67
Chapter 122C - Mental Health, Developmental Disabilities, and Substance Abuse Act of 1985 (Continuation)	68
Chapter 122D - North Carolina Agricultural Finance Act	68

Chapter 122E - North Carolina Housing Trust and Oil Overcharge Act	68
Chapter 123 - Impeachment	69
Chapter 123A - Industrial Development [Repealed.]	69
Chapter 124 - Internal Improvements	69
Chapter 125 - Libraries	69
Chapter 126 - State Personnel System	69
Chapter 127 - Militia [Repealed.]	69
Chapter 127A - Militia	69
Chapter 127B - Military Affairs	69
Chapter 127C - Advisory Commission on Military Affairs	69
Chapter 128 - Offices and Public Officers	69
Chapter 128 - Offices and Public Officers (Continuation)	70
Chapter 129 - Public Buildings and Grounds	70
Chapter 130 - Public Health [Repealed.]	70
Chapter 130A - Public Health	70
Chapter 130A - Public Health (Continuation)	71
Chapter 130A - Public Health (Continuation)	72
Chapter 130B - Hazardous Waste Management Commission [Repealed.]	72
Chapter 131 - Public Hospitals [Repealed.]	72
Chapter 131A - Health Care Facilities Finance Act	72
Chapter 131B - Licensing of Ambulatory Surgical Facilities [Repealed.]	72
Chapter 131C - Charitable Solicitation Licensure Act [Repealed.]	72
Chapter 131D - Inspection and Licensing of Facilities	72
Chapter 131E - Health Care Facilities and Services	72
Chapter 131E - Health Care Facilities and Services (Continuation)	73
Chapter 131F - Solicitation of Contributions	73
Chapter 132 - Public Records	73
Chapter 133 - Public Works	74
Chapter 134 - Youth Development [Recodified.]	74
Chapter 134A - Youth Services [Repealed.]	74
Chapter 135 - Retirement System for Teachers and State Employees; Social Security; Health Insurance Program for Children	74
Chapter 135 - Retirement System for Teachers and State Employees; Social Security; Health Insurance Program for Children	75
Chapter 136 - Transportation	75
Chapter 136 - Transportation (Continuation)	76
Chapter 137 - Rural Rehabilitation [Repealed.]	76
Chapter 138 - Salaries, Fees and Allowances	76
Chapter 138A - State Government Ethics Act	76
Chapter 139 - Soil and Water Conservation Districts	76

Chapter 140 - State Art Museum; Symphony and Art Societies	76
Chapter 140A - State Awards System	76
Chapter 141 - State Boundaries	76
Chapter 142 - State Debt	76
Chapter 143 - State Departments, Institutions, and Commissions	77
Chapter 143 - State Departments, Institutions, and Commissions (Continuation)	78
Chapter 143 - State Departments, Institutions, and Commissions (Continuation)	79
Chapter 143 - State Departments, Institutions, and Commissions (Continuation)	80
Chapter 143A - State Government Reorganization	80
Chapter 143B - Executive Organization Act of 1973	80
Chapter 143B - Executive Organization Act of 1973 (Continuation)	81
Chapter 143B - Executive Organization Act of 1973 (Continuation)	82
Chapter 143C - State Budget Act	83
Chapter 143D - The State Governmental Accountability and Internal Control Act	83
Chapter 144 - State Flag, Official Governmental Flags, Motto, and Colors	83
Chapter 145 - State Symbols and Other Official Adoptions.	83
Chapter 146 - State Lands	83
Chapter 147 - State Officers	83
Chapter 148 - State Prison System	84
Chapter 149 - State Song and Toast	84
Chapter 150 - Uniform Revocation of Licenses [Repealed.]	84
Chapter 150A - Administrative Procedure Act [Recodified.]	84
Chapter 150B - Administrative Procedure Act	84
Chapter 151 - Constables [Repealed.]	84
Chapter 152 - Coroners	84
Chapter 152A - County Medical Examiner [Repealed.]	84
Chapter 152A - County Medical Examiner [Repealed.] (Continuation)	85
Chapter 153 - Counties and County Commissioners [Repealed.]	85
Chapter 153A - Counties	85
Chapter 153B - Mountain Resources Planning Act	85
Chapter 153C - Uwharrie Regional Resources Act	85
Chapter 154 - County Surveyor [Repealed.]	85
Chapter 155 - County Treasurer [Repealed.]	85
Chapter 156 - Drainage	85
Chapter 156 – Drainage (Continuation)	86

Chapter 157 - Housing Authorities and Projects	86
Chapter 157A - Historic Properties Commissions [Transferred.]	86
Chapter 158 - Local Development	86
Chapter 159 - Local Government Finance	86
Chapter 159 - Local Government Finance (Continuation)	87
Chapter 159A - Pollution Abatement and Industrial Facilities Financing Act [Unconstitutional.]	87
Chapter 159B - Joint Municipal Electric Power and Energy Act	87
Chapter 159C - Industrial and Pollution Control Facilities Financing Act	87
Chapter 159D - The North Carolina Capital Facilities Financing Act	87
Chapter 159E - Registered Public Obligations Act	87
Chapter 159F - North Carolina Energy Development Authority [Repealed.]	87
Chapter 159G - Water Infrastructure	87
Chapter 159H - [Reserved.]	87
Chapter 159I - Solid Waste Management Loan Program and Local Government Special Obligation Bonds	87
Chapter 160 - Municipal Corporations [Repealed And Transferred.]	87
Chapter 160A - Cities and Towns	88
Chapter 160A - Cities and Towns (Continuation)	89
Chapter 160B - Consolidated City-County Act	89
Chapter 160C - Baseball Park Districts [Repealed.]	90
Chapter 161 - Register of Deeds	90
Chapter 162 - Sheriff	90
Chapter 162A - Water and Sewer Systems	90
Chapter 162B Continuity of Local Government in Emergency.	90
Chapter 163 Elections and Election Laws.	90
Chapter 163 Elections and Election Laws. (Continuation)	91
Chapter 164 Concerning the General Statutes of North Carolina.	92
Chapter 165 Veterans.	92
Chapter 166 Civil Preparedness Agencies [Repealed.]	92
Chapter 166A North Carolina Emergency Management Act.	92
Chapter 167 State Civil Air Patrol [Repealed.]	92
Chapter 168 Persons with Disabilities.	92
Chapter 168A Persons With Disabilities Protection Act.	92

Chapter 54B

Savings and Loan Associations.

Article 1.

General Provisions.

§ 54B-1. Title.

This Chapter shall be known and may be cited as "Savings and Loan Associations." (1981, c. 282, s. 3.)

§ 54B-2. Purpose.

The purpose of this Chapter is:

(1) To provide for the safe and sound conduct of the business of savings and loan associations, the conservation of their assets and the maintenance of public confidence in savings and loan associations;

(2) To provide for the protection of the interests of customers and members, and the public interest in the soundness of the savings and loan industry;

(3) To provide the opportunity for savings and loan associations to remain competitive with each other and with other savings and financial institutions existing under other laws of this and other states and the United States;

(4) To provide the opportunity for savings and loan associations to serve effectively the convenience and advantage of customers and members, and to improve and expand their services and facilities for such purposes;

(5) To provide the opportunity for the management of savings and loan associations to exercise prudent business judgment in conducting the affairs of savings and loan associations to the extent compatible with the purposes recited in this section; and

(6) To provide adequate rulemaking power and administrative discretion so that the regulation and supervision of savings and loan associations are readily

responsive to changes in economic conditions and in savings and loan practices. (1981, c. 282, s. 3.)

§ 54B-3. Applicability of Chapter.

The provisions of this Chapter, unless the context otherwise specifies, shall apply to all State associations. (1981, c. 282, s. 3.)

§ 54B-4. Definitions and application of terms.

(a) The terms "building and loan association" and "savings and loan association" when used in the General Statutes, shall mean an association and shall be interchangeable. Use of either term shall be construed to include the other unless a different intention is expressly provided.

(b) As used in this Chapter, unless the context otherwise requires, the term:

(1) Repealed by Session Laws 2001-193, s. 3, effective July 1, 2001.

(2) "Aggregate withdrawal value of withdrawable accounts" means the total value of all withdrawable accounts held by an association.

(3) "Application" means the completed package of the application to organize a State association, establish a branch office or conversion of structure of a savings and loan association which the Commissioner of Banks considers in making his recommendation.

(3a) "Affiliate" means a person or corporation that controls, is controlled by, or is under common control with an association.

(4) "Associate" when used to indicate a relationship with any person, means (i) any corporation or organization (other than the applicant or a majority-owned subsidiary of the applicant) of which such person is an officer or partner or is, directly or indirectly, the beneficial owner of ten percent (10%) or more of any class of equity securities, (ii) any trust or other estate in which such person has a substantial beneficial interest or as to which such person serves as trustee or in a similar fiduciary capacity, and (iii) any relative or spouse who lives in the

same house as that person, or any relative of that person's spouse who lives in the same house as that person, or who is a director or officer of the applicant or any of its parents or subsidiaries.

(5) "Association" includes a State association or a federal association unless limited by use of the words "State" or "federal."

(6) "Borrowers" means those who borrow funds from or in any other way become obligated on a loan to an association.

(7) "Branch office" means an office of an association other than its principal office which renders savings and loan services.

(8) "Capital stock" means securities which represent ownership of a stock association.

(9) "Certificate of approval" means a document signed by the Commissioner of Banks informing the North Carolina Secretary of State that the Commission has approved the certificate of incorporation of a proposed association.

(10) Repealed by Session Laws 1985, c. 659, s. 1.

(11) "Certificate of incorporation or charter" means the document which represents the corporate existence of a State association.

(12) "Certified copy" means a copy of an original document or paper which has been signed by the person or persons who certify such document to be an exact copy of the original.

(13) "This Chapter" means Chapter 54B of the North Carolina General Statutes.

(14) "Commission" means the State Banking Commission of the Department of Commerce.

(14a) "Commissioner" means the Commissioner of Banks authorized pursuant to Article 2 of Chapter 53C of the General Statutes.

(15) "Conflict of interest" means a matter before the board of directors in which one or more of the directors, officers or employees has a direct or indirect financial interest in its outcome.

(16) "Conformed copies" means photocopies or carbon copies or other mechanical reproductions of an original document or paper.

(16a) "Control" means the power, directly or indirectly, to direct the management or policies of an association or to vote twenty-five percent (25%) or more of any class of voting securities for an association.

(17) "Court of competent jurisdiction" means a court in North Carolina which is qualified to hear the case at hand.

(18) "Disinterested directors" means those directors who have absolutely no direct or indirect financial interest in the matter before them.

(19) "Dividends on stock" means the earnings of an association paid out to holders of capital stock in a stock association.

(20) "Dividends on withdrawable accounts" means the consideration paid by an association to a holder of a withdrawable account for the use of his money.

(21) "Division" means the Savings Institutions Division of the North Carolina Department of Commerce.

(22) "Entrance fee per withdrawable account" means the amount to be paid by each person, firm or corporation when he or it pledges to a proposed mutual association to deposit funds in a withdrawable account.

(23) "Examination and investigation" means a supervisory inspection of an association or proposed association which may include inspection of every relevant piece of information including subsidiary or affiliated businesses.

(24) "Federal association" means a corporation or association organized and operated under the provisions of federal law and regulation to conduct a savings and loan business.

(25) "Financial institution" means a person, firm or corporation engaged in the business of receiving, soliciting or accepting money or its equivalent on deposit and/or lending money or its equivalent.

(26) Repealed by Session Laws 1985, c. 659, s. 1.

(27) "General reserve" means appropriated or restricted funds in the form of cash or investments to be used solely for the purpose of absorbing losses.

(28) "Guaranty association" means a mutual deposit guaranty association which is a corporation organized under this Chapter or its predecessor and operated under the provisions of Article 12 of this Chapter.

(29) "Immediate family" means one's spouse, father, mother, children, brothers, sisters, and grandchildren; and the father, mother, brothers, and sisters of one's spouse; and the spouse of one's child, brother or sister.

(30) "Initial pledges for withdrawable accounts" means those pledges of funds by persons who promise to a proposed mutual association to deposit such amount if and when such proposed association becomes established.

(31) "Insurance of withdrawable accounts" means insurance on an association's withdrawable accounts when the beneficiary is the holder of such insured account.

(32) "Liquidity fund" means that portion of the assets of an association which is required to be held in readily marketable form.

(32a) "Interim association" means an association formed to facilitate the acquisition of one hundred percent (100%) of the voting shares of an existing stock association by a newly-formed association or an existing savings and loan holding company or to facilitate any other transaction the Commissioner of Banks may approve.

(33) "Members" means withdrawable account holders and borrowers in a State mutual association.

(34) "Minimum amount of consideration" means the amount of money a stock association shall be required to have received on the sale of its stock, before it shall commence business.

(35) "Minimum amount on deposit in withdrawable accounts" means the amount of money which a mutual association must have on hand prior to its commencement of business.

(36) "Mutual association" means all mutual savings and loan associations owned by members of the association, and organized under the provisions of this Chapter or its predecessor for the primary purpose of promoting thrift and home financing.

(37) "Net withdrawal value of withdrawable accounts" means the aggregate of the withdrawal value of an association's withdrawable accounts less the amount of any pledged withdrawable account which serves as security for a loan.

(38) "Net worth" means an association's total assets less total liabilities.

(39) "Original incorporators" means the organizers of a State association responsible for the business of a proposed association from the filing of the application to the Commission's final decision on such application.

(40) "Plan of conversion" means a detailed outline of the procedure of the conversion of an association from one to another regulatory authority or from one to another form of ownership.

(41) "Principal office" means the office which houses the headquarters of an association.

(42) "Proposed association" means an entity in organizational procedures prior to the Commission's final decision on its charter application.

(43) "Registered agent" means the person named in the certificate of incorporation upon whom service of legal process shall be deemed binding upon the association.

(44) "Rules and regulations" means those regulatory procedures and guidelines issued by the Commissioner of Banks and approved by the Commission.

(44a) Repealed by Session Laws 1991, c. 680, s. 2.

(45) "Service corporation" means a corporation operating under the provision of Article 8 of this Chapter which engages in activities determined by the Commissioner of Banks by rules and regulations to be incidental to the conduct of a savings and loan business as provided in this Chapter or activities which

further or facilitate the corporate purposes of an association, or which furnishes services to an association or subsidiaries of an association, the voting stock of which is owned directly or indirectly by one or more associations.

(46) "Specific reserve account" means an account held by an association as a loss reserve for coverage on specific loans and investments.

(47) "This State" means the State of North Carolina.

(48) "State association" means a corporation or association organized under this Chapter or its predecessor and operated under the provisions of this Chapter to conduct the savings and loan business; or a corporation organized under the provisions of the predecessors to this Chapter and operated under the provisions of this Chapter; or a corporation organized under the provisions of federal law and so converted as to be operated under the provisions of this Chapter.

(49) "Stock association" means any corporation or company owned by holders of capital stock and organized under the provisions of this Chapter for the primary purpose of promoting thrift and home financing.

(50) "Subscriptions" means the promise to purchase capital stock in a stock association and payment of a portion of the selling price.

(51) "Total assets" means the aggregate amount of assets of any and every kind held by an association.

(52) "Voluntary dissolution" means the dissolution and liquidation of an association initiated by its ownership.

(53) "Withdrawable accounts" means accounts in which a customer or member places funds with an association which may be withdrawn by the account holder.

(54) Repealed by Session Laws 1989, c. 76, s. 1. (1981, c. 282, s. 3; 1981 (Reg. Sess., 1982), c. 1238, s. 1; 1983, c. 144, ss. 1, 2; 1985, c. 659, ss. 1, 9(a); c. 677, s. 1; 1989, c. 76, s. 1; c. 751, s. 7(3); 1991, c. 680, s. 2; 1991 (Reg. Sess., 1992), c. 829, s. 1; c. 959, ss. 5, 5.1; 2001-193, ss. 3, 4, 17; 2012-56, s. 36.)

Article 2.

Incorporation and Organization.

§ 54B-5. Severability.

If any section or subsection of this Chapter, or the application thereof to any person is held invalid, the remaining sections or subsections of this Chapter, and the application of such section or subsection to any other person, shall not be invalidated or affected thereby. (1981, c. 282, s. 3.)

§ 54B-6. Hearings.

Any hearing required to be held by this Chapter shall be conducted in accordance with the applicable provisions of Article 3 of Chapter 150B of the General Statutes. (1981, c. 282, s. 3; 1987, c. 827, s. 1.)

§ 54B-7. Application of Chapter on business corporations.

All the provisions of law relating to private corporations, and particularly those enumerated in Chapter 55, of the General Statutes, entitled "North Carolina Business Corporation Act," which are not inconsistent with this Chapter, or with the proper business of savings and loan associations shall be applicable to all State associations. (1981, c. 282, s. 3; 1989 (Reg. Sess., 1990), c. 1024, s. 3.)

§ 54B-8. Scope and prohibitions; existing charters; injunctions.

(a)   Nothing in this Chapter shall be construed to invalidate any charter that was valid prior to the enactment of this Chapter. All such associations shall continue operation in full force, but such associations shall be operated in accordance with the provisions of this Chapter.

(b) Repealed by Session Laws 1985, c. 659, s. 2.

(c) No person or group of persons, nor any corporation, company, or association except one incorporated and licensed in accordance with the provisions of this Chapter to operate a State association, shall operate as a State association. Unless so authorized as a State or federal association and actually engaged in transacting a savings and loan business, no person or group of persons, nor any corporation, company, or association domiciled and doing business in this State shall:

(1) Use in its name the terms "building and loan association" or "savings and loan association" or words of similar import or connotation that lead the public reasonably to believe that the business so conducted is that of a savings and loan association; or

(2) Use any sign, or circulate or use any letterhead, billhead, circular or paper whatsoever, or advertise or communicate in any manner that would lead the public reasonably to believe that it is conducting the business of a savings and loan association.

(d) Upon application by the Commissioner of Banks or by any savings and loan association, a court of competent jurisdiction may issue an injunction to restrain any person or entity from violating or from continuing to violate any of the foregoing provisions of subsection (c). (1981, c. 282, s. 3; 1985, c. 659, s. 2; 1987, c. 237, s. 1; 2001-193, s. 16.)

§ 54B-9. Application to organize a savings and loan association.

(a) It shall be lawful for any five or more natural persons (hereinafter referred to as the "incorporators"), who are domiciled in this State, to organize and establish a savings and loan association in order to promote thrift and home financing, subject to approval as hereinafter provided in this Chapter. The incorporators shall file with the Commissioner of Banks a preliminary application to organize a State association, in the form to be prescribed by the Commissioner of Banks, together with the proper nonrefundable application fee.

(b) The application to organize a State association shall be received by the Commissioner of Banks not less than 60 days prior to the scheduled consideration of the application by the Commission, and it shall contain:

(1) The original of the certificate of incorporation, which shall be signed by the original incorporators, or a majority of them, but not less than five, and shall be properly acknowledged by a person duly authorized by this State to take proof or acknowledgment of deeds; and two conformed copies;

(2) The names and addresses of the incorporators; and the names and addresses of the initial members of the board of directors;

(3) Statements of the anticipated receipts, expenditures, earnings and financial condition of the association for its first two years of operation, or such longer period as the Commissioner of Banks may require;

(4) A showing satisfactory to the Commission that:

a. The public convenience and advantage will be served by the establishment of the proposed association;

b. There is a reasonable demand and necessity in the community which will be served by the establishment of the proposed association;

c. The proposed association will have a reasonable probability of sustaining profitable and beneficial operations within a reasonable time in the community in which the proposed association intends to locate;

d. The proposed association, if established, will promote healthy and effective competition in the community in the delivery to the public of savings and loan services;

(5) The proposed bylaws;

(6) Statements, exhibits, maps and other data which may be prescribed or requested by the Commissioner of Banks, which data shall be sufficiently detailed and comprehensive so as to enable the Commissioner of Banks to pass upon the criteria set forth in this Article.

(c) The application shall be signed by the original incorporators or a majority of them but not less than five, and shall be properly acknowledged by a person duly authorized by this State to take proof and acknowledgement of deeds. (1981, c. 282, s. 3; 1989, c. 76, s. 2; 2001-193, s. 16.)

§ 54B-10. Certificate of incorporation.

(a)   The certificate of incorporation of a proposed mutual savings and loan association shall set forth:

(1)   The name of the association, which must not so closely resemble the name of an existing association doing business under the laws of this State as to be likely to mislead the public;

(2)   The county and city or town where its principal office is to be located in this State; and the name of its registered agent and the address of its registered office, including county and city or town, and street and number;

(3)   The period of duration, which may be perpetual. When the certificate of incorporation fails to state the period of duration, it shall be considered perpetual;

(4)   The purposes for which the association is organized, which shall be limited to purposes permitted under the laws of this State for savings and loan associations;

(5)   The amount of the entrance fee per withdrawable account based upon the amount pledged;

(6)   The minimum amount on deposit in withdrawable accounts before it shall commence business;

(7)   Any provision not inconsistent with this Chapter and the proper operation of a savings and loan association, which the incorporators shall set forth in the certificate of incorporation for the regulation of the internal affairs of the association;

(8)   The number of directors, which shall not be less than seven, constituting the initial board of directors (which may be classified in the certificate of incorporation), and the name and addresses of each person who is to serve as a director until the first meeting of members, or until his successor be elected and qualified;

(9)   The names and addresses of the incorporators.

(b) The certificate of incorporation of a proposed stock savings and loan association shall set forth:

(1) The name of the association, which must not so closely resemble the name of an existing association doing business under the laws of this State as to be likely to mislead the public;

(2) The county and city or town where its principal office is to be located in this State; and the name of its registered agent and the address of its registered office, including county and city or town, and street and number;

(3) The period of duration, which may be perpetual. When the certificate of incorporation fails to state the period of duration, it shall be considered perpetual;

(4) The purposes for which the association is organized, which shall be limited to purposes permitted under the laws of this State for savings and loan associations;

(5) With respect to the shares of stock which the association shall have authority to issue:

a. If the stock is to have a par value, the number of such shares of stock and the par value of each;

b. If the stock is to be without par value, the number of such shares of stock;

c. If the stock is to be of both kinds mentioned in paragraphs a and b of subdivision (5) of this subsection, particulars in accordance with those paragraphs;

d. If the stock is to be divided into classes, or into series within a class of preferred or special shares of stock, the certificate of incorporation shall also set forth a designation of each class, with a designation of each series within a class, and a statement of the preferences, limitations, and relative rights of the stock of each class or series;

(6) The minimum amount of consideration to be received for its shares of stock before it shall commence business;

(7)   A statement as to whether stockholders have preemptive rights to acquire additional or treasury shares of the association and any provision limiting or denying said rights;

(8)   Any provision not inconsistent with this Chapter or the proper operation of a savings and loan association, which the incorporators shall set forth in the certificate of incorporation for the regulation of the internal affairs of the association;

(9)   The number of directors, which shall not be less than seven, constituting the initial board of directors (which may be classified in the certificate of incorporation) and the name and address of each person who is to serve as a director until the first meeting of the stockholders, or until his successor be elected and qualified;

(10)   The names and addresses of the incorporators.

(c)   The certificate of incorporation, whether for a mutual association or stock association, shall be signed by the original incorporators, or a majority of them, but not less than 10, and shall be acknowledged before an officer duly authorized under the law of this State to take proof or acknowledgement of deeds, and shall be filed along with two conformed copies in the office of the Commissioner of Banks as provided in G.S. 54B-9. (1981, c. 282, s. 3; 1983, c. 144, s. 3; 1989 (Reg. Sess., 1990), c. 806, s. 17; 1991, c. 707, s. 1; 2001-193, s. 16.)

§ 54B-11. Commissioner of Banks to consider application.

Upon receipt of an application to organize and establish a savings and loan association, the Commissioner of Banks shall examine or cause to be examined all the relevant facts connected with the formation of the proposed association. If it appears to the Commissioner of Banks that the proposed association has complied with all the requirements set forth in this Chapter and the rules and regulations for the formation of a savings and loan association and is otherwise lawfully entitled to be organized and established as a savings and loan association, the Commissioner of Banks shall present the application to the Commission for its consideration. (1981, c. 282, s. 3; 1983, c. 144, s. 4; 2001-193, s. 16.)

§ 54B-12. Criteria to be met before the Commissioner of Banks may recommend approval of an application.

(a) The Commissioner of Banks may recommend approval of an application to form a mutual association only when all of the following criteria are met:

(1) The proposed association has an operational expense fund, from which to pay organizational and incorporation expenses, in an amount determined by the Commissioner of Banks to be sufficient for the safe and proper operation of the association, but in no event less than seventy-five thousand dollars ($75,000). The moneys remaining in such expense fund shall be held by the association for at least one year from its date of licensing. No portion of such fund shall be released to an incorporator or director who contributed to it, nor to any other contributor, nor to any other person and no dividends shall be accrued or paid on such funds without the prior approval of the Commissioner of Banks.

(2) The proposed association has pledges for withdrawable accounts in an amount determined by the Commissioner of Banks to be sufficient for the safe and proper operation of the association, but in no event less than four million dollars ($4,000,000).

(3) All entrance fees for withdrawable accounts of the proposed association have been made with legal tender of the United States.

(4) All initial pledges for withdrawable accounts of the proposed association are made by residents of North Carolina.

(5) The name of the proposed association will not mislead the public and is not the same as an existing association or so similar to the name of an existing association as to mislead the public.

(6) The character, general fitness and responsibility of the incorporators and the initial board of directors of the proposed association who shall be residents of North Carolina are such as to command the confidence of the community in which the proposed association intends to locate.

(7) There is a reasonable demand and necessity in the community which will be served by the establishment of the proposed association.

(8) The public convenience and advantage will be served by the establishment of the proposed association.

(9) The proposed association will have a reasonable probability of sustaining profitable and beneficial operations in the community.

(10) The proposed association, if established, will promote healthy and effective competition in the community in the delivery to the public of savings and loan services.

(b) The Commissioner of Banks may recommend approval of an application to form a stock association only when all of the following criteria are met:

(1) The proposed association has prepared a plan to solicit subscriptions for capital stock in an amount determined by the Commissioner of Banks to be sufficient for the safe and proper operation of the association, but in no event less than three million dollars ($3,000,000).

(2) Repealed by Session Laws 1989, c. 76, s. 3.

(3) All subscriptions for capital stock of the proposed association have been purchased with legal tender of the United States.

(4) to (7) Repealed by Session Laws 1983, c. 144, s. 5.

(8) The name of the proposed association will not mislead the public and is not the same as an existing association or so similar to the name of an existing association as to mislead the public; and contains the wording "corporation," "incorporated," "limited," or "company," an abbreviation of one of such words or other words sufficient to distinguish stock associations from mutual associations.

(9) The character, general fitness, and trustworthiness of the incorporators, initial board of directors, and initial stockholders of the proposed association are such as to command the confidence of the community in which the proposed association intends to locate.

(10) There is a reasonable demand and necessity in the community which will be served by the establishment of the proposed association.

(11) The public convenience and advantage will be served by the establishment of the proposed association.

(12) The proposed association will have a reasonable probability of sustaining profitable and beneficial operations in the community.

(13) The proposed association, if established, will promote healthy and effective competition in the community in the delivery to the public of savings and loan services.

(c) The minimum amount of pledges for withdrawable accounts or subscriptions for capital stock may be adjusted in the discretion of the Commissioner of Banks if he determines that a greater requirement is necessary or that a smaller requirement will provide a sufficient capital base. Such a finding and recommendation to the Commission shall be based upon due consideration of (i) the population of the proposed trade area, (ii) the total deposits of the depository financial institutions operating in the proposed trade area, (iii) the economic conditions of and projections for the proposed trade area, (iv) the business experience and reputation of the proposed management, (v) the business experience and reputation of the proposed incorporators and directors, and (vi) the projected deposit growth, capitalization, and profitability of the proposed association. (1981, c. 282, s. 3; 1983, c. 144, s. 5; 1985, c. 659, s. 3; 1989, c. 76, s. 3; 2001-193, s. 16.)

§ 54B-13. State Banking Commission to review findings and recommendations of Commissioner of Banks.

(a) If the Commissioner of Banks does not have the completed application within 120 days of the filing of the preliminary application, the application shall be returned to the applicants.

(b) When the Commissioner of Banks has completed his examination and investigation of the facts relevant to the establishment of the proposed association, he shall present his findings and recommendations to the Commission at a public hearing. The State Banking Commission must approve or reject an application within 180 days of the submission of the preliminary application.

(c)   Not less than 45 days prior to the public hearing held for the consideration of the application to establish a savings and loan association, the incorporators shall cause to be published a notice in a newspaper of general circulation in the area to be served by the proposed association. Such notice shall contain:

(1)   A statement that the application has been filed with the Commissioner of Banks;

(2)   The name of the community where the principal office of the proposed association intends to locate;

(3)   A statement that a public hearing shall be held to consider the application; and

(4)   A statement that any interested or affected party may file a written statement either favoring or protesting the creation of the proposed association. Such statement must be filed with the Commissioner of Banks within 30 days of the date of publication.

(d)   The Commission, at the public hearing, shall consider the findings and recommendation of the Commissioner of Banks and shall hear such oral testimony as he may wish to give or be called upon to give, and shall also receive information and hear testimony from the incorporators of the proposed association and from any and all other interested or affected parties. The Commission shall hear only testimony and receive only information which is relevant to the consideration of the application and the operation of the proposed association. (1981, c. 282, s. 3; 1989, c. 76, s. 4; 2001-193, ss. 16, 17.)

§ 54B-14. Grounds for approval or denial of application.

(a)   After consideration of the findings and recommendation of the Commissioner of Banks and his oral testimony, if any, and the consideration of such other information and evidence, either written or oral, as has come before it at the public hearing, the Commission shall approve or disapprove the application within 30 days after the public hearing. The Commission shall approve the application if it finds that the certificate of incorporation is in compliance with the provisions of G.S. 54B-10, that all the criteria set out in G.S.

54B-12 have been complied with, and that all other applicable provisions of this Chapter, rules and regulations, and the General Statutes have been complied with.

(b) If the Commission approves the application, the Commissioner of Banks shall so notify the Secretary of State with a certificate of approval, accompanied by the original of the certificate of incorporation and the two conformed copies.

(c) Upon receipt of the certificate of approval, the original of the certificate of incorporation, and the two conformed copies, the Secretary of State shall, upon the payment by the newly chartered association of the appropriate organization tax and fees, file the certificate of incorporation in accordance with G.S. 55-1-20. He shall certify under his official seal the two conformed copies of the certificate of incorporation, one of which shall forthwith be forwarded to the incorporators or their representative, for the purpose of recordation in the office of the register of deeds of the county where the principal office of the association shall be located, the other of which shall be forwarded to the office of the Commissioner of Banks for filing. Upon the recordation of the certificate of incorporation by the Secretary of State, the association shall be a body politic and corporate under the name stated in such certificate, and shall be authorized to begin the savings and loan business when duly licensed by the Commissioner of Banks.

(d) The said certificate of incorporation, or a copy thereof, duly certified by the Secretary of State, or by the register of deeds of the county where the association is located, or by the Commissioner of Banks, under their respective seals, shall be evidence in all courts and places, and shall, in all judicial proceedings, be deemed prima facie evidence of the complete organization and incorporation of the association purporting thereby to have been established. (1981, c. 282, s. 3; 1983, c. 144, s. 9; 1985, c. 369; 1989 (Reg. Sess., 1990), c. 806, s. 18; 2001-193, s. 16.)

§ 54B-15. Final decision.

The Commission shall present the Commissioner of Banks with a final decision which shall be in accordance with the applicable provisions of Chapter 150B of the General Statutes. (1981, c. 282, s. 3; 1987, c. 827, s. 1; 2001-193, s. 16.)

§ 54B-16. Appeal.

The final decision of the Commission may be appealed in accordance with Chapter 150B of the General Statutes. (1981, c. 282, s. 3; 1987, c. 827, s. 1.)

§ 54B-17. Insurance of accounts required.

All State associations must obtain and maintain insurance on all members' and customers' withdrawable accounts. Contracts for such insurance may be made only with an insurance corporation created by an act of Congress. Prior to the licensing of an association, a certificate of incorporation duly recorded under the provisions of G.S. 54B-14(c), shall be deemed to be sufficient certification to the insuring corporation that the association is a legal corporate entity. Such insurance must be obtained within the time limit prescribed in G.S. 54B-18. (1981, c. 282, s. 3; 1987, c. 237, s. 2.)

§ 54B-18. Time allowed to commence business.

A newly chartered association shall commence business within six months after the date upon which its corporate existence shall have begun. An association which shall not commence business within such time, shall forfeit its corporate existence, unless the Commissioner of Banks, before the expiration of such six-month period, shall have approved an extension of the time within which the association may commence business, upon a written request stating the reasons for which such request is made. Upon such forfeiture, the certificate of incorporation shall expire, and any and all action taken in connection with the incorporation and chartering of the association, with the exception of fees paid to the Division, shall become null and void. The Commissioner of Banks shall determine if an association has failed to commence business within six months, without extension as provided in this section, and shall notify the Secretary of State and the register of deeds in the county in which the association is located that the certificate of incorporation has expired. (1981, c. 282, s. 3; 2001-193, s. 16.)

§ 54B-19. Licensing.

A newly chartered association shall be entitled to a license to operate upon payment to the Division of the appropriate license fee as prescribed by the Commissioner of Banks, when it shows to the satisfaction of the Commissioner of Banks evidence of capable, efficient and equitable management, and when it passes a final inspection by the Commissioner of Banks or his representatives preceding the opening of its doors for business. (1981, c. 282, s. 3; 2001-193, s. 16.)

§ 54B-20. Amendments to certificate of incorporation.

(a) Any addition, alteration or amendment to the certificate of incorporation of any State association shall be made at any annual or special meeting of such association, held in accordance with the provisions of G.S. 54B-106 and G.S. 54B-107, by a majority of votes or shares cast by members or stockholders present in person or by proxy at such meeting. Any such addition, alteration or amendment shall be signed, submitted to the Commissioner of Banks for his approval or rejection, and if approved, then certified by the Commissioner of Banks and recorded as provided in G.S. 54B-14 for certificates of incorporation.

(b) Notwithstanding the provisions of subsection (a) of this section, any State association may change its registered office or its registered agent or both in accordance with the provisions of G.S. 55D-31. A copy of the statement or certificate certified by the Secretary of State shall be filed in the office of the Commissioner of Banks. (1981, c. 282, s. 3; 1981 (Reg. Sess., 1982), c. 1238, s. 4; 1985, c. 659, s. 17; 1989 (Reg. Sess., 1990), c. 806, s. 19; 2001-193, s. 16; 2001-358, s. 47(g); 2001-387, s. 173; 2001-413, s. 6.)

§ 54B-21. List of stockholders to be maintained.

Every stock association organized and operated under the provisions of this Chapter or its predecessor shall at all times cause to be kept an up-to-date list of the names of all its stockholders. Whenever called upon by the Commissioner of Banks, a stock association shall file in the office of the Commissioner of Banks a correct list of all its stockholders, the resident address of each, the number of shares of stock held by each, and the dates of issue. (1981, c. 282, s. 3; 1983, c. 144, s. 10; 2001-193, s. 16.)

§ 54B-22. Branch offices.

(a)   Any State association may apply to the Commissioner of Banks for permission to establish a branch office. The application shall be in such form as may be prescribed by the Commissioner of Banks and shall be accompanied by the proper branch application fee. Branch applications shall be approved or denied by the Commissioner of Banks within 120 days of filing.

(b)   The Commissioner of Banks shall approve a branch application when all of the following criteria are met:

(1)   The applicant has gross assets of at least ten million dollars ($10,000,000);

(2)   The applicant has evidenced financial responsibility;

(3)   The applicant has a net worth equal to or exceeding the amount required by the insurer of the applicant's withdrawable accounts;

(4)   The applicant has an acceptable internal control system. Such a system would include certain basic internal control requirements essential to the protection of assets and the promotion of operational efficiency regardless of the size of the applicant. Some of the factors which require extensive internal control requirements such as the use of the controller or internal auditor and more distinctive placement responsibilities include the applicant's size, number of personnel and history of and anticipated plans for expansion.

(c)   Upon receipt of a branch application, the Commissioner of Banks shall examine or cause to be examined all the relevant facts connected with the establishment of the proposed branch office. If it appears to the satisfaction of the Commissioner of Banks that the applicant has complied with all the requirements set forth in this section and the regulations for the establishment of a branch office and that the association is otherwise lawfully entitled to establish such branch office, then the administrator shall approve the branch application.

(d)   Not more than 10 days following the filing of the branch application with the Commissioner of Banks, the applicant shall cause a notice to be published in a newspaper of general circulation in the area to be served by the proposed branch office. Such notice shall contain:

(1) A statement that the branch application has been filed with the Commissioner of Banks;

(2) The proposed address of the branch office, including city or town and street; and

(3) A statement that any interested or affected party may file a written statement with the Commissioner of Banks, within 30 days of the date of the publication of the notice, protesting the establishment of the proposed branch office and requesting a hearing before the Commissioner of Banks on the application.

(e) Any interested or affected party may file a written statement with the Commissioner of Banks within 30 days of the date of initial publication of the branch application notice, protesting the establishment of the proposed branch office and requesting a hearing before the Commissioner of Banks on the application. If a hearing is held on the branch application, the Commissioner of Banks shall only receive information and hear testimony from the applicant and from any interested or affected party which is relevant to the branch application and the operation of the proposed branch office. The Commissioner of Banks shall issue his final decision on the branch application within 30 days following the hearing. Such final decision shall be in accordance with the applicable provisions of Chapter 150B of the General Statutes.

(f) If a hearing is not held on the branch application, the Commissioner of Banks shall issue his final decision within 120 days of the filing of the application. Such final decision shall be in accordance with the applicable provisions of Chapter 150B of the General Statutes.

(g) to (i) Repealed by Session Laws 1981 (Regular Session, 1982), c. 1238, s. 3.

(j) Any party to a branch application may appeal the final decision of the to the Commission at any time after final decision, but not later than 30 days after a written copy of the final decision is served upon the party and his attorney of record by personal service or by certified mail. Failure to file such appeal within the time stated shall operate as a waiver of the right of such party to review by the Commission and by a court of competent jurisdiction in accordance with

Chapter 150B of the General Statutes, relating to judicial review. (1981, c. 282, s. 3; 1981 (Reg. Sess., 1982), c. 1238, s. 3; 1987, c. 827, s. 1; 2001-193, s. 16.)

§ 54B-23. Application to change location of a branch or principal office.

(a) The board of directors of a State association may change the location of a branch office or the principal office of the association by submitting to the Commissioner of Banks an application for such change on forms prescribed by the Commissioner of Banks.

(b) Upon receipt of an application accompanied by the proper application fee, the Commissioner of Banks shall conduct, or cause to be conducted, an examination and investigation of the facts and circumstances connected with the consideration of the application. After such examination and investigation, the Commissioner of Banks shall approve or deny the application.

(c) If an application filed under this section is approved by the Commissioner of Banks and the association fails to change the location of such branch office or principal office within six months after the date of the order approving such application, such approval shall be revoked. Such a six-month period may be extended upon a showing to the satisfaction of the Commissioner of Banks of good cause. (1981, c. 282, s. 3; 1983, c. 144, s. 11; 2001-193, s. 16.)

§ 54B-24. Approval revoked; branch office.

The Commission may, for good cause and after a hearing, order the closing of a branch office. Such order shall be made in writing to the association and shall fix a reasonable time after which the association shall close the branch office. (1981, c. 282, s. 3.)

§ 54B-25. Branch offices closed.

The board of a State association may discontinue the operation of a branch office upon giving at least 90 days' prior written notice to the Commissioner of

Banks and depositors, the notice to include the date upon which the branch office shall be closed. (1981, c. 282, s. 3; 1983, c. 144, s. 12; 1989, c. 76, s. 5; 1991 (Reg. Sess., 1992), c. 829, s. 2; 2001-193, s. 16.)

§ 54B-26: Repealed by Session Laws 1991, c. 680, s. 3.

§§ 54B-27 through 54B-29. Reserved for future codification purposes.

Article 3.

Fundamental Changes.

§ 54B-30. Conversion from State to federal association.

Any State savings and loan association, stock or mutual, organized and operated under the provisions of this Chapter, may convert into a federal savings and loan association in accordance with the provisions of the laws and regulations of the United States and with the same force and effect as though originally incorporated under such laws, and the procedure to effect such conversion shall be as follows:

(1) The association shall submit a plan of conversion to the Commissioner of Banks, and he may approve the same, with or without amendment, or refuse to approve the plan. If he approves the plan, then the plan shall be submitted to the members or stockholders as provided in the next subdivision. If he refuses to approve the plan, he shall state his objections in writing and give the converting association an opportunity to amend the plan to obviate such objections or to appeal his decision to the Commission.

(2) A meeting of the members or stockholders shall be held upon not less than 15 days' notice to each member or stockholder. Notice can be made either by mailing such to each member or stockholder, postage prepaid, to the last known address or by the board of directors causing to be published once a week for two weeks preceding such meeting, in a newspaper of general circulation published in the county where such association has its principal

office, a notice of the meeting. It shall be regarded as sufficient notice of the purpose of the meeting if the notice contains the following statement: "The purpose of this meeting is to consider the conversion of this State-chartered association into a federally chartered association, pursuant to the laws of the United States." An appropriate officer of the association shall make proof by affidavit at such meeting of due service of the notice or call for said meeting.

(3) At the meeting of the members or stockholders of such association, such members or stockholders may by affirmative vote of a majority of votes or shares present, in person or by proxy, resolve to convert said association to a federal savings and loan association. A copy of the minutes of the meeting of the members or stockholders certified by an appropriate officer of the association shall be filed in the office of the Commissioner of Banks. The said certified copy when so filed shall be prima facie evidence of the holding and the action of the meeting.

(4) Within a reasonable time after the receipt of a certified copy of the minutes, the Commissioner of Banks shall either approve or disapprove the proceedings of the meeting for compliance with the procedure set forth in this section. If the Commissioner of Banks approves the proceedings he shall endorse the certified copy of the minutes, and shall issue a certificate of his approval of the conversion and proceedings and send the same to the association. Such certificate shall be recorded in the office of the Secretary of State and in the office of the register of deeds of the county in which the association has its principal office, and the original shall be held by the association. If the Commissioner of Banks disapproves the proceedings he shall note his disapproval on the certified copy of the minutes and notify the Commission and the association of his disapproval. The association may appeal a disapproval to the Commission.

(5) Within 60 days after approval of the proceedings by the Commissioner of Banks, the association shall file an application, in the manner prescribed or authorized by the laws and regulations of the United States, to consummate the conversion to a federal association. A copy of the charter or authorization issued to such association by the federal regulatory authority, or a certificate showing the organization or conversion of such association into a federal savings and loan association, and upon such filing with the Commissioner of Banks the association shall cease to be a State association and shall be a federal association.

(6) Whenever any such association shall convert into a federal savings and loan association it shall cease to be an association under the laws of this State, except that its corporate existence shall be deemed to be extended for the purpose of prosecuting or defending suits by or against it and of enabling it to close its business affairs as a State association, and to dispose of and convey its property. At the time when such conversion becomes effective, all the property of the state association including all its rights, title and interest in and to all property of whatever kind, whether real, personal or mixed, and things in action, and every right, privilege, interest and asset of any conceivable value or benefit then existing, belonging or pertaining to it, or which would inure to it, shall immediately by act of law and without any conveyance or transfer, and without any further act or deed, be vested in and become the property of the federal association, which shall have, hold and enjoy the same in its own right as fully and to the same extent as the same was possessed, held and enjoyed by the State association; and the federal association as of the effective time of such conversion shall succeed to all the rights, obligations and relations of the State association. (1981, c. 282, s. 3; 1981 (Reg. Sess., 1982), c. 1238, s. 5; 1989, c. 76, s. 6; 1989 (Reg. Sess., 1990), c. 806, s. 1; 2001-193, s. 16.)

§ 54B-31. Conversion from federal to State association.

Any federal savings and loan association, stock or mutual, organized and existing under the laws and regulations of the United States and duly authorized to operate and actually operating in North Carolina may convert into a State savings and loan association operating under the provisions of this Chapter, with the same force and effect as though originally incorporated under the provisions of this Chapter, by complying with the rules and regulations of the federal regulatory authority, and also by following the procedure as set forth in this section:

(1) The federal association shall submit a plan of conversion to the Commissioner of Banks. When such plan, either with or without amendment, has been approved by the Commissioner of Banks, it shall be submitted to the members or stockholders of the association as provided in the next subdivision.

(2) A meeting of the members or stockholders shall be held upon not less than 15 days' notice to each member or stockholder. Notice can be made either by mailing such to each member or stockholder, postage prepaid, to the last known address or by the board of directors causing to be published once a

week for two weeks preceding such meeting, in a newspaper of general circulation published in the county where such association has its principal office, a notice of the meeting. It shall be regarded as sufficient notice of the purpose of the meeting if the call contains the following statement: "The purpose of this meeting is to consider the conversion of this federally chartered association to a State-chartered savings and loan association, pursuant to the provisions of the laws of the State of North Carolina." An appropriate officer of the association shall make proof by affidavit at such meeting of the due service of the notice or call for said meeting.

(3) At the meeting of the members or stockholders of such association, such members or stockholders may by affirmative vote of a majority of votes or shares present, in person or by proxy, resolve to convert said association to a State association. A copy of the minutes of the meeting of the members or stockholders, certified by an appropriate officer of the association, shall be filed with the Commissioner of Banks, accompanied by a conversion fee. The certified copy when so filed shall be prima facie evidence of the holding of and the action taken at the meeting.

(4) Within 30 days after the approval of the proceedings by the Commissioner of Banks, the association shall file with the Commissioner of Banks, the Secretary of State, and the register of deeds of the county where such association intends to operate a copy of the certificate of incorporation of such association, signed by at least seven directors. The certificate of incorporation shall conform to the provisions of the laws of this State. The Secretary of State and the register of deeds of the county where the association has its principal office shall not issue or record the certificate of incorporation until authorized to do so by the Commissioner of Banks. Upon receipt of a copy of the certificate of incorporation the Commissioner of Banks shall cause to be made a careful examination and investigation of the facts connected with the conversion of the association, including an examination of its affairs generally and a determination of its assets and liabilities. The reasonable cost and expenses of the examination and investigation shall be paid by the association. If it appears that the association, if converted, will lawfully be entitled to conduct business as a State association pursuant to the provisions of this Chapter, the Commissioner of Banks shall so certify to the Secretary of State and the register of deeds in the county in which the association is located, who shall thereupon issue and record such certificate of incorporation. Upon issuance and recordation of the certificate of incorporation the association shall file with the appropriate federal regulatory authority a certified copy of same. Upon such

filing, the association shall cease to be a federal association and shall be converted to a State association.

(5) Upon conversion, all the property of the federal association, including all its rights, title and interest in and to all property of whatsoever kind whether real, personal or mixed, and things in action, and every right, privilege, interest and asset of any conceivable value or benefit then existing, belonging or pertaining to it, or which would inure to it, shall immediately by act of law and without any conveyance or transfer, and without any further act or deed, be vested in and become the property of the State association, which shall have, hold, and enjoy the same in its own right as fully and to the same extent as if the same was possessed, held or enjoyed by said federal association; and such State association shall be deemed to be a continuation of the entity and the identity of said federal association, operating under and pursuant to the provisions of this Chapter, and all rights, obligations and relations of said federal association to or in respect to any person, estate, or creditor, depositor, trustee or beneficiary of any trust, and to or in respect to any executorship or trusteeship or other trust or fiduciary function, shall remain unimpaired, and the State association, shall by operation of this section succeed to all such rights, obligations, relations and trusts, and the duties and liabilities connected therewith, and shall execute and perform each and every such right, obligation, trust and relation in the same manner as if such State association had itself assumed the trust or relation, including the obligations and liabilities connected therewith. (1981, c. 282, s. 3; 1981 (Reg. Sess., 1982), c. 1238, s. 6; 1985, c. 659, s. 4; 1989, c. 76, s. 7; 2001-193, s. 16.)

§ 54B-32. Simultaneous charter and ownership conversion.

(a) In the event of a State charter to federal charter conversion, when the form of ownership will also simultaneously be changed from stock to mutual, or from mutual to stock, the conversion shall proceed initially as if it involves only a charter conversion, under G.S. 54B-30. After the association becomes a federal association, then the federal regulatory authority shall govern the continuing conversion of the form of ownership of such newly converted association.

(b) In the event of a federal charter to State charter conversion, when the form of ownership will also simultaneously be changed from stock to mutual or from mutual to stock, the conversion shall proceed initially as if it involves only a charter conversion, under G.S. 54B-31. After the association becomes a State association, the provisions of G.S. 54B-33 or 54B-34 shall govern the continuing conversion of the form of ownership of such newly converted association.

(c)   The provisions of this section shall not apply to any simultaneous charter and ownership conversion accomplished in conjunction with a merger under the provisions of G.S. 54B-39. (1981, c. 282, s. 3; 1981 (Reg. Sess., 1982), c. 1238, s. 9.)

§ 54B-33. Conversion of mutual to stock association.

(a)   Any mutual association may convert from mutual to the stock form of ownership as provided in this section.

(b)   A mutual association may apply to the Commissioner of Banks for permission to convert to a stock association and for certification of appropriate amendments to the association's certificate of incorporation. Upon receipt of an application to convert from mutual to stock form the Commissioner of Banks shall examine all facts connected with the requested conversion. The expenses and cost of such examination, monitoring and supervision shall be paid by the association applying for permission to convert.

(c)   The association shall submit a plan of conversion as a part of the application to the Commissioner of Banks, and he may approve it with or without amendment, if it appears that:

(1)   After conversion the association will be in sound financial condition and will be soundly managed;

(2)   The conversion will not impair the capital of the association nor adversely affect the association's operations;

(3)   The conversion will be fair and equitable to the members of the association and no person whether member, employee or otherwise, will receive any inequitable gain or advantage by reason of the conversion;

(4)   The savings and loan services provided to the public by the association will not be adversely affected by the conversion;

(5) The substance of the plan has been approved by a vote of two thirds of the board of directors of the association;

(6) All shares of stock issued in connection with the conversion are offered first to the members of the association; except that any one or more tax qualified stock benefit plan may first purchase in the aggregate not more than ten percent (10%) of the total offering of shares;

(7) All stock shall be offered to members of the association and others in prescribed amounts and otherwise pursuant to a formula and procedure which is fair and equitable and will be fairly disclosed to all interested persons;

(8) The plan provides a statement as to whether stockholders shall have preemptive rights to acquire additional or treasury shares of the association and any provision limiting or denying said rights; and

(9) The conversion shall not be complete until all stock offered in connection with the conversion has been subscribed.

If the Commissioner of Banks approves the plan, then the plan shall be submitted to the members as provided in subsection (d) of this section. If the Commissioner of Banks refuses to approve the plan, the Commissioner of Banks shall state the objections in writing and give the converting association an opportunity to amend the plan to obviate the objections or to appeal the Commissioner of Banks' decision to the Commission.

(d) After lawful notice to the members of the association and full and fair disclosure, the substance of the plan must be approved by a majority of the total votes which members of the association are eligible and entitled to cast. Such a vote by the members may be in person or by proxy. Following the vote of the members, the results of the vote certified by an appropriate officer of the association shall be filed with the Commissioner of Banks. The Commissioner of Banks shall then either approve or disapprove the requested conversion. After approval of the conversion, the Commissioner of Banks shall supervise and monitor the conversion process and he shall ensure that the conversion is conducted pursuant to law and the association's approved plan of conversion.

(e) Upon conversion of a mutual association to the stock form of ownership, the legal existence of the association shall not terminate but the converted stock association shall be a continuation of the mutual association. The conversion shall be deemed a mere change in identity or form of organization. All rights, liabilities, obligations, interest and relations of whatever kind of the mutual association shall continue and remain in the stock-owned association. All actions and legal proceedings to which the association was a party prior to conversion shall be unaffected by the conversion and proceed as if the conversion had not taken place.

(f) The Commissioner of Banks may promulgate such rules and regulations as may be necessary to govern conversions; provided, however, that such rules and regulations as may be promulgated by the Commissioner of Banks shall be equal to or exceed the requirements for conversion imposed by the rules and regulations governing conversions of federal chartered mutual savings and loan associations.

(g) Repealed by Session Laws 1987, c. 237, s. 3(d). (1981, c. 282, s. 3; 1981 (Reg. Sess., 1982), c. 1238, s. 7; 1983, c. 144, s. 6; 1987, c. 237, s. 3; 1989 (Reg. Sess., 1990), c. 806, s. 2; 1991 (Reg. Sess., 1992), c. 829, s. 3; 2001-193, s. 16.)

§ 54B-34. Conversion of stock associations to mutual associations.

Any stock savings and loan association organized and operating under the provisions of this Chapter may, subject to the approval of the Commission, convert to a mutual savings and loan association under the provisions of this section. The Commissioner of Banks may promulgate rules and regulations governing the conversion of stock associations to mutual associations. Such rules and regulations shall include, but shall not be limited to requirements that:

(1) The conversion neither impair the capital of the converting association nor adversely affect its operations;

(2) The conversion shall be fair and equitable to all stockholders of the converting associations;

(3) The public shall not be adversely affected by the conversion;

(4) Conversion of an association shall be accomplished only pursuant to a plan approved by the Commissioner of Banks. Said plan must have been approved by an affirmative vote of two thirds of the members of the board of directors of the converting association, and only after a full and fair disclosure to

the stockholders, by an affirmative vote [of] a majority of the total votes which stockholders of the association are eligible and entitled to cast;

(5) The plan of conversion provides that:

a. Withdrawable accounts be issued in connection with the conversion to the stockholders of the converting association;

b. A uniform date be fixed for the determination of the stockholders to whom, and the amount to each stockholder of which, withdrawable accounts shall be made available;

c. Withdrawable accounts so made available to stockholders be based upon a fair and equitable formula approved by the Commissioner of Banks and fully and fairly disclosed to the stockholders of the converting association. (1981, c. 282, s. 3; 2001-193, s. 16.)

§ 54B-34.1. Conversion to State association.

(a) A savings bank or State or national bank, upon a majority vote of its board of directors, may apply to the Commissioner of Banks for permission to convert to a State association and for certification of appropriate amendments to its certificate of incorporation to effect the change. Upon receipt of an application to convert to a State association, the Commissioner of Banks shall examine all facts connected with the conversion. The depository institution applying for permission to convert shall pay all the expenses and costs of examination.

(b) The converting depository institution shall submit a plan of conversion as a part of the application to the Commissioner of Banks. The Commissioner of Banks may approve it with or without amendment. If the Commissioner of Banks approves the plan, then the plan shall be submitted to the members or stockholders as provided in subsection (c) of this section. If the Commissioner of Banks refuses to approve the plan, the Commissioner of Banks' objections shall be stated in writing and the converting depository institution shall be given an opportunity to amend its plan to obviate the objections or to appeal the Commissioner of Banks' decision to the Commission.

(c)   After lawful notice to the members or stockholders of the converting depository institution and full and fair disclosure, the substance of the plan shall be approved by a majority of the votes or shares present, in person or by proxy. Following the vote of the members or stockholders, the results of the vote certified by an appropriate officer of the converting depository institution shall be filed with the Commissioner of Banks. The Commissioner of Banks shall then either approve or disapprove the requested conversion to a State association. After approval of the conversion, the Commissioner of Banks shall supervise and monitor the conversion process and shall ensure that the conversion is conducted lawfully and under the approved plan of conversion. (1993, c. 163, s. 5; 2001-193, s. 16.)

§ 54B-34.2. Conversion to bank.

(a)   A savings and loan association, upon a majority vote of its board of directors, may apply to the Commissioner of Banks for permission to convert to a bank, as defined under G.S. 53C-1-4(4), or to a national bank or other form of depository institution and for certification of appropriate amendments to its certificate of incorporation to effect the change. Upon receipt of an application to so convert, the Commissioner of Banks shall examine all facts connected with the conversion including receipt of approval of the converting institution's plan of conversion by other federal or state regulatory agencies having jurisdiction over the institution upon completion of its conversion. The depository institution applying for permission to convert shall pay all the expenses and costs of examination.

(b)   The converting depository institution shall submit a plan of conversion as a part of the application to the Commissioner of Banks. The Commissioner of Banks may approve it with or without amendment. If the Commissioner of Banks approves the plan, then the plan shall be submitted to the members or stockholders as provided in subsection (c) of this section. If the Commissioner of Banks refuses to approve the plan, the Commissioner of Banks' objections shall be stated in writing and the converting depository institution shall be given an opportunity to amend its plan to obviate the objections or to appeal the Commissioner of Banks' decision to the Commission.

(c)   After lawful notice to the members or stockholders of the converting depository institution and full and fair disclosure, the substance of the plan shall be approved by the members or the shareholders at a duly called and properly convened meeting of the members or shareholders. Following the meeting of the members or shareholders, the results of the vote certified by an appropriate officer of the converting depository institution shall be filed with the Commissioner of Banks. The Commissioner of Banks shall then either approve or disapprove the requested conversion to a bank, national bank, or other form of depository institution. After approval of the conversion, the Commissioner of Banks shall supervise and monitor the conversion process and shall ensure that the conversion is conducted lawfully and under the approved plan of conversion. (1993, c. 163, s. 5; 2001-193, s. 16; 2012-56, s. 37.)

§ 54B-35. Merger of like savings and loan associations.

Any two or more mutual associations or any two or more stock associations organized and operating, may merge or consolidate into a single association which may be either one of said merging associations, and the procedure to effect such merger shall be as follows:

(1)   The directors, or a majority of them, of such associations as desire to merge, may, at separate meetings, enter into a written agreement of merger signed by them and under the corporate seals of the respective associations, specifying each association to be merged and the association which is to receive into itself the merging association or associations, and prescribing the terms and conditions of the merger and the mode of carrying it into effect. Such merger agreement must provide the manner and basis of converting or exchanging the withdrawable accounts in the mutual association or associations so merged for withdrawable accounts of the same or a different class of the receiving association, or of converting or exchanging the stock in the stock association or associations so merged into stock or other securities or obligations of the receiving association. The merger agreement may provide for such other provisions with respect to the merger as appear necessary or desirable, or as the Commissioner of Banks may require by regulation to enable him to discharge his duties with respect to such merger.

(2)   Such merger agreement together with copies of the minutes of the meetings of the respective boards of directors verified by the secretaries of the respective associations shall be submitted to the Commissioner of Banks, who shall cause a careful investigation and examination to be made of the affairs of the associations proposing to merge, including a determination of their respective assets and liabilities. The reasonable cost and expenses of such

examination shall be defrayed by each association so investigated and examined. If, as a result of such investigation, he shall conclude that the members or stockholders of each of the associations proposing to merge will be benefited thereby, he shall, in writing, approve same. If he deems that the proposed merger will not be in the interest of all members or stockholders of the associations so merging, he shall, in writing, disapprove the same. If he approves the merger agreement, then same shall be submitted, within 45 days after notice of such associations of such approval, to the members or stockholders of each of such association, as provided in the next subdivision. Such disapproval may be appealed by the association to the Commission.

(3) A special meeting of the members or stockholders of each of the associations shall be held separately upon written notice of not less than 20 days to members or stockholders of each association. The notice shall specify the time, place, and purpose for the calling of the meeting. Notice may be given to members of mutual associations by one or more of the following methods: (i) personal service, (ii) postage prepaid mail to the last address of each member appearing upon the records of the association, or (iii) publication of notice at least once a week for four successive weeks in one or more newspapers published in the county or counties where each association has its principal or a branch office, or in a newspaper published in an adjoining county if none is published in the county. Notice may be given to stockholders by personal service or prepaid mail to the last address of each stockholder appearing upon the records of the association. The Commissioner of Banks may approve notice to stockholders by publication in the same manner as provided to members of mutual associations. The secretary or other officer of the association shall make proof by affidavit at such meeting of the due service of the notice or call for said meeting.

(4) At separate meetings of the members or stockholders of the respective associations, the members or stockholders may adopt, by an affirmative vote of a majority of the votes or shares present, in person or by proxy, a resolution to merge into a single association upon the terms of the merger agreement as shall have been agreed upon by the directors of the respective associations and as approved by the Commissioner of Banks. Upon the adoption of the resolution, a copy of the minutes of the proceedings of the meetings of the members or stockholders of the respective associations, certified by the president or vice-president and secretary or assistant secretary of the merging associations, shall be filed in the office of the Commissioner of Banks. Within 15 days after the receipt of a certified copy of the minutes of such meetings the Commissioner of Banks shall either approve or disapprove the proceedings for

compliance with this section. If the proceedings are approved by him, he shall issue a certificate of his approval of the merger and send it to each of the associations. The certificate shall be filed and recorded in the office of the Secretary of State. When the certificate is so filed, the merger agreement shall take effect according to its terms and shall be binding upon all the members or stockholders of the associations merging, and it shall be deemed to be the act of merger of such constituent savings and loan associations under the laws of this State, and the certificate or certified copy thereof shall be evidence of the agreement and act of merger of the savings and loan associations and the observance and performance of all acts and conditions necessary to have been observed and performed precedent to such merger. Within 60 days after its receipt from the Secretary of State, the certified copy of the certificate shall be filed with the register of deeds of the county or counties in which the respective associations so merged have recorded their original certificates of incorporation. Failure to so file shall only subject the association to a penalty of one hundred dollars ($100.00) to be collected by the Secretary of State. The only fees that shall be collected in connection with the merger of the associations shall be filing and recording fees. If the Commissioner of Banks disapproves the proceedings, he shall mark the certified copies of the meetings in his office as disapproved and notify the associations to that effect. Such disapproval may be appealed by the association to the Commission.

(5) Upon the merger of any association, as above provided, into another:

a. Its corporate existence shall be merged into that of the receiving association; and all and singular its rights, powers, privileges and franchises, and all of its property, including all right, title, interest in and to all property of whatsoever kind, whether real, personal or mixed, and things in action, and every right, privilege, interest or asset of any conceivable value or benefit then existing, belonging or pertaining to it, or which would inure to it under an unmerged existence, shall immediately by act of law and without any conveyance or transfer, and without any further act or deed, be vested in and become the property of such receiving association which shall have, hold and enjoy the same in its own right as fully and to the same extent as if the same were possessed, held or enjoyed by the association or associations so merged; and such receiving association shall absorb fully and completely the association or associations so merged.

b. Its rights, liabilities, obligations and relations to any person shall remain unchanged and the association into which it has been merged shall, by the merger, succeed to all the relations, obligations and liabilities as though it had itself assumed or incurred the same. No obligation or liability of a member, customer or stockholder in an association which is a party to the merger shall be affected by the merger, but obligations and liabilities shall continue as they existed before the merger, unless otherwise provided in the merger agreement.

c.   A pending action or other judicial proceeding to which any association that shall be so merged is a party, shall not be deemed to have abated or to have discontinued by reason of the merger, but may be prosecuted to final judgment, order or decree in the same manner as if the merger had not been made; or the receiving association may be substituted as a party to such action or proceeding, and any judgment, order or decree may be rendered for or against it that might have been rendered for or against such other association if the merger had not occurred.

(6)   Notwithstanding any other provision of this section, the Commissioner of Banks may waive any or all of the foregoing requirements upon finding that such waiver would be in the best interest of the members or stockholders of the merging associations. (1981, c. 282, s. 3; c. 670, s. 1; 1981 (Reg. Sess., 1982), c. 1238, s. 8; 1983, c. 144, s. 13; 1985, c. 659, s. 5; 1989, c. 76, s. 8; 2001-193, s. 16.)

§ 54B-36. Merger of associations where ownership is converted.

(a)   Any two or more State mutual associations organized or operating may merge to form a single State stock association. The procedure to effect such a merger and conversion of ownership shall be as follows:

(1)   The merging associations shall merge (to form a mutual association), as provided under G.S. 54B-35.

(2)   The surviving association shall then convert to a stock association, as provided under G.S. 54B-33.

(b)   Any two or more State stock associations organized or operating may merge to form a single mutual association. The procedure to effect such a merger and conversion of ownership shall be as follows:

(1)   The merging associations shall merge (to form a stock association), as provided under G.S. 54B-35.

(2) The surviving association shall then convert to a mutual association, as provided under G.S. 54B-34.

(b1) Nothing in this section shall be construed to prevent a simultaneous merger-conversion in subsections (a) and (b) of this section.

(c) The Commissioner of Banks may promulgate rules and regulations to facilitate the transition from two or more associations to a single association under a new form of ownership. (1981, c. 282, s. 3; 1985, c. 659, s. 6; 2001-193, s. 16.)

§ 54B-37. Merger of mutual and stock associations.

(a) Any State mutual association and any State stock association, organized or operating, may merge to form a single stock association. The procedure to effect such a merger shall be as follows:

(1) The mutual association involved shall convert separately to a stock association, as provided under G.S. 54B-33.

(2) The two stock associations shall then merge to form a single stock association, as provided in G.S. 54B-35.

(b) Any State mutual association, and any State stock association organized or operating may merge to form a mutual association. The procedure to effect such merger shall be as follows:

(1) The stock association involved shall convert separately to a mutual association, as provided under G.S. 54B-34.

(2) The two mutual associations shall then merge to form a single mutual association, as provided in G.S. 54B-35.

(b1) Nothing in this section shall be construed to prevent a simultaneous conversion-merger in subsections (a) and (b) of this section.

(c) The Commissioner of Banks is hereby empowered to promulgate rules and regulations to facilitate such a merger of mutual with stock associations. (1981, c. 282, s. 3; 1985, c. 659, s. 7; 2001-193, s. 16.)

§ 54B-37.1. Simultaneous conversion/merger.

(a) The Commissioner of Banks shall not approve any application for the conversion of an association from mutual to stock form and its simultaneous (i) merger into a stock-owned savings institution or bank or (ii) acquisition by an operating financial institution holding company except as authorized in subsection (b) of this section. As used in this section, "simultaneous conversion/merger" shall mean a transaction in which the members of a mutual association proposing to convert to stock form are offered the opportunity to purchase (i) stock in the savings institution or bank into which it will be merged or (ii) stock in the holding company by which it will be acquired.

(b) The Commissioner of Banks shall approve a plan of simultaneous conversion/merger only if:

(1) The transaction is proposed to address supervisory concerns of the Commissioner of Banks as to the safety and soundness of the mutual association; or

(2) The mutual association:

a. Operates in a local market area in which long-term trends make reasonable growth, continued profitability, and safe and sound operation appear unlikely;

b. Furnishes evidence concerning its asset size, capital to assets ratio, and other factors, which may include a cost/benefit analysis, satisfactory to the Commissioner of Banks that a simultaneous conversion/merger is more likely than remaining independent, merging with a mutual institution, converting to stock ownership, or other alternatives available to the association, to result in deposit, credit, and other financial services being provided within the local community safely and soundly on a long-term basis; and

c. Furnishes evidence satisfactory to the Commissioner of Banks that no director, officer, or other person associated with the parties to the proposed transaction will receive benefits as a result of the simultaneous conversion/merger which in the aggregate exceed those permitted under federal regulations governing similar transactions.

(c) The Commissioner of Banks may adopt rules to govern simultaneous conversion/mergers, which rules shall contain restrictions or limitations which equal or exceed the limitations or restrictions contained in the rules of federal regulatory agencies governing similar transactions. No plan of a simultaneous conversion/merger shall be approved by the Commissioner of Banks unless it includes notification by first class mail to the members of the association to be acquired explaining the details of the plan including economic benefits or incentives to be received by officers and directors of the association, if any. Shares of stock in the acquiring entity purchased at a discount or otherwise by members of the association as part of the simultaneous conversion/merger shall be without limitation on subsequent sales by such members: provided, however, rules adopted by the Commissioner of Banks may place limitations of the sale of such stock purchased by officers and directors of the association. (1995, c. 479, s. 4; 2001-193, s. 16.)

§ 54B-38. Repealed by Session Laws 1985, c. 659, s. 8.

§ 54B-39. Merger of federal with State associations.

(a) Any two or more associations, when one or more is a State association and one or more is a federal association operating in North Carolina, may merge to form one association under either a State or federal charter.

(b) The Commissioner of Banks shall promulgate rules and regulations to facilitate the merger of federal and State associations. (1981, c. 282, s. 3; 1981 (Reg. Sess., 1982), c. 1238, s. 10; 2001-193, s. 16.)

§ 54B-40. Voluntary dissolution by directors.

A State association may be voluntarily dissolved by a majority vote of the board of directors when substantially all of the assets have been sold for the purpose of terminating the business of the association or as provided in G.S. 55-14-01, and when a certificate of dissolution is recorded in the manner required by this Chapter for the recording of certificates of incorporation. (1981, c. 282, s. 3; 1989 (Reg. Sess., 1990), c. 806, s. 20; 1991, c. 707, s. 2.)

§ 54B-41. Voluntary dissolution by stockholders or members.

At any annual or special meeting called for such purpose, an association may, by an affirmative vote in person or by proxy of at least two thirds of the total number of shares or votes which all members or stockholders of the association are entitled to cast, resolve to dissolve and liquidate the association and adopt a plan of voluntary dissolution. Upon adoption of such resolution and plan of voluntary dissolution, the members or stockholders shall proceed to elect not more than three liquidators who shall post bond as required by the Commissioner of Banks. The liquidators shall have full power to execute the plan; and the procedure thereafter shall be as follows:

(1) A copy of the resolution certified by the president or secretary of the association, together with the minutes of the meeting of members or stockholders, the plan of liquidation, and an itemized statement of the association's assets and liabilities sworn to by a majority of its board of directors, shall be filed with the Commissioner of Banks. The minutes of the meeting of members or stockholders shall be certified by the president or secretary of the association, and shall set forth the notice given and the time of mailing thereof, the vote on the resolution and the total number of shares or votes which all members of the association were entitled to cast thereon, and the names of the liquidators elected.

(2) If the Commissioner of Banks finds that the proceedings are in accordance with the provisions of this Chapter, and that the plan of liquidation is not unfair to any person affected, he shall attach his certificate of approval to the plan and shall forward one copy to the liquidators and one copy to the association's withdrawable account insurance corporation. Once the Commissioner of Banks has approved the resolution and the plan of liquidation it shall thereafter be unlawful for such association to accept any additional withdrawable accounts or additions to withdrawable accounts or make any additional loans, but all its income and receipts in excess of actual expenses of liquidation of the association shall be applied to the discharge of its liabilities.

(3) The liquidator or liquidators so appointed shall be paid a reasonable compensation by the liquidating association subject to the approval of the Commissioner of Banks.

(4) The plan shall become effective upon the recording of the Commissioner of Banks' certificate of approval in the manner required by this Chapter for the recording of the certificate of incorporation.

(5) The liquidation of the association shall be subject to the supervision and examination of the Commissioner of Banks. (1981, c. 282, s. 3; 2001-193, s. 16.)

§ 54B-42. Rules, regulations and reports of voluntary dissolution.

(a) The Commissioner of Banks shall promulgate rules and regulations governing the dissolution and liquidation of State associations. These rules and regulations shall include, but not be limited to, provisions with respect to:

(1) The protection and liquidation of assets;

(2) The plan of liquidation;

(3) Notice to file claims;

(4) Claims of members;

(5) Payments of claims and distribution; and

(6) Final distribution and liquidation.

(b) Upon completion of liquidation, the liquidators shall file with the Commissioner of Banks a final report and accounting of the liquidation. The approval of the report by the Commissioner of Banks shall operate as a complete and final discharge of the liquidators, the board of directors, and each member or stockholder in connection with the liquidation of such association. Upon approval of the report, the Commissioner of Banks shall issue a certificate of dissolution of the association and shall record same in the manner required by this Chapter for the recording of certificates of incorporation; and upon such recording, the dissolution shall be effective. (1981, c. 282, s. 3; 2001-193, s. 16.)

§ 54B-43. Stock dividends.

No dividend on stock shall be paid unless the association has the prior written approval of the Commissioner of Banks. (1981, c. 282, s. 3; 1983, c. 144, s. 7; 1989, c. 76, s. 9; 2001-193, s. 16.)

§ 54B-44. Supervisory mergers, consolidations, conversions, and combination mergers and conversions.

(a) Notwithstanding any other provision of this Chapter, in order to protect the public, including members, depositors and stockholders of a State association, the Commissioner of Banks, upon making a finding that a State association is unable to operate in a safe and sound manner, may authorize or require a short form merger, consolidation, conversion, or combination merger and conversion of the State association, or any other transaction, as to which the finding is made.

(b) The Commissioner of Banks shall promulgate rules and regulations to govern supervisory mergers, consolidations, conversions, and combination mergers and conversions authorized by this section. (1981, c. 670, s. 2; 1981 (Reg. Sess., 1982), c. 1238, s. 11; 1985, c. 659, s. 18; 1985 (Reg. Sess., 1986), c. 948, s. 2; 2001-193, s. 16.)

§ 54B-45. Interim associations.

(a) Article 2 of this Chapter shall not apply to applications for permission to organize an interim State association so long as the application is approved by the Commissioner of Banks.

(b) Preliminary approval of an application for permission to organize an interim State association shall be conditional upon the Commissioner of Banks' approval of an application to merge the interim association and an existing stock association or on the Commissioner of Banks' approval of any other transaction.

(c)   The Commissioner of Banks shall promulgate rules and regulations to govern the formation of interim associations authorized by this section. (1985, c. 659, s. 9(b); 2001-193, s. 16.)

§ 54B-46. Conversion of bank to stock association.

(a)   Any bank, as defined in G.S. 53C-1-4(4), may convert to a stock association as provided in this section.

(b)   Any bank, upon a majority vote of its board of directors, may apply to the Commissioner of Banks for permission to convert to a stock association and for certification of appropriate amendments to the bank's certificate of incorporation to effect the conversion.

(c)   The bank shall submit a plan of conversion as a part of the application to the Commissioner of Banks. The Commissioner of Banks may recommend approval of the plan of conversion with or without amendment. The Commissioner of Banks shall recommend approval of the plan of conversion if upon examination and investigation he finds that:

(1)   The resulting stock association will operate in a safe, sound, and prudent manner with adequate capital, liquidity, and earnings prospects;

(2)   The directors, officers, and other managerial officials of the bank are qualified by character and financial responsibility to control and operate in a legal and proper manner the stock association proposed to be formed as a result of the conversion;

(3)   The interest of the depositors, the creditors, and the public generally will not be jeopardized by the proposed conversion; and

(4)   The proposed name will not mislead the public as to the character or purpose of the resulting stock association, and the proposed name is not the same as one already adopted or appropriated by an existing association in this State or so similar as to be likely to mislead the public.

(d)   Any action taken by the Commissioner of Banks pursuant to this section shall be subject to review by the Commission which may approve, modify, or disapprove any action taken or recommended by the Commissioner of Banks.

The Commission may promulgate rules to govern conversions undertaken pursuant to this section. The requirements for a converting bank shall be no more stringent than those provided by rule or regulation applicable to other FDIC-insured stock associations. The requirements for a converting bank shall be no less stringent than those provided by rule or regulation applicable to other FDIC-insured stock associations, except as may be allowed during transition periods permitted by subdivisions (e)(4) and (h)(2) of this section.

(e)   In the absence of the promulgation of rules under subsection (d), the conditions to be met for approval of the application for conversion should include the following:

(1)   Condition. The applicant's general condition must reflect adequate capital, liquidity, reserves, earnings, and asset composition necessary for safe and sound operation of the resulting stock association.

(2)   Management. The management and the board of directors must be capable of supervising a sound stock association operation and overseeing the changes that must be accomplished in the conversion from a bank to a stock association.

(3)   Public Convenience. The Commission must determine that the conversion will have a positive impact on the convenience of the public and will not substantially reduce the services available to the public in the market area.

(4)   Transition. Within a reasonable time after the effective date of the conversion, the resulting stock association must divest itself of all assets and liabilities that do not conform to State banking law or rules. The length of this transition period shall be determined by the Commissioner of Banks and shall be specified when the application for conversion is approved.

In evaluating each of these conditions, the Commission shall consider a comparison of the relevant financial ratios of the applicant with the average ratios of North Carolina stock associations of similar asset size. The Commission may not approve a conversion where the applicant presents an undue supervisory concern or has not been operated in a safe and sound manner.

(f)   If the Commissioner of Banks approves the plan of conversion, then the bank shall submit the plan to the stockholders as provided in subsection (g). After approval of the plan of conversion, the Commissioner of Banks shall supervise and monitor the conversion process and shall ensure that the conversion is conducted pursuant to law and the bank's approved plan of conversion.

(g)   After lawful notice to the stockholders of the bank and full and fair disclosure of the plan of conversion, the plan must be approved by a majority of the total votes that stockholders of the bank are eligible and entitled to cast. The vote by the stockholders may be in person or by proxy. Following the vote of the stockholders, the bank shall file with the Commissioner of Banks the results of the vote certified by an appropriate officer of the bank. The Commissioner of Banks shall approve the requested conversion and the bank shall file with the Secretary of State amended articles of incorporation with the certificate of the Commissioner of Banks attached. The conversion of the bank to a stock association shall be effective upon this filing.

(h)   The Commissioner of Banks may authorize the resulting stock association to do the following:

(1)   Wind up any activities legally engaged in by the bank at the time of conversion but not permitted to stock associations.

(2)   Retain for a transitional period any assets and deposit liabilities legally held by the bank at the effective date of the conversion that may not be held by stock associations.

The length, terms, and conditions of the transitional periods under subdivisions (1) and (2) are subject to the discretion of the Commissioner of Banks, but may not exceed five years after the effective date of the conversion.

(i)   Upon conversion of a bank to a stock association, the legal existence of the bank does not terminate, and the resulting stock association is a continuation of the bank. The conversion shall be a mere change in identity or form of organization. All rights, liabilities, obligations, interest, and relations of whatever kind of the bank shall continue and remain in the resulting stock association. Except as may be authorized during a transitional period by the Commissioner of Banks pursuant to subsection (h), a stock association resulting from the conversion of a bank shall have only those rights, powers, and duties which are authorized for stock associations by the laws of this State and the United States. All actions and legal proceedings to which the bank was a party prior to conversion shall be unaffected by the conversion and proceed as if the conversion had not taken place. (1989 (Reg. Sess., 1990), c. 845, s. 2; 2001-193, s. 16; 2012-56, s. 38.)

§ 54B-47. Merger of banks and associations.

(a)   Any State association, upon a majority vote of its board of directors, may apply to the Commissioner of Banks for permission to merge with any bank, as defined in G.S. 53C-1-4(4).

(b)   The State association shall submit a plan of merger as a part of the application to the Commissioner of Banks. The Commissioner of Banks may recommend approval of the plan of merger with or without amendment.

If he approves the plan, then the plan shall be submitted to the stockholders or members as provided in the next subsection. If he refuses to approve the plan, he shall state his objections in writing and give the merging association an opportunity to amend the plan to obviate such objections or to appeal his decision to the commission.

(c)   After lawful notice to the stockholders or members of the association and full and fair disclosure, the substance of the plan must be approved by a majority of the total votes which stockholders or members of the association are eligible and entitled to cast. Such a vote by the stockholders or members may be in person or by proxy. Following the vote of the stockholders or members, the results of the vote certified by an appropriate officer of the association shall be filed with the Commissioner of Banks. The Commissioner of Banks shall then either approve or disapprove the requested merger.

(d)   The Commissioner of Banks may promulgate such rules and regulations as may be necessary to govern such mergers. (1991, c. 707, s. 7; 2001-193, s. 16; 2012-56, s. 39.)

§ 54B-48: Reserved for future codification purposes.

Article 3A.

North Carolina Regional Reciprocal Savings and Loan Acquisition Act.

§ 54B-48.1. Title.

This Article shall be known and may be cited as the North Carolina Regional Reciprocal Savings and Loan Acquisition Act. (1983 (Reg. Sess., 1984), c. 1087, s. 1.)

§ 54B-48.2. Definitions.

Notwithstanding the provisions of G.S. 54B-4, as used in this Article, unless the context requires otherwise:

(1) "Acquire", as applied to an association or a savings and loan holding company, means any of the following actions or transactions:

a. The merger or consolidation of an association with another association or savings and loan holding company or a savings and loan holding company with another savings and loan holding company.

b. The acquisition of the direct or indirect ownership or control of voting shares of an association or savings and loan holding company if, after the acquisition, the acquiring association or savings and loan holding company will directly or indirectly own or control more than five percent (5%) of any class of voting shares of the acquired association or savings and loan holding company.

c. The direct or indirect acquisition of all or substantially all of the assets of an association or savings and loan holding company.

d. The taking of any other action that would result in the direct or indirect control of an association or savings and loan holding company.

(2) "Commissioner of Banks" means the Commissioner of Banks.

(3) "Association" means a mutual or capital stock savings and loan association, building and loan association or savings bank chartered under the laws of any one of the states or under the laws of the United States.

(4) "Branch office" means any office at which an association accepts deposits. The term branch office does not include:

a. Unmanned automatic teller machines, point-of-sale terminals, or similar unmanned electronic banking facilities at which deposits may be accepted;

b. Offices located outside the United States; and

c. Loan production offices, representative offices, service corporation offices, or other offices at which deposits are not accepted.

(5) "Company" means that which is set forth in the Federal Savings and Loan Holding Company Act, 12 U.S.C. Section 1730a(a)(1)(C), as amended.

(6) "Control" means that which is set forth in the Federal Savings and Loan Holding Company Act, 12 U.S.C. Section 1730a(a)(2), as amended.

(7) "Deposits" means all demand, time, and savings deposits, without regard to the location of the depositor: Provided, however, that "deposits" shall not include any deposits by associations. For purposes of this Article, determination of deposits shall be made with reference to regulatory reports of condition or similar reports made by or to State and federal regulatory authorities.

(8) "Federal association" means an association chartered under the laws of the United States.

(9) "North Carolina association" means an association organized under the laws of the State of North Carolina or under the laws of the United States and that:

a. Has its principal place of business in the State of North Carolina;

b. Which if controlled by an organization, the organization is either a North Carolina association, Southern Region association, North Carolina savings and loan holding company, or a Southern Region savings and loan holding company; and

c. More than eighty percent (80%) of its total deposits, other than deposits located in branch offices acquired pursuant to Section 123 of the Garn-St. Germain Depository Institutions Act of 1982 (12 U.S.C. 1730a(m)) or comparable state law, are in its branch offices located in one or more of the Southern Region states.

(10) "North Carolina Savings and Loan Holding Company" means a savings and loan holding company that:

a. Has its principal place of business in the State of North Carolina;

b. Has total deposits of its Southern Region association subsidiaries and North Carolina association subsidiaries that exceed eighty percent (80%) of the total deposits of all association subsidiaries of the savings and loan holding company other than those association subsidiaries held pursuant to Section 123 of the Garn-St. Germain Depository Institutions Act of 1982 (12 U.S.C. 1730a(m)) or comparable state law.

(11) "Principal place of business" of an association means the state in which the aggregate deposits of the association are the largest. For the purposes of this Article, the principal place of business of a savings and loan holding company is the state where the aggregate deposits of the association subsidiaries of the holding company are the largest.

(12) "Savings and loan holding company" means any company which directly or indirectly controls an association or controls any other company which is a savings and loan holding company.

(13) "Service Corporation" means any corporation, the majority of the capital stock of which is owned by one or more associations and which engages, directly or indirectly, in any activities which may be engaged in by a service corporation in which an association may invest under the laws of one of the states or under the laws of the United States.

(14) "Southern Region association" means an association other than a North Carolina association organized under the laws of one of the Southern Region states or under the laws of the United States and that:

a. Has its principal place of business only in a Southern Region state other than North Carolina;

b. Which if controlled by an organization, the organization is either a Southern Region association or a Southern Region savings and loan holding company; and

c. More than eighty percent (80%) of its total deposits, other than deposits located in branch offices acquired pursuant to Section 123 of the Garn-St. Germain Depository Institutions Act of 1982 (12 U.S.C. 1730a(m)) or comparable state law, are in its branch offices located in one or more of the Southern Region states.

(15) "Southern Region savings and loan holding company" means a savings and loan holding company that:

a. Has its principal place of business in a Southern Region state other than the State of North Carolina;

b. Has total deposits of its Southern Region association subsidiaries and North Carolina association subsidiaries that exceed eighty percent (80%) of the total deposits of all association subsidiaries of the savings and loan holding company other than those association subsidiaries held pursuant to Section 123 of the Garn-St. Germain Depository Institutions Act of 1982 (12 U.S.C. 1730a(m)) or comparable state law.

(16) "Southern Region states" means the states of Alabama, Arkansas, Florida, Georgia, Kentucky, Louisiana, Maryland, Mississippi, North Carolina, South Carolina, Tennessee, Virginia, West Virginia, and the District of Columbia.

(17) "State" means any state of the United States and the District of Columbia.

(18) "State association" means an association organized under the laws of one of the states.

(19) "Subsidiary" means that which is set forth in the Federal Savings and Loan Holding Company Act, 12 U.S.C. Section 1730a(a)(1)(H), as amended. (1983 (Reg. Sess., 1984), c. 1087, s. 1; 1989, c. 76, s. 15; 1989 (Reg. Sess., 1990), c. 806, s. 3; 2001-193, s. 16.)

§ 54B-48.3. Acquisitions by Southern Region savings and loan holding companies and Southern Region associations.

(a) A Southern Region savings and loan holding company or a Southern Region association that does not have a North Carolina association subsidiary (other than a North Carolina association subsidiary that was acquired either pursuant to Section 123 of the Garn-St. Germain Depository Institutions Act of 1982 (12 U.S.C. 1730a(m)), or comparable provisions in state law, or in the regular course of securing or collecting a debt previously contracted in good faith) may acquire a North Carolina savings and loan holding company or a North Carolina association with the approval of the Commissioner of Banks. The Southern Region savings and loan holding company or Southern Region association shall submit to the Commissioner of Banks an application for approval of such acquisition, which application shall be approved only if:

(1) The Commissioner of Banks determines that the laws of the state in which the Southern Region savings and loan holding company or Southern Region association making the acquisition has its principal place of business permit North Carolina savings and loan holding companies and North Carolina associations to acquire associations and savings and loan holding companies in that state;

(2) The Commissioner of Banks determines that the laws of the state in which the Southern Region savings and loan holding company or Southern Region association making the acquisition has its principal place of business permit such Southern Region savings and loan holding company or Southern Region association to be acquired by the North Carolina savings and loan holding company or North Carolina association sought to be acquired;

(3) The Commissioner of Banks determines either that the North Carolina association sought to be acquired has been in existence and continuously operating for more than five years or that all of the association subsidiaries of the North Carolina savings and loan holding company sought to be acquired have been in existence and continuously operating for more than five years: Provided, that the Commissioner of Banks may approve the acquisition by a Southern Region savings and loan holding company or Southern Region association of all or substantially all of the shares of an association organized solely for the purpose of facilitating the acquisition of an association that has been in existence and continuously operating as an association for more than five years; and

(4)   The Commissioner of Banks makes the acquisition subject to any conditions, restrictions, requirements or other limitations that would apply to the acquisition by a North Carolina savings and loan holding company or North Carolina association of an association or savings and loan holding company in the state where the Southern Region savings and loan holding company or Southern Region association making the acquisition has its principal place of business but that would not apply to the acquisition of an association or savings and loan holding company in such state by an association or a savings and loan holding company all the association subsidiaries of which are located in that state;

(5)   With respect to acquisitions involving the merger or consolidation of two associations resulting in a Southern Region association, the application includes a business plan extending for an initial period of at least three years from the date of the acquisition which shall be renewed thereafter for as long as may be required by the Commissioner of Banks. The association may not deviate without the prior written approval of the Commissioner of Banks from the business plan which shall address such matters as the Commissioner of Banks may deem appropriate for the protection of the depositors and members of the acquired North Carolina association and the general public. The business plan shall address, without limitation:

a.   Insurance of depositors' accounts.

b.   Limitation of services and activities to those permitted under this Chapter to North Carolina associations.

c.   Conversion of corporate form or other fundamental changes.

d.   Closing, selling or divesting any or all North Carolina branches.

e.   Protection of the voting rights of North Carolina members.

(b)   A Southern Region savings and loan holding company or Southern Region association that has a North Carolina association subsidiary (other than a North Carolina association subsidiary that was acquired either pursuant to Section 123 of the Garn-St. Germain Depository Institutions Act of 1982 (12 U.S.C. 1730a(m)), or comparable provisions in North Carolina law, or in the regular course of securing or collecting a debt previously contracted in good faith) may acquire any North Carolina association or North Carolina savings and loan holding company with the approval of the Commissioner of Banks. The Southern Region savings and loan holding company shall submit to the Commissioner of Banks an application for approval of such acquisition, which application shall be approved only if:

(1) The Commissioner of Banks determines either that the North Carolina association sought to be acquired has been in existence and continuously operating for more than five years or that all of the association subsidiaries of the North Carolina savings and loan holding company sought to be acquired have been in existence and continuously operating for more than five years: Provided, that the Commissioner of Banks may approve the acquisition by a Southern Region savings and loan holding company or Southern Region association of all or substantially all of the shares of an association organized solely for the purpose of facilitating the acquisition of an association that has been in existence and continuously operating as an association for more than five years; and

(2) The Commissioner of Banks makes the acquisition subject to any conditions, restrictions, requirements or other limitations that would apply to the acquisition by the North Carolina savings and loan holding company or North Carolina association of an association or savings and loan holding company in the State where the Southern Region savings and loan holding company or Southern Region association making the acquisition has its principal place of business but that would not apply to the acquisition of an association or savings and loan holding company in such state by a savings and loan holding company all the association subsidiaries of which are located in that state.

(3) With respect to acquisitions involving the merger or consolidation of two associations resulting in a Southern Region association, the application includes a business plan extending for an initial period of at least three years from the date of the acquisition which shall be renewed thereafter for as long as may be required by the Commissioner of Banks. The association may not deviate without the prior written approval of the Commissioner of Banks from the business plan which shall address such matters as the Commissioner of Banks may deem appropriate for the protection of the depositors and members of the acquired North Carolina association and the general public. The business plan shall address, without limitation:

a. Insurance of depositors' accounts.

b. Limitation of services and activities to those permitted under this Chapter to North Carolina associations.

c. Conversion of corporate form or other fundamental changes.

d. Closing, selling or divesting any or all North Carolina branches.

e. Protection of the voting rights of North Carolina members.

(b1) A North Carolina savings and loan holding company or a North Carolina association may acquire any Southern Region association or Southern Region savings and loan holding company with the approval of the Commissioner of Banks. The North Carolina savings and loan holding company or North Carolina association shall submit to the Commissioner of Banks an application for approval of the acquisition, which application shall be approved only if the application includes a business plan extending for an initial period of at least three years from the date of the acquisition which shall be renewed thereafter for as long as may be required by the Commissioner of Banks. The association may not deviate without the prior written approval of the Commissioner of Banks from the business plan which shall address such matters as the Commissioner of Banks may deem appropriate for the protection of the depositors and members of the North Carolina association and the general public. The business plan shall address, without limitation:

(1) Insurance of depositors' accounts.

(2) Conversion of corporate form or other fundamental changes.

(3) Closing, selling, or divesting any or all North Carolina branches.

(c) The Commissioner of Banks shall rule on any application submitted under this section not later than 90 days following the date of submission of a complete application. If the Commissioner of Banks fails to rule on the application within the requisite 90-day period, the failure to rule shall be deemed a final decision of the Commissioner of Banks approving the application. (1983 (Reg. Sess., 1984), c. 1087, s. 1; 1989 (Reg. Sess., 1990), c. 806, s. 4; 2001-193, s. 16.)

§ 54B-48.4. Exceptions.

A North Carolina savings and loan holding company, a North Carolina association, a Southern Region savings and loan holding company, or a Southern Region association may acquire or control, and shall not cease to be a North Carolina savings and loan holding company, a North Carolina association, a Southern Region savings and loan holding company, or a Southern Region association, as the case may be, by virtue of its acquisition or control of:

(1) An association having branch offices in a state not within the region, if such association has been acquired pursuant to the provisions of Section 123 of the Garn-St. Germain Depository Institutions Act of 1982 (12 U.S.C. 1730a(m)), or comparable provisions of state law;

(2) An association which is not a Southern Region association if such association has been acquired in the regular course of securing or collecting a debt previously contracted in good faith, and if the association or savings and loan holding company divests the securities or assets acquired within two years of the date of acquisition. A North Carolina association, a North Carolina savings and loan holding company, or a Southern Region association may retain these interests for up to three additional periods of one year if the Commissioner of Banks determines that the required divestiture would create undue financial difficulties for that association or savings and loan holding company. (1983 (Reg. Sess., 1984), c. 1087, s. 1; 2001-193, s. 16.)

§ 54B-48.5. Prohibitions.

(a) Except as may be expressly permitted by federal law, no savings and loan holding company that is not either a North Carolina savings and loan holding company or a Southern Region savings and loan holding company shall acquire a North Carolina savings and loan holding company or a North Carolina association.

(b) Except as required by federal law, a North Carolina savings and loan holding company or a Southern Region savings and loan holding company that ceases to be a North Carolina savings and loan holding company or a Southern Region savings and loan holding company shall as soon as practicable and, in all events, within one year after such event divest itself of control of all North Carolina savings and loan holding companies and all North Carolina associations: Provided, however, that such divestiture shall not be required if the North Carolina savings and loan holding company or the Southern Region savings and loan holding company ceases to be a North Carolina savings and loan holding company or a Southern Region savings and loan holding company, as the case may be, because of an increase in the deposits held by association subsidiaries not located within the region and if such increase is not the result of the acquisition of an association or savings and loan holding company. Provided further that nothing in this Article shall be construed to permit interstate branching by associations nor to require the divestiture of a North Carolina association or a North Carolina savings and loan holding company by a savings and loan holding company which acquired its subsidiary North Carolina association or North Carolina savings and loan holding company prior to the effective date of this Article. Nor shall anything in this Article be construed to prohibit any savings and loan holding company which has acquired a North Carolina association or North Carolina savings and loan holding company prior to the effective date of this Article from acquiring additional North Carolina associations or North Carolina savings and loan holding companies. Nor shall anything in this Article be construed to limit the authority of the Commissioner of Banks pursuant to G.S. 54B-44. (1983 (Reg. Sess., 1984), c. 1087, s. 1; 2001-193, s. 16.)

§ 54B-48.6. Applicable laws, rules and regulations.

(a) Any North Carolina association that is controlled by a savings and loan holding company that is not a North Carolina savings and loan holding company shall be subject to all laws of this State and all rules and regulations under such laws that are applicable to North Carolina associations that are controlled by North Carolina savings and loan holding companies.

(b) The Commissioner of Banks may promulgate rules, including the imposition of a reasonable application and administration fee, to implement and effectuate the provisions of this Article. (1983 (Reg. Sess., 1984), c. 1087, s. 1; 2001-193, s. 16.)

§ 54B-48.7. Appeal of Commissioner of Banks' decision.

Notwithstanding any other provision of law, any aggrieved party in a proceeding under G.S. 54B-48.3 or G.S. 54B-48.4(2) may, within 30 days after final decision of the Commissioner of Banks and by written notice to the Commissioner of Banks, appeal directly to the North Carolina Court of Appeals for judicial review on the record. In the event of an appeal, the Commissioner of Banks shall certify the record to the Clerk of the Court of Appeals within 30 days after filing of the appeal. (1983 (Reg. Sess., 1984), c. 1087, s. 1; 2001-193, s. 16.)

§ 54B-48.8. Periodic reports; interstate agreements.

(a) The Commissioner of Banks may from time to time require reports under oath in such scope and detail as he may reasonably determine of each Southern Region savings and loan holding company or Southern Region association subject to this Article for the purpose of assuring continuing compliance with the provisions of this Article.

(b) The Commissioner of Banks may enter into cooperative agreements with other savings and loan regulatory authorities for the periodic examination of any Southern Region savings and loan holding company or Southern Region association that has a North Carolina association subsidiary and may accept reports of examination and other records from such authorities in lieu of conducting its own examinations. The Commissioner of Banks may enter into joint actions with other savings and loan regulatory authorities having concurrent jurisdiction over any Southern Region savings and loan holding company or Southern Region association that has a North Carolina association subsidiary or may take such actions independently to carry out his responsibilities under this Chapter and assure compliance with the provisions of this Article and the applicable laws of this State. (1983 (Reg. Sess., 1984), c. 1087, s. 1; 2001-193, s. 16.)

§ 54B-48.9. Enforcement.

The Commissioner of Banks shall have the power to enforce the provisions of this Article, including the divestiture requirement of G.S. 54B-48.5(b), through an action in any court of this State or any other state or in any court of the United States for the purpose of obtaining an appropriate remedy for violation of any provision of this Article, including such criminal penalties as are contemplated by G.S. 54B-66. (1983 (Reg. Sess., 1984), c. 1087, s. 1; 2001-193, s. 16.)

§§ 54B-49 through 54B-51. Reserved for future codification purposes.

Article 4.

Supervision and Regulation.

§ 54B-52. Commissioner of Banks.

The Commissioner of Banks of the State is hereby empowered and directed to perform all the duties and exercise all the powers as to savings and loan associations organized or operated under this Chapter, unless herein otherwise provided. (1981, c. 282, s. 3; 1989, c. 76, s. 16; 2001-193, s. 16.)

§ 54B-53: Repealed by Session Laws 2001-193, s. 3.

§ 54B-54. Deputy commissioner of Savings Institutions Division.

There shall be a deputy commissioner of the Savings Institutions Division as appointed by the Commissioner in G.S. 53C-2-2. The deputy commissioner authorized by this section shall perform any duties and exercise any powers directed by the Commissioner. (1981, c. 282, s. 3; 1989, c. 76, s. 18; 2001-193, s. 5; 2012-56, s. 40.)

§ 54B-55. Power of Commissioner of Banks to promulgate rules and regulations; reproduction of records.

(a)   The Commissioner of Banks shall have the right, and is empowered, to promulgate rules, instructions and regulations as may be necessary to the discharge of his duties and powers as to savings and loan associations for the supervision and regulation of said associations, and for the protection of the public investing in said savings and loan associations.

(b) Without limiting the generality of the foregoing paragraph, rules, instructions, and regulations may be promulgated with respect to:

(1) Reserve requirements;

(2) Stock ownership and dividends;

(3) Stock transfers;

(4) Incorporators, stockholders, directors, officers and employees of an association;

(5) Bylaws;

(6) Repealed by Session Laws 2001-193, s. 3.

(7) The structure of the office of the Commissioner of Banks;

(8) The operation of associations;

(9) Withdrawable accounts, bonus plans, and contracts for savings programs;

(10) Loans and loan expenses;

(11) Investments;

(12) Forms and definitions;

(13) Types of financial records to be maintained by associations;

(14) Retention periods of various financial records;

(15) Internal control procedures of associations;

(16) Conduct and management of associations;

(17) Chartering and branching;

(18) Liquidations;

(19) Mergers;

(20) Conversions;

(21) Reports which may be required by the Commissioner of Banks;

(22) Conflicts of interest;

(23) Collection of State savings and loan taxes;

(24) Service corporations; and

(25) Savings and loan holding companies.

(c) Repealed by Session Laws 1983, c. 144, s. 14.

(d) Any association may cause any or all records by it to be recorded, copied or reproduced by any photographic, photostatic or miniature photographic process which correctly, accurately, permanently copies, reproduces or forms a medium for copying or reproducing the original record on a film or other durable material.

(e) Any such photographic, photostatic or miniature photographic copy or reproduction shall be deemed to be an original record in all courts and administrative agencies for the purpose of its admissibility in evidence. A facsimile, exemplification or certified copy of any such photographic copy or reproduction shall, for all purposes, be deemed a facsimile, exemplification or certified copy of the original record.

(f) The provisions of this section with reference to the retention and disposition of records shall apply to any federal savings and loan association operating in North Carolina unless in conflict with regulations prescribed by its supervisory authority. (1981, c. 282, s. 3; 1983, c. 144, s. 14; 1989, c. 76, s. 19; 2001-193, ss. 3, 16.)

§ 54B-56. Examinations by Commissioner of Banks; report.

(a) If at any time the Commissioner of Banks deems it prudent, it shall be his duty to examine and investigate everything relating to the business of a State association or a savings and loan holding company, and to appoint a suitable and competent person to make such investigation, who shall file with the Commissioner of Banks a full report of his finding in such case, including in his report any violation of law or any unauthorized or unsafe practices of the association disclosed by his examination.

(b) The Commissioner of Banks shall furnish a copy of the report to the association examined and may, upon request, furnish a copy of or excerpts from the report to the appropriate federal regulatory authorities.

(c) No association may willfully delay or willfully obstruct an examination in any fashion. Any person failing to comply with this subsection shall be guilty of a Class 1 misdemeanor.

(d) No person having in his possession or control any books, accounts or papers of any State association shall refuse to exhibit same to the Commissioner of Banks or his agents on demand, or shall knowingly or willingly make any false statement in regard to the same. Any person failing to comply with this subsection shall be guilty of a Class 1 misdemeanor. (1981, c. 282, s. 3; 1989 (Reg. Sess., 1990), c. 806, s. 5; 1993, c. 539, ss. 431, 432; 1994, Ex. Sess., c. 24, s. 14(c); 2001-193, s. 16.)

§ 54B-57. Supervision and examination fees.

(a) Every State association, including associations in process of voluntary liquidation or savings and loan holding company, shall pay into the office of the Commissioner of Banks each July a supervisory fee. Examination fees shall be paid promptly upon an association's receipt of the examination billing. The Commissioner of Banks, subject to the advice and consent of the Commission, shall, on or before June 1 of each year:

(1) Determine and fix the scale of supervisory and examination fees to be assessed and collected during the next fiscal year;

(2) Determine and fix the amount of the fee and set the fee collection schedule for the fees to be assessed to and collected from applicants to defray

the cost of processing their charter, branch, merger, conversion, location change, savings and loan holding company acquisition, and name change applications.

(b)   All funds and revenue collected by the Division under the provisions of this section and the provisions of all other sections of this Chapter which authorize the collection of fees and other funds shall be deposited with the State Treasurer of North Carolina and expended under the terms of the Executive Budget Act, solely to defray expenses incurred by the office of the Commissioner of Banks in carrying out its supervisory and auditing functions.

(c)   Notwithstanding any of the provisions of subsections (a) and (b) of this section, whenever the Commissioner of Banks under the provisions of G.S. 54B-56 appoints a suitable and competent person, other than a person employed by the Commissioner of Banks' office, to make an examination and investigation of the business of a State association, all costs and expenses relative to such examination and investigation shall be paid by such association. (1981, c. 282, s. 3; 1983, c. 144, s. 15; 1985, c. 659, s. 10; 2001-193, s. 16.)

§ 54B-58. Prolonged audit, examination or revaluation; payment of costs.

(a)   If, in the opinion of the Commissioner of Banks, an examination conducted under the provisions of G.S. 54B-57 fails to disclose the complete financial condition of an association, he may in order to ascertain its complete financial condition:

(1)   Make an extended audit or examination of the association or cause such an audit or examination to be made by an independent auditor;

(2)   Make an extended revaluation of any of the assets or liabilities of the association or cause an independent appraiser to make such revaluation.

(b)   The Commissioner of Banks shall collect from the association a reasonable sum for actual or necessary expenses of such an audit, examination or revaluation. (1981, c. 282, s. 3; 2001-193, s. 16.)

§ 54B-59. Cease and desist orders.

(a) If any person or association is engaging in, or has engaged in, any unsafe or unsound practice or unfair and discriminatory practice in conducting the association's business, or of any other law, rule, regulation, order or condition imposed in writing by the Commissioner of Banks, the Commissioner of Banks may issue a notice of charges to such person or association. A notice of charges shall specify the acts alleged to sustain a cease and desist order, and state the time and place at which a hearing shall be held. A hearing before the Commission on the charges shall be held no earlier than seven days, and no later than 14 days after issuance of the notice. The charged institution is entitled to a further extension of seven days upon filing a request with the Commissioner of Banks. The Commissioner of Banks may also issue a notice of charges if he has reasonable grounds to believe that any person or association is about to engage in any unsafe or unsound business practice, or any violation of this Chapter, or any other law, rule, regulation or order. If, by a preponderance of the evidence, it is shown that any person or association is engaged in, or has been engaged in, or is about to engage in, any unsafe or unsound business practice, or unfair and discriminatory practice or any violation of this Chapter, or any other law, rule, regulation, or order, a cease and desist order shall be issued. The Commission may issue a temporary cease and desist order to be effective for 14 days and may be extended once for a period of 14 days.

(b) If any person or State association is engaging in, has engaged in, or is about to engage in any unsafe or unsound practice in conducting the association's business, or any violation of this Chapter or of any other law, rules, regulation, order, or condition imposed in writing by the Commissioner of Banks, and the Commissioner of Banks has determined that immediate corrective action is required, the Commissioner of Banks may issue a temporary cease and desist order. A temporary cease and desist order shall be effective immediately upon issuance for a period of 14 days, and may be extended once for a period of 14 days. Such an order shall state its duration on its face and the words, "Temporary Cease and Desist Order." A hearing before the Commission shall be held within such time as such an order remains effective, at which time a temporary order may be dissolved or made permanent. (1981, c. 282, s. 3; 2001-193, s. 16.)

§ 54B-60. Commissioner of Banks to have right of access to books and records of association; right to issue subpoenas, administer oaths, examine witnesses.

(a) The Commissioner of Banks and his agents:

(1) Shall have free access to all books and records of an association, or a service corporation thereof, that relate to its business, and the books and records kept by an officer, agent or employee relating to or upon which any record is kept;

(2) May subpoena witnesses and administer oaths or affirmations in the examination of any director, officer, agent, or employee of an association, or a service corporation thereof or of any other person in relation to its affairs, transactions and conditions;

(3) May require the production of records, books, papers, contracts and other documents; and

(4) May order that improper entries be corrected on the books and records of an association.

(b) The Commissioner of Banks may issue subpoenas duces tecum.

(c) If a person fails to comply with a subpoena so issued or a party or witness refuses to testify on any matters, a court of competent jurisdiction, on the application of the Commissioner of Banks, shall compel compliance by proceedings for contempt as in the case of disobedience of the requirements of a subpoena issued from such court or a refusal to testify in such court. (1981, c. 282, s. 3; 2001-193, s. 16.)

§ 54B-61. Test appraisals of collateral for loans; expense paid.

(a) The Commissioner of Banks may direct the making of test appraisals of real estate and other collateral securing loans made by associations doing business in this State, employ competent appraisers, or prescribe a list from which competent appraisers may be selected, for the making of such appraisals by the Commissioner of Banks, and do any and all other acts incident to the making of such test appraisals.

(b)   In lieu of causing such appraisals to be made, the Commissioner of Banks may accept an appraisal caused to be made by the appropriate federal regulatory authority.

(c)   The expense and cost of test appraisals made pursuant to this section shall be defrayed by the association subjected to such test appraisals, and each association doing business in this State shall pay all reasonable costs and expenses of such test appraisals when it shall be directed. (1981, c. 282, s. 3; 1989 (Reg. Sess., 1990), c. 806, s. 6; 2001-193, s. 16.)

§ 54B-62. Relationship of savings and loan associations with the Savings Institutions Division.

(a)   Except as provided by subsection (b) of this section, a savings and loan association or any director, officer, employee, or representative thereof shall not grant or give to any employee of the Savings Institutions Division, or to their spouses, any loan or gratuity, directly or indirectly.

(b)   No person on the staff of the Savings Institutions Division shall:

(1)   Hold an office or position in any State association or exercise any right to vote on any State association matter by reason of being a member of the association;

(2)   Be interested, directly or indirectly in any savings and loan association organized under the laws of this State; or

(3)   Undertake any indebtedness, as a borrower directly or indirectly or endorser, surety or guarantor, or sell or otherwise dispose of any loan or investment to any savings and loan association organized under the laws of this State.

(c)   Notwithstanding subsection (b) of this section, any person employed in or by the Savings Institutions Division may be a withdrawable account holder and receive earnings on such account.

(d)   Any employee of the Savings Institutions Division shall dispose of any right or interest in a savings and loan association, held either directly or indirectly, that is prohibited under subsection (b) of this section, within 60 days after the date of the employee's appointment or employment. If that person is indebted as borrower directly or indirectly, or is an endorser, surety or guarantor on a note, at the time of his appointment or employment, he may continue in such capacity until such loan is paid off.

(e) If any employee of the Division has a loan or other note acquired by a State savings and loan association through the secondary market, he may continue with the debt until such loan or note is paid off. (1981, c. 282, s. 3; 1989, c. 76, s. 20; 1991, c. 707, s. 3; 2001-193, s. 6.)

§ 54B-63. Confidential information.

(a) The following records or information of the Commission, the Commissioner of Banks or the agent(s) of either shall be confidential and shall not be disclosed:

(1) Information obtained or compiled in preparation of or anticipation of, or during an examination, audit or investigation of any association;

(2) Information reflecting the specific collateral given by a named borrower, the specific amount of stock owned by a named stockholder, or specific withdrawable accounts held by a named member or customer;

(3) Information obtained, prepared or compiled during or as a result of an examination, audit or investigation of any association by an agency of the United States, if the records would be confidential under federal law or regulation;

(4) Information and reports submitted by associations to federal regulatory agencies, if the records or information would be confidential under federal law or regulation;

(5) Information and records regarding complaints from the public received by the Division which concern associations when the complaint would or could result in an investigation, except to the management of those associations;

(6) Any other letters, reports, memoranda, recordings, charts or other documents or records which would disclose any information of which disclosure is prohibited in this subsection.

(b) A court of competent jurisdiction may order the disclosure of specific information.

(c) The information contained in an application shall be deemed to be public information. Disclosure shall not extend to the financial statement of the incorporators nor to any further information deemed by the Commissioner of Banks to be confidential.

(d) Nothing in this section shall prevent the exchange of information relating to associations and the business thereof with the representatives of the agencies of this State, other states, or of the United States, or with reserve or insuring agencies for associations. The private business and affairs of an individual or company shall not be disclosed by any person employed by the Savings Institutions Division, any member of the Commission, or by any person with whom information is exchanged under the authority of this subsection.

(e) Any official or employee violating this section shall be liable to any person injured by disclosure of such confidential information for all damages sustained thereby. Penalties provided shall not be exclusive of other penalties. (1981, c. 282, s. 3; 1989, c. 76, s. 21; 2001-193, s. 16.)

§ 54B-63.1. Confidential records.

(a) As used in this section:

(1) "Compliance review committee" means:

a. An audit, loan review, or compliance committee appointed by the board of directors of an association or any other person to the extent the person acts at the direction of or reports to a compliance review committee; and

b. Whose functions are to audit, evaluate, report, or determine compliance with any of the following:

1. Loan underwriting standards;

2. Asset quality;

3. Financial reporting to federal or State regulatory agencies;

4. Adherence to the association's investment, lending, accounting, ethical, and financial standards; or

5. Compliance with federal or State statutory requirements.

(2) "Compliance review documents" means documents prepared for or created by a compliance review committee.

(3) "Loan review committee" means a person or group of persons who, on behalf of an association, reviews assets, including loans held by the association, for the purpose of assessing the credit quality of the loans or the loan application process, compliance with the association's investment and loan policies, and compliance with applicable laws and regulations.

(4) "Person" means an individual, group of individuals, board, committee, partnership, firm, association, corporation, or other entity.

(b) Associations chartered under the laws of North Carolina or of the United States shall maintain complete records of compliance review documents, and the documents shall be available for examination by any federal or State association regulatory agency having supervisory jurisdiction. Notwithstanding Chapter 132 of the General Statutes, compliance review documents in the custody of an association or regulatory agency are confidential, are not open for public inspection, and are not discoverable or admissible in evidence in a civil action against an association, its directors, officers, or employees, unless the court finds that the interests of justice require that the documents be discoverable or admissible in evidence. (1995, c. 408, s. 2.)

§ 54B-64. Civil penalties; State associations.

(a) Except as otherwise provided in this Article, any association which is found to have violated any provision of this Article may be ordered to forfeit and pay a civil penalty of up to twenty thousand dollars ($20,000). Any association which is found to have violated or failed to comply with any cease and desist order issued under the authority of this Article may be ordered to forfeit or pay a civil penalty of up to twenty thousand dollars ($20,000) for each day that the violation or failure to comply continues.

The clear proceeds of civil penalties provided for in this section shall be remitted to the Civil Penalty and Forfeiture Fund in accordance with G.S. 115C-457.2.

(b) To enforce the provisions of this section, the Commissioner of Banks is authorized to assess such a penalty and to appear in a court of competent jurisdiction and to move the court to order payment of the penalty. Prior to the assessment of the penalty, a hearing shall be held by the Commissioner of Banks which shall comply with the provisions of Article 3 of Chapter 150B of the General Statutes.

(c) If the Commissioner of Banks determines that, as a result of a violation of any provision of this Article, or of a failure to comply with any cease and desist order issued under the authority of this Article, a situation exists requiring immediate corrective action, the Commissioner of Banks may impose the civil penalty in this section on the association without a prior hearing, and said penalty shall be effective as of the date of notice to the association. Imposition of such penalty may be directly appealed to the Wake County Superior Court.

(d) Nothing in this section shall prevent anyone damaged by a State association from bringing a separate cause of action in a court of competent jurisdiction. (1981, c. 282, s. 3; 1987, c. 827, s. 1; 1998-215, s. 36; 2001-193, s. 16.)

§ 54B-65. Civil penalties; directors, officers and employees.

(a) Any person, whether a director, officer or employee, who is found to have violated any provision of this Article, whether willfully or as a result of gross negligence, gross incompetency, or recklessness, may be ordered to forfeit and pay a civil penalty of up to five thousand dollars ($5,000) per violation. Any person who is found to have violated or failed to comply with any cease and desist order issued under the authority of this Article, may be ordered to forfeit and pay a civil penalty of up to five thousand dollars ($5,000) per violation for each day that the violation or failure to comply continues.

The clear proceeds of civil penalties provided for in this section shall be remitted to the Civil Penalty and Forfeiture Fund in accordance with G.S. 115C-457.2.

(b) To enforce the provisions of this section, the Commissioner of Banks is authorized to assess such a penalty and to appear in a court of competent jurisdiction and to move the court to order payment of the penalty. Prior to the assessment of the penalty, a hearing shall be held by the Commissioner of Banks which shall comply with the provisions of Article 3 of Chapter 150B of the General Statutes.

(c) Whenever the Commissioner of Banks shall determine that an emergency exists which requires immediate corrective action, the Commissioner of Banks, either before or after instituting any other action or proceeding authorized by this Article, may request the Attorney General to institute a civil action in a court of competent jurisdiction, in the name of the State upon the relation of the Commissioner of Banks seeking injunctive relief to restrain or enjoin the violation or threatened violation of this Article and for such other and further relief as the court may deem proper. Instituting an action for injunctive relief shall not relieve any party to such proceedings from any civil or criminal penalty prescribed for violation of this Article.

(d) Nothing in this section shall prevent anyone damaged by a director, officer or employee of a State association from bringing a separate cause of action in a court of competent jurisdiction. (1981, c. 282, s. 3; 1987, c. 827, s. 1; 1998-215, s. 37; 2001-193, s. 16.)

§ 54B-66. Criminal penalties.

(a) The provisions of this section shall in no event extend to persons who are found to have acted only with gross negligence, simple negligence, recklessness or incompetence.

(b) In addition to any of the other penalties or remedies provided by this Article, the following shall be deemed to be Class 1 misdemeanors:

(1) The willful or knowing violation of the provisions of this Article by any employee of the Savings Institutions Division.

(2) The willful or knowing violation of a cease and desist order which has become final in that no further administrative or judicial appeal is available.

(c) In addition to any of the other penalties or remedies provided by this Article, the willful omission, making, or concurrence in making or publishing a written report, exhibit, or entry in a financial statement on the books of the association, which contains a material statement known to be false shall be deemed to be a Class 1 misdemeanor. For purposes of this section, "material" shall mean "so substantial and important as to influence a reasonable and prudent businessman or investor."

(d) The Commissioner of Banks is authorized to enforce this section in a court of competent jurisdiction. (1981, c. 282, s. 3; 1989, c. 76, s. 22; 1993, c. 539, s. 433; 1994, Ex. Sess., c. 24, s. 14(c); 2001-193, s. 16.)

§ 54B-67. Primary jurisdiction.

Whenever an agency of the United States government shall defer to the Commissioner of Banks, or notify the Commissioner of Banks of pending action against an association chartered by this State or fail to exercise its authority over any State-or federally-chartered association doing business in this State, the Commissioner of Banks shall have the authority to exercise jurisdiction over such association. (1981, c. 282, s. 3; 2001-193, s. 16.)

§ 54B-68. Supervisory control.

(a) Whenever the Commissioner of Banks determines that an association is conducting its business in an unsafe or unsound manner or in any fashion which threatens the financial integrity or sound operation of the association, the Commissioner of Banks may serve a notice of charges on the association, requiring it to show cause why it should not be placed under supervisory control. Such notice of charges shall specify the grounds for supervisory control, and set the time and place for a hearing. A hearing before the Commission pursuant to such notice shall be held within 15 days after issuance of the notice of charges, and shall comply with the provisions of Article 3 of Chapter 150B of the General Statutes.

(b) If, after the hearing provided above, Commission determines that supervisory control of the association is necessary to protect the association's members, customers, stockholders or creditors, or the general public, the

Commissioner of Banks shall issue an order taking supervisory control of the association. An appeal may be filed in the Wake County Superior Court.

(c)   If the order taking supervisory control becomes final, the Commissioner of Banks may appoint an agent to supervise and monitor the operations of the association during the period of supervisory control. During the period of supervisory control, the association shall act in accordance with such instructions and directions as may be given by the Commissioner of Banks directly or through his supervisory agent and shall not act or fail to act except when to do so would violate an outstanding cease and desist order.

(d)   Within 180 days of the date the order taking supervisory control becomes final, the Commissioner of Banks shall issue an order approving a plan for the termination of supervisory control. The plan may provide for:

(1)   The issuance by the association of capital stock;

(2)   The appointment of one or more officers and/or directors;

(3)   The reorganization, merger, or consolidation of the association;

(4)   The dissolution and liquidation of the association.

The order approving the plan shall not take effect for 30 days during which time period an appeal may be filed in the Wake County Superior Court.

(e)   The costs incident to this proceeding shall be paid by the association, provided such costs are found to be reasonable.

(f)   For the purposes of this section, an order shall be deemed final if:

(1)   No appeal is filed within the specific time allowed for the appeal, or

(2)   After all judicial appeals are exhausted. (1981, c. 282, s. 3; 1987, c. 827, s. 1; 2001-193, s. 16.)

§ 54B-69. Removal of directors, officers and employees.

(a) If, in the Commissioner of Banks' opinion, one or more directors, officers or employees of any association has participated in or consented to any violation of this Chapter, or any other law, rule, regulation or order, or any unsafe or unsound business practice in the operation of any association; or any insider loan not specifically authorized by or pursuant to this Chapter; or any repeated violation of or failure to comply with any association's bylaws, the Commissioner of Banks may serve a written notice of charges upon the director, officer or employee in question, and the association, stating his intent to remove said director, officer or employee. Such notice shall specify the conduct and place for the hearing before the Commission to be held. A hearing shall be held no earlier than 15 days and no later than 30 days after the notice of charges is served, and it shall comply with the provisions of Article 3 of Chapter 150B of the General Statutes. If, after the hearing, the Commission determines that the charges asserted have been proven by a preponderance of the evidence, the Commissioner of Banks may issue an order removing the director, officer or employee in question. Such an order shall be effective upon issuance and may include the entire board of directors or all of the officers of the association.

(b) If it is determined that any director, officer or employee of any association has knowingly participated in or consented to any violation of this Chapter, or any other law, rule, regulation or order, or engaged in any unsafe or unsound business practice in the operation of any association, or any repeated violation of or failure to comply with any association's bylaws, and that as a result, a situation exists requiring immediate corrective action, the Commissioner of Banks may issue an order temporarily removing such person or persons pending a hearing. Such an order shall state its duration on its face and the words, "Temporary Order of Removal," and shall be effective upon issuance, for a period of 15 days, and may be extended once for a period of 15 days. A hearing must be held within 10 days of the expiration of a temporary order, or any extension thereof, at which time a temporary order may be dissolved or converted to a permanent order.

(c) Any removal pursuant to subsections (a) or (b) of this section shall be effective in all respects as if such removal had been made by the board of directors, the members or the stockholders of the association in question.

(d) Without the prior written approval of the Commissioner of Banks, no director, officer or employee permanently removed pursuant to this section shall be eligible to be elected, reelected or appointed to any position as a director, officer or employee of that association, nor shall such a director, officer or employee be eligible to be elected to or retain a position as a director, officer or employee of any other State association. (1981, c. 282, s. 3; 1987, c. 827, s. 1; 2001-193, s. 16.)

§ 54B-70. Involuntary liquidation.

(a) The Commissioner of Banks with prior approval of the Commission may take custody of the books, records and assets of every kind and character of any association organized and operated under the provisions of this Chapter for any of the purposes hereinafter enumerated, if it reasonably appears from examinations or from reports made to the Commissioner of Banks that:

(1) The directors, officers, or liquidators have neglected, failed or refused to take such action which the Commissioner of Banks may deem necessary for the protection of the association, or have impeded or obstructed an examination; or

(2) The withdrawable capital of the association is impaired to the extent that the realizable value of its assets is insufficient to pay in full its creditors and holders of withdrawable accounts; or its liquidity fund or general reserve account is impaired; or

(3) The business of the association is being conducted in a fraudulent, illegal or unsafe manner, or that the association is in an unsafe or unsound condition to transact business; (any association which, except as authorized in writing by the Commissioner of Banks, fails to make full payment of any withdrawal when due is in an unsafe or unsound condition to transact business, notwithstanding such provisions of the certificate of incorporation or such statutes or regulations with respect to payment of withdrawals in event an association does not pay all withdrawals in full); or

(4) The officers, directors, or employees have assumed duties or performed acts in excess of those authorized by statute or regulation or charter, or without supplying the required bond; or,

(5) The association has experienced a substantial dissipation of assets or earnings due to any violation or violations of statute or regulation, or due to any unsafe or unsound practice or practices; or

(6) The association is insolvent, or is in imminent danger of insolvency or has suspended its ordinary business transactions due to insufficient funds; or

(7)   The association is unable to continue operations.

(b)   Unless the Commissioner of Banks finds that such an emergency exists which may result in loss to members, withdrawable account holders, stockholders, or creditors, and which requires that he take custody immediately, he shall first give written notice to the directors and officers specifying the conditions criticized and allowing a reasonable time in which corrections may be made before a receiver shall be appointed as outlined in subsection (d) below.

(c)   The purposes for which the Commissioner of Banks may take custody of an association include examination or further examination; conservation of its assets; restoration of impaired capital; the making of any reasonable or equitable adjustment deemed necessary by the Commissioner of Banks under any plan of reorganization.

(d)   If the Commissioner of Banks after taking custody of an association, finds that one or more of the reasons for having taken custody continue to exist through the period of his custody, with little or no likelihood of amelioration of the situation, then he shall appoint as receiver or co-receiver any qualified person, firm or corporation for the purpose of liquidation of the association, which receiver shall furnish bond in form, amount and with surety as the Commissioner of Banks may require. The Commissioner of Banks may appoint the association's withdrawable account insurance corporation or its nominee as the receiver, and such insuring corporation shall be permitted to serve without posting bond.

(e)   In the event the Commissioner of Banks appoints a receiver for an association, he shall mail a certified copy of the appointment order by certified mail to the address of the association as it shall appear on the records of the Division, and to any previous receiver or other legal custodian of the association, and to any court or other authority to which such previous receiver or other legal custodian is subject. Notice of such appointment shall be published in a newspaper of general circulation in the county where such association has its principal office.

(f)   Whenever a receiver for an association is appointed pursuant to subsection (d) above the association may within 30 days thereafter bring an action in the Superior Court of Wake County, for an order requiring the Commissioner of Banks to remove such receiver.

(g)   The duly appointed and qualified receiver shall take possession promptly of the association for which he or it has been so appointed, in accordance with the terms of such appointment, by service of a certified copy of the Commissioner of Banks' appointment order upon the association at its principal office through the officer or employee who is present and appears to be in charge. Immediately upon taking possession of the association, the receiver shall take possession and title to books, records and assets of every description of such association. The receiver, by operation of law and without any conveyance or other instrument, act or deed, shall succeed to all the rights, titles, powers and privileges of the association, its members or stockholders, holders of withdrawable accounts, its officers and directors or any of them; and to the titles to the books, records and assets of every description of any previous receiver or other legal custodian of such association. Such members, stockholders, holders of withdrawable accounts, officers or directors, or any of them, shall not thereafter, except as hereinafter expressly provided, have or exercise any such rights, powers or privileges or act in connection with any assets or property of any nature of the association in receivership: Provided however, that any officer, director, member, stockholder, withdrawable account holder, or borrower of such association shall have the right to communicate with the Commissioner of Banks with respect to such receivership. The Commissioner of Banks, with the approval of the Commission, may at any time, direct the receiver to return the association to its previous or a newly constituted management. The Commissioner of Banks may provide for a meeting or meetings of the members or stockholders for any purpose, including, without any limitation on the generality of the foregoing, the election of directors or an increase in the number of directors, or both, or the election of an entire new board of directors; and may provide for a meeting or meetings of the directors for any purpose including, without any limitation on the generality of the foregoing, the filling of vacancies on the board, the removal of officers and the election of new officers, or for any of such purposes. Any such meeting of members or stockholders, or of directors, shall be supervised or conducted by a representative of the Commissioner of Banks.

(h)   A duly appointed and qualified receiver shall have power and authority to:

(1)   Demand, sue for, collect, receive and take into his possession all the goods and chattels, rights and credits, moneys and effects, lands and tenements, books, papers, choses in action, bills, notes, and property of every description of the association;

(2) Foreclose mortgages, deeds of trust, and other liens executed to the association to the extent the association would have had such right;

(3) Institute suits for the recovery of any estate, property, damages, or demands existing in favor of the association, and he shall, upon his own application, be substituted as party plaintiff in the place of the association in any suit or proceeding pending at the time of his appointment;

(4) Sell, convey, and assign all the property rights and interest owned by the association;

(5) Appoint agents to serve at his pleasure;

(6) Examine and investigate papers and persons, and pass on claims as provided in the regulations as prescribed by the Commissioner of Banks;

(7) Make and carry out agreements with the insuring corporation or with any other financial institution for the payment or assumption of the association liabilities, in whole or in part, and to sell, convey, transfer, pledge, or assign assets as security or otherwise and to make guarantees in connection therewith; and

(8) Perform all other acts which might be done by the employees, officers and directors.

Such powers shall be continued in effect until liquidation and dissolution or until return of the association to its prior or newly constituted management.

(i) A receiver may at any time during the receivership and prior to final liquidation be removed and a replacement appointed by the Commissioner of Banks.

(j) The Commissioner of Banks may determine that such liquidation proceedings should be discontinued. He shall then remove the receiver and restore all the rights, powers, and privileges of its members and stockholders, customers, employees, officers and directors, or restore such rights, powers, and privileges to its members, stockholders and customers, and grant such rights, powers and privileges to a newly constituted management, all as of the time of such restoration of the association to its management unless another time for such restoration shall be specified by the Commissioner of Banks. The return of an association to its management or to a newly constituted management from the possession of a receiver shall, by operation of law and without any conveyance or other instrument, act or deed, vest in such association the title to all property held by the receiver in his capacity as receiver for such association.

(k) A receiver may also be appointed under the authority of G.S. 1-502. No judge or court, however, shall appoint a receiver for any State association unless five days' advance notice of the motion, petition or application for appointment of a receiver shall have been given to such association and to the Commissioner of Banks.

(l) Following the appointment of a receiver, the Commissioner of Banks shall request the Attorney General to institute an action in the name of the Commissioner of Banks in the superior court against the association for the orderly liquidation and dissolution of the association, and for an injunction to restrain the officers, directors and employees from continuing the operation of the association.

(m) Claims against a State association in receivership shall have the following order of priority for payment:

(1) Costs, expenses and debts of the association incurred on or after the date of the appointment of the receiver, including compensation for the receiver;

(2) Claims of holders of special purpose or thrift accounts;

(3) Claims of holders of withdrawable accounts;

(4) Claims of general creditors;

(5) Claims of stockholders of a stock association;

(6) All remaining assets to members and stockholders in an amount proportionate to their holdings as of the date of the appointment of the receiver.

(n) All claims of each class described within subsection (m) above shall be paid in full so long as sufficient assets remain. Members of the class for which the receiver cannot make payment in full because assets will be depleted during payment to such class shall be paid an amount proportionate to their total claims.

(o) The Commissioner of Banks shall have the authority to direct the payment of claims for which no provision is herein made, and may direct the payment of claims within a class. The Commissioner of Banks shall have the authority to promulgate rules and regulations governing the payment of claims by an association in receivership.

(p) When all assets of the association have been fully liquidated, and all claims and expenses have been paid or settled, and the receiver shall recommend a final distribution, the dissolution of the association in receivership shall be accomplished in the following manner:

(1) The receiver shall file with the Commissioner of Banks a detailed report, in a form to be prescribed by the Commissioner of Banks, of his acts and proposed final distribution, and dissolution.

(2) Upon the Commissioner of Banks' approval of the final report of the receiver, the receiver shall provide such notice and thereafter shall make such final distribution, in such manner as the Commissioner of Banks may direct.

(3) When a final distribution has been made except as to any unclaimed funds, the receiver shall deposit such unclaimed funds with the Commissioner of Banks and shall deliver to the Commissioner of Banks all books and records of the dissolved association.

(4) Upon completion of the foregoing procedure, and upon the joint petition of the Commissioner of Banks and receiver to the superior court, the court may find that the association should be dissolved, and following such publication of notice of dissolution as the court may direct, the court may enter a decree of final resolution and the association shall thereby be dissolved.

(5) Upon final dissolution of the association in receivership or at such time as the receiver shall be otherwise relieved of his duties, the Commissioner of Banks shall cause an audit to be conducted, during which the receiver shall be available to assist in such. The accounts of the receiver shall then be ruled upon by the Commissioner of Banks and Commission and if approved, the receiver shall thereupon be given a final and complete discharge and release. (1981, c. 282, s. 3; 1987, c. 237, s. 4; 2001-193, s. 16.)

§ 54B-71. Judicial review.

Any person or State association against whom a cease and desist order is issued or a fine is imposed may have such order or fine reviewed by a court of competent jurisdiction. Except as otherwise provided, an appeal may be made only within 30 days of the issuance of the order or the imposition of the fine, whichever is later. (1981, c. 282, s. 3.)

§ 54B-72. Indemnity.

No person who is fined or penalized for a violation of any criminal provision of this Article shall be reimbursed or indemnified in any fashion by the association for such fine or penalty. (1981, c. 282, s. 3.)

§ 54B-73. Cumulative penalties.

All penalties, fines, and remedies provided by this Article shall be cumulative. (1981, c. 282, s. 3.)

§ 54B-74. Annual license fees.

All State associations shall pay an annual license fee set by the Commissioner of Banks, subject to the advice and consent of the Commission. Such license fee shall be used to defray the expenses incurred by the Division in supervising State associations. The Commissioner of Banks may license each State association upon receipt of the license fee and filing of an application in such form as the Commissioner of Banks may prescribe. (1981, c. 282, s. 3; 1985, c. 659, s. 11; 2001-193, s. 16.)

§ 54B-75. Statement; fees.

Every State association shall file in the office of the Commissioner of Banks, on or before the first day of February in each year, in such form as the Commissioner of Banks shall prescribe, a statement of the business standing and financial condition of such association on the preceding 31st day of December. This statement shall be signed and sworn to by the secretary or other officer duly authorized by the board of directors of the association before a notary public. The statement shall be accompanied by a filing fee set by the Commissioner of Banks, subject to the advice and consent of the Commission. The filing fees shall be used to defray the expenses incurred by the Division in supervising State associations. (1981, c. 282, s. 3; 1985, c. 659, s. 12; 1993, c. 163, s. 1; 2001-193, s. 16.)

§ 54B-76. Statement examined, approved, and published.

It shall be the duty of the Commissioner of Banks to receive and thoroughly examine each annual statement required by G.S. 54B-75, and if made in compliance with the requirements thereof, each State association shall at its own expense, publish an abstract of the same in a newspaper having general circulation within each market area of the association as selected by the managing officer. (1981, c. 282, s. 3; 1993, c. 163, s. 2; 2001-193, s. 16.)

§ 54B-77. Certain powers granted to State associations.

(a) In addition to the powers granted under this Chapter, any savings and loan association incorporated or operated under the provisions of this Chapter is herein authorized to:

(1) Establish off the premises of any principal office or branch a customer communications terminal, point-of-sale terminal, automated teller machine, automated or other direct or remote information-processing device or machine, whether manned or unmanned, through or by means of which funds or information relating to any financial service or transaction rendered to the public is stored and transmitted, instantaneously or otherwise to or from an association terminal or terminals controlled or used by or with other parties; and the establishment and use of such a device or machine shall not be deemed to constitute a branch office and the capital requirements and standards for approval of a branch office as set forth in the statutes and regulations, shall not be applicable to the establishment of any such off-premises terminal, device or machine; and associations may through mutual consent share on-premises unmanned automated teller machines and cash dispensers. The Commissioner

of Banks may prescribe rules and regulations with regard to the application for permission for use, maintenance and supervision of said terminals, devices and machines;

(2) Subject to such regulations as the Commissioner of Banks may prescribe, a state-chartered association is authorized to issue credit cards, extend credit in connection therewith, and otherwise engage in or participate in credit card operations;

(3) Subject to such regulations as the Commissioner of Banks may prescribe, a state-chartered association may act as a trustee, executor, administrator, guardian or in any other fiduciary capacity permitted for federal savings and loan associations;

(4) a. In accordance with rules and regulations issued by the Commissioner of Banks, mutual capital certificates may be issued by state-chartered associations and sold directly to subscribers or through underwriters, and such certificates shall constitute part of the general reserve and net worth of the issuing association. The Commissioner of Banks, in the rules and regulations relating to the issuance and sale of mutual capital certificates, shall provide that such certificates:

1. Shall be subordinate to all savings accounts, savings certificates, and debt obligations;

2. Shall constitute a claim in liquidation on the general reserves, surplus and undivided profits of the association remaining after the payment of all savings accounts, savings certificates, and debt obligations;

3. Shall be entitled to the payment of dividends; and

4. May have a fixed or variable dividend rate.

b. The Commissioner of Banks shall provide in the rules and regulations for charging losses to the mutual capital certificate, reserves, and other net worth accounts.

(b) To such extent as the Commissioner of Banks may authorize by regulation or advice in writing, a State association may issue notes, bonds, debentures, or other obligations or securities. (1981, c. 282, s. 3; 1983, c. 144, s. 16; 1989 (Reg. Sess., 1990), c. 806, s. 7; 2001-193, s. 16.)

§ 54B-78. Prohibited practices.

Any person or association who shall engage in any of the following acts or practices shall be guilty of a Class 1 misdemeanor:

(1) Defamation: Making, publishing, disseminating, or circulating, directly or indirectly, or aiding, abetting, or encouraging the making, publishing, disseminating, or circulating of any oral, written, or printed statement which is false regarding the financial condition of any association.

(2) False information and advertising: Making, publishing, disseminating, or circulating or causing, directly or indirectly, to be made published, disseminated, circulated, or otherwise placed before the public in any publication, media, notice, pamphlet, letter, poster, or any other way, an advertisement, announcement, or statement containing any assertion, representation, or statement with respect to the savings and loan business or with respect to any person in the conduct of the savings and loan business which is untrue, deceptive, or misleading. (1985, c. 659, s. 13; 1993, c. 539, s. 434; 1994, Ex. Sess., c. 24, s. 14(c).)

§§ 54B-79 through 54B-99. Reserved for future codification purposes.

Article 5.

Corporate Administration.

§ 54B-100. Membership of a mutual association.

The membership of a mutual association organized or operated under the provisions of this Chapter shall consist of:

(1) Those who hold withdrawable accounts in an association; and

(2)   Those who borrow funds and those who become obligated on a loan from the association, for such time as the loan remains unpaid and the borrower remains liable to the association for the payment thereof.

Any person in his own right, or in a trust or other fiduciary capacity, or any partnership, association, corporation, political subdivision or public or governmental unit or entity may become a member of a mutual association. Members shall be possessed of such voting rights and such other rights as are provided by an association's certificate of incorporation and bylaws as approved by the Commissioner of Banks. Members are the owners of a mutual association. (1981, c. 282, s. 3; 2001-193, s. 16.)

§ 54B-101. Directors.

(a)   The directors of a mutual association shall be elected by the members at an annual meeting, held pursuant to the terms of G.S. 54B-106, for such terms as the bylaws of the association may provide. Directors' terms may be classified in the certificate of incorporation. Voting for directors by withdrawable account holders shall be weighted according to the total amount of withdrawable accounts held by such members, subject to any maximum number of votes per member which an association may choose to prescribe in the bylaws of the association. Such requirements shall be fully prescribed in a detailed manner in the bylaws of the association.

(b)   The directors of a stock association shall be elected by the stockholders at an annual meeting, held pursuant to the terms of G.S. 54B-106, for such terms as the bylaws of the association may provide. Directors' terms may be classified in the certificate of incorporation.

   (c) Every State association shall have no less than five directors. (1981, c. 282, s. 3; 1983, c. 144, s. 17; 1991, c. 707, s. 4.)

§ 54B-102. Employment policies.

Employment policies appropriate for the transaction of the business of a State association may be set forth in the bylaws or established by resolution of the board of directors. (1981, c. 282, s. 3; 1981 (Reg. Sess., 1982), c. 1238, s. 22.)

§ 54B-103. Duties and liabilities of officers and directors to their associations.

Officers and directors of a State association shall act in a fiduciary capacity towards the association and its members or stockholders. They shall discharge duties of their respective positions in good faith, and with that diligence and care which ordinarily prudent men would exercise under similar circumstances in like positions. (1981, c. 282, s. 3.)

§ 54B-104. Conflicts of interest.

Each director, officer and employee of a State association has a fundamental duty to avoid placing himself in a position which creates, or which leads to or could lead to a conflict of interest or appearance of a conflict of interest having adverse effects on the interests of members, customers or stockholders of the association, the soundness of the association, and the provision of economical home financing for this State. (1981, c. 282, s. 3.)

§ 54B-105. Voting rights.

Voting rights in the affairs of a State association may be exercised by members and stockholders by voting either in person or by proxy. The Commissioner of Banks shall promulgate rules and regulations governing forms of proxies, holders of proxies and proxy solicitation. (1981, c. 282, s. 3; 2001-193, s. 16.)

§ 54B-106. Annual meetings; notice required.

(a)   Each association shall hold an annual meeting of its members or stockholders. The annual meeting shall be held at a time and place as shall be provided in the bylaws or determined by the board of directors.

(b) The board of directors of a mutual association shall cause to be published once a week for two weeks preceding such meeting, in a newspaper of general circulation published in the county where such association has its principal office, a notice of the meeting, signed by the association's secretary, and stating the time and place where it is to be held. In addition to the foregoing notice, each association shall disseminate additional notice of any annual meeting by notice made available to all members entering the premises of any office or branch of the association in the regular course of business by posting therein, in full view of the public and such members, one or more conspicuous signs or placards announcing the pending meeting, the time, date and place of the meeting and the availability of additional information. Printed matter shall be freely available to said members containing any information as may be prescribed in rules and regulations issued by the Commissioner of Banks. Such additional notice shall be given at any time within the period of 60 days prior to and 14 days prior to the meeting and shall continue through the time of the meeting.

(c) The board of directors of a stock association shall cause a written or printed notice signed by the association's secretary, and stating the time and place of the annual meeting to be delivered not less than 10 days nor more than 50 days before the date of the meeting, either personally or by mail to each stockholder of record entitled to vote at the meeting. If mailed, such notice shall be deemed to be delivered when deposited in the United States postal service addressed to the stockholder at his address as it appears on the record of stockholders of the corporation, with postage thereon prepaid. (1981, c. 282, s. 3; 2001-193, s. 16.)

§ 54B-107. Special meetings; notice required.

(a) Special meetings of members or stockholders of an association may be called by the president or the board of directors or by such other officers or persons as may be provided for in the charter or bylaws of the association.

(b) Notice of any special meeting of members or stockholders shall be given in the same manner as provided for annual meetings under G.S. 54B-106. (1981, c. 282, s. 3.)

§ 54B-108. Quorum.

Unless otherwise provided in the association's charter or bylaws, 50 holders of withdrawable accounts in a mutual association or 50 stockholders or a majority of shares eligible to vote in a stock association, present in person or represented by proxy, shall constitute a quorum at any annual or special meeting. (1981, c. 282, s. 3.)

§ 54B-109. Indemnification.

(a)   An association shall maintain a blanket indemnity bond of at least a minimum amount as prescribed by the Commissioner of Banks.

(b)   An association which employs collection agents, who for any reason are not covered by the bond as hereinabove required, shall provide for the bonding of each such agent in an amount equal to at least twice the average monthly collections of such agent. Such agents shall be required to make settlement with the association at least once monthly. No such coverage by bond will be required of any agent which is a federally insured depository institution. The amount and form of such bonds and the sufficiency of the surety thereon shall be approved by the board of directors and the Commissioner of Banks before such is valid. All such bonds shall provide that a cancellation thereof either by the surety or by the insured shall not become effective unless and until 30 days' notice in writing shall have been given to the Commissioner of Banks.

(c)   The Commissioner of Banks may require every member of the board of directors, officer or employee of an association who shall knowingly make, approve, participate in, or assent to, or who knowingly shall permit any of the officers or agents of the association to make investments not authorized by this Chapter, to deposit with the association an indemnity bond, insurance or collateral of a kind and amount sufficient to indemnify the association against damage which the association or its members or stockholders sustain in consequence of such unauthorized investment.

(d)   The amount considered sufficient to indemnify the association shall, in the case of an unauthorized loan, be the difference between the book value of the loan and the amount that could legally have been made under the provisions of this Chapter. The amount considered sufficient to indemnify the association shall, in the case of an unauthorized other investment, be the difference between the book value and the market value of the investment at the time when the Commissioner of Banks makes his determination that such investment is unauthorized. Whenever an unauthorized investment has been sold or disposed of without recourse, the Commissioner of Banks shall release such part of the indemnity as remains after deducting any loss, which amount shall be retained by the association. Whenever the balance of an unauthorized loan has been reduced to an amount which would permit such loan to be made in compliance with the provisions of this Chapter, the indemnity shall be released. The Commissioner of Banks, in making such determination may require an independent appraisal of the security.

(e)   The Commissioner of Banks shall cause to be examined annually all such bonds and pass on their sufficiency and either the board of directors or the Commissioner of Banks may require new or additional bonds at any time.

(f)   The Commissioner of Banks is empowered to promulgate rules and regulations with respect to litigation expenses and other indemnity matters. (1981, c. 282, s. 3; 1989 (Reg. Sess., 1990), c. 806, s. 8; 2001-193, s. 16.)

§ 54B-110. Days and hours of operation.

Any association may operate on such days and during such hours, and may observe such holidays, as the association's board of directors shall designate. (1987, c. 853, s. 3; 1995 (Reg. Sess., 1996), c. 556, s. 3.)

§§ 54B-111 through 54B-120. Reserved for future codification purposes.

Article 6.

Withdrawable Accounts.

§ 54B-121. Creation of withdrawable accounts.

(a) Every State association shall be authorized to raise capital through the solicitation of investments from any person, natural or corporate, except as restricted or limited by law, or by such regulations as the Commissioner of Banks may prescribe.

(b) Such funds obtained through the solicitation of investments shall be held by an association in accounts designated generally as withdrawable accounts.

(c) An association may establish as many classes of withdrawable accounts as may be provided for in its certificate of incorporation or bylaws, subject to such regulations and limitations as the Commissioner of Banks may prescribe.

(1) At least one class of withdrawable accounts shall be established by which the holder, upon notice to the association, shall be able to withdraw the entire balance of such account without any penalty. The required period of notice, not to exceed 30 days, shall be determined by the board of directors of each association.

(2) For any additional classes of withdrawable accounts that may be established, the board may require a fixed minimum amount of money and a fixed minimum term, at the end of which, the account holder, without any notice on his part, shall be entitled to payment of the final balance of the funds in such account. Such minimum amount and minimum term and the rate of dividends on withdrawable accounts shall be agreed upon prior to the transfer to the association of any funds by the account holder and shall be evidenced by an executed contract.

a. An association may impose a penalty upon the holder of such account to be assessed at the time of any withdrawal from the account prior to the date of termination of the minimum term for which the account holder contracted.

b. An association may require that the holder of such an account provide the association with not less than 30 days' notice of an intended withdrawal prior to the date of the termination of the account contract.

c. When the date of termination of such an account is passed and the account is mature and payable, all payments thereon by the holder and all dividends on withdrawable account credits thereto by the association shall cease. However, if the holder shall notify the association, prior to the termination date of the account, that he wishes to extend the life of the account, the association shall renew the account and continue to accept payments and/or make dividends on withdrawable account credits or cancel the account as provided under the original contract.

d. Unless the association receives notification within the proper time period and renews the account, then upon the date of termination, it shall either pay to the holder of the account the final value thereof, or mail a notice to the holder at his last address as it appears on the records of the association to the effect that he is entitled to receive payment for the account.

e. If the association does not make payment to the holder of the account upon the date of termination and instead mails a notice to him as provided in paragraph d above, then until such time as the holder is paid, the account shall earn dividends on withdrawable accounts at a rate not less than the rate which the association is paying on its account or accounts established under subdivision (1) above, unless provided otherwise by the account contract.

f. Whenever an association has funds in an amount insufficient to make immediate payment upon the date of termination of an account, or upon an application for withdrawal, the maturity shall be paid in accordance with the provisions of G.S. 54B-124. Whenever such a situation arises, dividends on withdrawable accounts shall be credited to the account at a rate not less than the rate provided for in the account contract.

(3) An association may establish demand deposit accounts as a class of withdrawable accounts. The association shall not permit any overdraft, including an intraday overdraft, on behalf of an affiliate or incur any overdraft in the association's account at a federal reserve bank or federal home loan bank on behalf of an affiliate. (1981, c. 282, s. 3; 1981 (Reg. Sess., 1982), c. 1238, s. 12; 1989 (Reg. Sess., 1990), c. 806, s. 9; 2001-193, s. 16.)

§ 54B-122. Additional requirements.

Withdrawable accounts shall be:

(1) Withdrawable upon demand, subject to the requisite advance notice to the association by the holder, as listed in G.S. 54B-121(c)(2)b and by such regulations as the Commissioner of Banks may prescribe;

(2)   Entitled to dividends as provided herein or in such regulations as the Commissioner of Banks may prescribe;

(3)   Evidenced by an executed contract setting forth any special terms and provisions applicable to the account and the conditions upon which withdrawal may be made. The form of such contract shall be subject to the prior approval of the Commissioner of Banks and shall be held by the association as part of its records pertaining to the account. (1981, c. 282, s. 3; 1981 (Reg. Sess., 1982), c. 1238, s. 13; 2001-193, s. 16.)

§ 54B-123. Dividends on withdrawable accounts.

(a)   An association shall compute and pay dividends on withdrawable accounts in accordance with such terms and conditions as are herein prescribed, and subject to additional limitation and restrictions as shall be set forth in its bylaws, or certificate of incorporation and resolutions of its board of directors.

(b)   Notwithstanding any other provisions of the General Statutes, savings and loan associations shall not be limited in the amount of dividends they may pay on withdrawable accounts. The Commissioner of Banks shall have the authority to insure that no association pays dividends on withdrawable accounts inconsistent with the association's continued solvency, and safe and proper operation. (1981, c. 282, s. 3; 2001-193, s. 16.)

§ 54B-124. Withdrawals from withdrawable accounts.

(a)   A withdrawable account holder may at any time make written application for withdrawal of all or any part of the withdrawal value thereof except to the extent the same may be pledged as security for a loan, as recorded by the association. The association shall number, date, and file every unpaid withdrawal application in the order of actual receipt.

(b)   An association shall pay the total amount of the withdrawal value of a withdrawable account upon application from the holder of the account, except as otherwise provided in this section. Payment shall be made in full, without exception, to holders of withdrawable accounts whose withdrawable account totals one hundred dollars ($100.00) or less.

(c)   If an association has funds in the treasury and from current receipts in an amount insufficient to pay all long term withdrawable accounts which are mature and due and all applications for withdrawal, then within seven days after such accounts mature or payment is due, the board of directors of such association shall provide by resolution:

(1)   A statement of the amount of money available in each calendar month to pay maturities and withdrawals, in accordance with safe and required operating procedures; provided, that after making provision for expenses, debts, obligations and cash dividends on withdrawable accounts, not less than one hundred percent (100%) of the remainder of cash treasury funds and current receipts shall be made available for the payment of outstanding applications for withdrawal and maturities;

(2)   A list of matured withdrawable accounts in order of their maturity, and if in the same series, in order of issuance within such series; and a list of applications for withdrawal in order of actual receipt;

(3)   For a maximum sum, set by the Commissioner of Banks which shall be paid to any one holder of a withdrawable account, for which a maturity or an application for withdrawal has not been paid, in any one month; and if the maturity or withdrawal due shall exceed the sum so fixed, then the holder shall be paid such sum in his turn according to the due date of the maturity or the filing date of the application; and his application shall be deemed refiled for payment in order in the next month; and such limited payment shall be made on a fixed date in each month for so long as any application or maturity remains unpaid.

(d)   A withdrawable account pledged by the holder as sole security or partial security for a loan shall be subject to the withdrawal provisions of this section, but an application for withdrawal from such account shall be paid only if the resulting balance in such account would equal or exceed the outstanding loan balance, or portion thereof, secured by the withdrawable account. However, withdrawal of any additional amount from the account may be permitted, provided that such payment of such withdrawal application shall be applied first to the outstanding balance of the loan.

(e)   The contents of a withdrawable account may be accepted by an association in payment or partial payment for any real property or other assets owned by the association and being sold.

(f)   The holder of a withdrawable account which is mature and payable or for which application for withdrawal has been made does not become a creditor of the association merely by reason of such payment due to him.

(g)   Any such resolution adopted by an association's board of directors pursuant to this section shall be submitted to the Commissioner of Banks for his approval or rejection. If he finds such to be fair to all affected parties, he shall approve it. If he determines otherwise, such resolution shall be rejected and the association shall not implement any of its provisions. The Commissioner of Banks shall issue his findings within 10 days after receipt of the resolution.

(h)   The membership in a mutual association of a withdrawable account holder who has filed an application for withdrawal or whose account is mature and due shall remain unimpaired for so long as any withdrawal value remains to his credit upon the books of the association.

(i)   An association may not obligate itself to pay maturities and withdrawals under any provisions other than the ones set forth in this section without prior approval of the Commissioner of Banks. (1981, c. 282, s. 3; 2001-193, s. 16.)

§ 54B-125. Emergency limitations.

The Commissioner of Banks, with the approval of the Governor, may impose a limitation upon the amounts withdrawable or payable from withdrawable accounts of State associations during any specifically defined period when such limitation is in the public interest and welfare. (1981, c. 282, s. 3; 2001-193, s. 16.)

§ 54B-126. Forced retirement of withdrawable accounts.

(a)   At any time that funds may be on hand and available for such a purpose, and the bylaws of an association and withdrawable account contracts so provide, an association shall have the authority and right to redeem all or any portion of its withdrawable accounts which have not been pledged as security for loans by forcing the retirement thereof. The number of and total amount of such withdrawable accounts to be retired by an association shall be determined by the board of directors.

(b)   An association shall give notice by certified mail to the last address of each holder of an affected withdrawable account of at least 30 days. The redemption price of withdrawable accounts so retired shall be the full withdrawal value of the account, as determined on the last dividend date, plus all dividends on withdrawable accounts credited or paid as of the effective retirement date. Dividends shall continue to accrue and be paid or credited by the association to the withdrawable accounts to be retired up to and including the effective retirement date.

(c)   If the required notice has been properly given, and if on the effective retirement date the funds necessary for payment have been set aside so as to be available, and shall continue to be available therefor, dividends on those withdrawable accounts called for forced retirement shall cease to accrue after the effective retirement date. All rights with respect to such account shall, after the effective retirement date, terminate, except only the right of the holder of the retired withdrawable account to receive the full redemption price.

(d)   No association may redeem withdrawable accounts by forced retirement whenever it has on file applications for withdrawal, or maturities which have not yet been acted upon and paid. No association may redeem withdrawable accounts by forced retirement until the maturity of any fixed minimum term which may be required for the class of withdrawable accounts to be retired. (1981, c. 282, s. 3.)

§ 54B-127. Negotiable orders of withdrawal.

Notwithstanding any other provisions of law, the Commissioner of Banks shall by regulation, authorize associations to accept deposits to withdrawable accounts which may be withdrawn or transferred on or by negotiable or transferable order or authorization to the association. (1981, c. 282, s. 3; 2001-193, s. 16.)

§ 54B-128. Option on nonnegotiable orders of withdrawal.

Notwithstanding any other provisions of law, the Commissioner of Banks may by regulation authorize State associations to establish nonnegotiable orders or authorizations of withdrawal. (1981, c. 282, s. 3; 2001-193, s. 16.)

§ 54B-129. Joint accounts.

(a) Any two or more persons may open or hold a withdrawable account or accounts. The withdrawable account and any balance thereof shall be held by them as joint tenants, with or without right of survivorship, as the contract shall provide; the account may also be held pursuant to G.S. 41-2.1 and have incidents set forth in that section, provided, however, if the account is held pursuant to G.S. 41-2.1 the contract shall set forth that fact as well. Unless the persons establishing the account have agreed with the association that withdrawals require more than one signature, payment by the association to, or on the order of, any persons holding an account authorized by this section shall be a total discharge of the association's obligation as to the amount so paid. Funds in a joint account established with right of survivorship shall belong to the surviving joint tenant or tenants upon the death of a joint tenant, and the funds shall be subject only to the personal representative's right of collection as set forth in G.S. 28A-15-10(a)(3), or as provided in G.S. 41-2.1 if the account is established pursuant to the provisions of that section. Payment by the association of funds in the joint account to a surviving joint tenant or tenants shall terminate the personal representative's authority under G.S. 28A-15-10(a)(3) to collect against the association for the funds so paid, but the personal representative's authority to collect such funds from the surviving joint tenant or tenants is not terminated. A pledge of such account by any holder or holders shall, unless otherwise specifically agreed upon, be a valid pledge and transfer of such account, or of the amount so pledged, and shall not operate to sever or terminate the joint ownership of all or any part of the account. Persons establishing an account under this section shall sign a statement showing their election of the right of survivorship in the account, and containing language set forth in a conspicuous manner and substantially similar to the following:

"SAVINGS AND LOAN (or name of institution)

JOINT ACCOUNT WITH RIGHT OF SURVIVORSHIP

G.S. 54B-129

We understand that by establishing a joint account under the provisions of North Carolina General Statute 54B-129 that:

1. The savings and loan association (or name of institution) may pay the money in the account to, or on the order of, any person named in the account unless we have agreed with the association that withdrawals require more than one signature; and

2. Upon the death of one joint owner the money remaining in the account will belong to the surviving joint owners and will not pass by inheritance to the heirs of the deceased joint owner or be controlled by the deceased joint owner's will.

We DO elect to create the right of survivorship in this account.

_____

    _____ "

(a1) This section shall not be deemed exclusive. Deposit accounts not conforming to this section shall be governed by other applicable provisions of the General Statutes or the common law as appropriate.

(b) This section does not repeal or modify any provisions of law relating to estate taxes. This section regulates and protects the association in its relationships with joint owners of deposit accounts.

(c) No addition to such account, nor any withdrawal or payment shall affect the nature of the account as a joint account, or affect the right of any tenant to terminate the account. (1981, c. 282, s. 3; 1987 (Reg. Sess., 1988), c. 1078, s. 5; 1989, c. 164, s. 1; 1989 (Reg. Sess., 1990), c. 866, s. 1; 1998-69, s. 16.)

§ 54B-130: Repealed by Session Laws 2011-236, s. 2, effective October 1, 2011.

§ 54B-130.1. Payable on Death (POD) accounts.

(a)   If any natural person or natural persons establishing a deposit account shall execute a written agreement with the association containing a statement that it is executed pursuant to the provisions of this section and providing for the account to be held in the name of the natural person or natural persons as owner or owners for one or more beneficiaries, the account and any balance thereof shall be held as a Payable on Death account. The account shall have the following incidents:

(1)   Any owner during the owner's lifetime may change any designated beneficiary by a written direction to the association.

(2)   If there are two or more owners of a Payable on Death account, the owners shall own the account as joint tenants with right of survivorship and, except as otherwise provided in this section, the account shall have the incidents set forth in G.S. 54B-129.

(3)   Any owner may withdraw funds by writing checks or otherwise, as set forth in the account contract, and receive payment in cash or check payable to the owner's personal order.

(4)   If the beneficiary or beneficiaries are natural persons, there may be one or more beneficiaries and the following shall apply:

a.   If only one beneficiary is living and of legal age at the death of the last surviving owner, the beneficiary shall be the owner of the account, and payment by the association to such owner shall be a total discharge of the association's obligation as to the amount paid. If two or more beneficiaries are living at the death of the last surviving owner, they shall be owners of the account as joint tenants with right of survivorship as provided in G.S. 54B-129, and payment by the association to the owners or any of the owners shall be a total discharge of the association's obligation as to the amount paid.

b.   If only one beneficiary is living and that beneficiary is not of legal age at the death of the last surviving owner, the association shall transfer the funds in the account to the general guardian or guardian of the estate, if any, of the minor beneficiary. If no guardian of the minor beneficiary has been appointed, the association shall hold the funds in a similar interest bearing account in the name of the minor until the minor reaches the age of majority or until a duly appointed guardian withdraws the funds.

(5)   If the beneficiary is an entity other than a natural person, there shall be only one beneficiary.

(6)   If one or more owners survive the last surviving beneficiary who was a natural person, or if a beneficiary who is an entity other than a natural person should cease to exist before the death of the owner, the account shall become an individual account of the owner, or a joint account with right of survivorship of the owners, and shall have the legal incidents of an individual account in a case of a single owner or a joint account with right of survivorship, as provided in G.S. 54B-129, in the case of multiple owners.

(7)   Prior to the death of the last surviving owner, no beneficiary shall have any ownership interest in a Payable on Death account. Funds in a Payable on Death account established pursuant to this subsection shall belong to the beneficiary or beneficiaries upon the death of the last surviving owner, and the funds shall be subject only to the personal representative's right of collection as set forth in G.S. 28A-15-10(a)(1). Payment by the association of funds in the Payable on Death account to the beneficiary or beneficiaries shall terminate the personal representative's authority under G.S. 28A-15-10(a)(1) to collect against the association for the funds so paid, but the personal representative's authority to collect such funds from the beneficiary or beneficiaries is not terminated.

The natural person or natural persons establishing an account under this subsection shall sign a statement containing language set forth in a conspicuous manner and substantially similar to the language set out below; the language may be on a signature card or in an explanation of the account that is set out in a separate document whose receipt is acknowledged by the person or persons establishing the account:

"SAVINGS AND LOAN (or name of institution)

PAYABLE ON DEATH ACCOUNT

G.S. 54B-130.1

I (or we) understand that by establishing a Payable on Death account under the provisions of North Carolina General Statute 54B-130.1 that:

1.   During my (or our) lifetime I (or we), individually or jointly, may withdraw the money in the account.

2.   By written direction to the association (or name of institution) I (or we), individually or jointly, may change the beneficiary or beneficiaries.

3.   Upon my (or our) death the money remaining in the account will belong to the beneficiary or beneficiaries, and the money will not be inherited by my (or our) heirs or be controlled by will.

_____

_____"

(b)   This section shall not be deemed exclusive. Deposit accounts not conforming to this section shall be governed by other applicable provisions of the General Statutes or the common law, as appropriate.

(c)   No addition to such accounts, nor any withdrawal, payment, or change of beneficiary, shall affect the nature of such accounts as Payable on Death accounts or affect the right of any owner to terminate the account.

(d)   This section does not repeal or modify any provisions of laws relating to estate taxes. (1981, c. 282, s. 3; 1987 (Reg. Sess., 1988), c. 1078, s. 6; 1989, c. 164, s. 4; 1989 (Reg. Sess., 1990), c. 866, s. 2; 1998-69, s. 17; 2001-267, s. 3; 2011-236, s. 2; 2012-168, s. 4; 2012-194, s. 63.)

§ 54B-131. Right of setoff on withdrawable accounts.

(a)   Every association shall have a right of setoff, without further agreement or pledge, upon all withdrawable accounts owned by any member or customer to whom or upon whose behalf the association has made an unsecured advance of money by loan; and upon the default in the repayment or satisfaction thereof the association may cancel on its books all or any part of the withdrawable accounts owned by such member or customer, and apply the value of such accounts in payment on account of such obligation.

(b) An association which exercises the right of setoff provided in this section shall first give 30 days' notice to the member or customer that such right will be exercised. Such accounts may be held or frozen, with no withdrawals permitted, during the 30-day notice period. Such accounts may not be canceled and the value thereof may not be applied to pay such obligation until the 30-day period has expired without the member or customer having cured the default on the obligation. The amount of any member's or customer's interest in a joint account or other account held in the names of more than one person shall be subject to the right of setoff provided in this section.

(c) This section is not exclusive, but shall be in addition to contract, common law and other rights of setoff. Such other rights shall not be governed in any fashion by this section. (1981, c. 282, s. 3; 1991, c. 707, s. 5.)

§ 54B-132. Minors as withdrawable account holders; safe deposit box lessees.

(a) An association may issue a withdrawable account to a minor as the sole and absolute owner, or as a joint owner, and receive payments, pay withdrawals, accept pledges and act in any other manner with respect to such account on the order of the minor with like effect as if he were of full age and legal capacity. Any payment to a minor shall be a discharge of the association to the extent thereof. The account shall be held for the exclusive right and benefit of the minor, and any joint owners, free from the control of all persons, except creditors.

(b) An association may lease a safe deposit box to a minor and, with respect to such lease, may deal with the minor in all regards as if the minor were of full age and legal capacity. A minor entering a lease agreement with an association pursuant to this subsection shall be bound by the terms of the agreement to the same extent as if the minor were of full age and legal capacity. (1981, c. 282, s. 3; 1989, c. 437; 1991, c. 707, s. 6.)

§ 54B-133. Withdrawable accounts as deposit of securities.

Notwithstanding any restrictions or limitations contained in any law of this State, the withdrawable accounts of any State association or of any federal association having its principal office in this State, may be accepted by any agency, department or official of this State in any case wherein such agency, department or official acting in its or his official capacity requires that securities be deposited with such agency, department or official. (1981, c. 282, s. 3.)

§ 54B-134. New account books.

A new account book or certificate or other evidence of ownership of a withdrawable account may be issued in the name of the holder of record at any time when requested by such holder or his legal representative upon proof satisfactory to the association that the original account book or certificate has been lost or destroyed. Such new account book or certificate shall expressly state that it is issued in lieu of the one lost or destroyed and that the association shall in no way be liable thereafter on account of the original book or certificate. The association may in its bylaws require indemnification against any loss that might result from the issuance of the new account book or certified certificate. (1981, c. 282, s. 3.)

§ 54B-135. Transfer of withdrawable accounts.

The owner of a withdrawable account may transfer his rights therein absolutely or conditionally to any other person eligible to hold the same but such transfer may be made on the books of the association only upon presentation of evidence of transfer satisfactory to the association, and accompanied by the proper application for transfer by the transferor and transferee, who shall accept such account subject to the terms and conditions of the savings contract, the bylaws of the association, the provisions of its certificate of incorporation, and all rules and regulations of the Commissioner of Banks. Notwithstanding the effectiveness of such a transfer between the parties thereto, the association may treat the holder of record of a withdrawable account as the owner thereof for all purposes, including payment and voting (in the case of a mutual association) until such transfer and assignment has been recorded by the association. (1981, c. 282, s. 3; 2001-193, s. 16.)

§ 54B-136. Authority of power of attorney.

An association may continue to recognize the authority of an individual holding a power of attorney in writing to manage or to make withdrawals either in whole or in part from the withdrawable account of a customer or member until it receives written or actual notice of death or of adjudication of incompetency of such member or revocation of the authority of such individual holding such power of attorney. Payment by the association to an individual holding a power of attorney prior to receipt of such notice shall be a total discharge of the association's obligation as to the amount so paid. (1981, c. 282, s. 3.)

§ 54B-137. Reserved for future codification purposes.

§ 54B-138. Reserved for future codification purposes.

§ 54B-139. Personal agency accounts.

(a)   A person may open a personal agency account by written contract containing a statement that it is executed pursuant to the provisions of this section. A personal agency account may be a checking account, savings account, time deposit, or any other type of withdrawable account or certificate. The written contract shall name an agent who shall have authority to act on behalf of the depositor in regard to the account as set out in this subsection. The agent shall have the authority to:

(1)   Make, sign or execute checks drawn on the account or otherwise make withdrawals from the account;

(2)   Endorse checks made payable to the principal for deposit only into the account; and

(3)   Deposit cash or negotiable instruments, including instruments endorsed by the principal, into the account.

A person establishing an account under this section shall sign a statement containing language substantially similar to the following in a conspicuous manner:

"SAVINGS AND LOAN (or name of institution)

PERSONAL AGENCY ACCOUNT

G.S. 54B-139

I understand that by establishing a personal agent account under the provisions of North Carolina General Statute 54B-139 that the agent named in the account may:

1. Sign checks drawn on the account; and

2. Make deposits into the account.

I also understand that upon my death the money remaining in the account will be controlled by my will or inherited by my heirs.

_____ "

(b) An account created under the provisions of this section grants no ownership right or interest in the agent. Upon the death of the principal there is no right of survivorship to the account and the authority set out in subsection (a) terminates.

(c) The written contract referred to in subsection (a) shall provide that the principal may elect to extend the authority of the agent set out in subsection (a) to act on behalf of the principal in regard to the account notwithstanding the subsequent incapacity or mental incompetence of the principal. If the principal so elects to extend such authority of the agent, then upon the subsequent incapacity or mental incompetence of the principal, the agent may continue to exercise such authority, without the requirement of bond or of accounting to any court, until such time as the agent shall receive actual knowledge that such authority has been terminated by a duly qualified guardian of the estate of the incapacitated or incompetent principal or by the duly appointed attorney-in-fact for the incapacitated or incompetent principal, acting pursuant to a durable power of attorney (as defined in G.S. 32A-8) which grants to the attorney-in-fact that authority in regard to the account which is granted to the agent by the written contract executed pursuant to the provisions of this section, at which time the agent shall account to such guardian or attorney-in-fact for all actions of the agent in regard to the account during the incapacity or incompetence of the principal. If the principal does not so elect to extend the authority of the agent, then upon the subsequent incapacity or mental incompetence of the principal, the authority of the agent set out in subsection (a) terminates.

(d) When an account under this section has been established all or part of the account or any interest or dividend thereon may be paid by the association on a check made, signed or executed by the agent. In the absence of actual knowledge that the principal has died or that the agency created by the account has been terminated, such payment shall be a valid and sufficient discharge to the association for payment so made. (1987 (Reg. Sess., 1988), c. 1078, s. 7; 1989, c. 164, s. 7; 1989 (Reg. Sess., 1990), c. 866, s. 3.)

§§ 54B-140 through 54B-146. Reserved for future codification purposes.

Article 6A.

Fee for Returned Checks.

§ 54B-147. Collection of processing fee for returned checks.

Notwithstanding any other provision of law, a processing fee may be charged and collected by any association for checks (including negotiable order of withdrawal drafts) on which payment has been refused by the payor depository institution. An association may also collect said fee for checks drawn on that association with respect to an account with insufficient funds. (1981 (Reg. Sess., 1982), c. 1238, s. 14; 1985, c. 224.)

§§ 54B-148 through 54B-149. Reserved for future codification purposes.

Article 7.

Loans.

§ 54B-150. Manner of making loans.

(a) The board of directors shall establish procedures by which loans are to be considered, approved, and made by the association.

(b) All actions on loan applications to the association shall be reported to the board of directors at its next meeting. (1981, c. 282, s. 3; 1983, c. 144, s. 18.)

§ 54B-151. Permitted loans.

(a) An association may lend funds on the sole security of pledged withdrawable accounts, but no loan so made shall exceed the withdrawal value of the pledged account. However, no such loan shall be made when an association has applications for withdrawals or maturities which have not been paid.

(b) An association may lend funds on the security of real property:

(1) Of such value, determined in accordance with the provisions of this Chapter and the rules and regulations concerning appraisals, sufficient to provide good and ample security for the loan; and

(2) Which has a fee simple title, totally free from encumbrances except as permitted within this Article; or

(3) Which has a leasehold title extending or renewable automatically or at the option of the holder or at the option of the association for a period of at least 10 years beyond the maturity of the loan; and

(4) Which has a clear title established by such evidence of title as is consistent with sound lending practices; and

(5) Where the security interest in such real property is evidenced by an appropriate written instrument creating or constituting a first and prior lien on real property, and the loan is evidenced by a note, bond or similar written instrument; or

(6) Where the security interest in such real property is evidenced by an appropriate written instrument creating or constituting a second or junior lien on real property which is subject only to a mortgage or deed of trust securing a commercial loan or a residential loan made by the association or another lender; and

(7) Where the security property may be subject also to taxes and special assessments not yet due and payable.

(c) An association may lend funds on the security of the whole of the beneficial interest in a trust in which the trust property consists of real property of the type upon which a loan would be permitted under G.S. 54B-151(b).

(d) An association may lend funds on the security of bonds issued as general obligations of or guaranteed by the United States, bonds issued as general obligations of this State, and bonds issued as general obligations of any county, city, town, village, school district, sanitation or park district, or other political subdivision or municipal corporation of this State. The amount of such loan made under the authority of this subsection shall not exceed ninety percent (90%) of the face value of the bonds which serve as security.

(e) An association may invest in construction loans, the proceeds of which, under the terms of a written contract between a lender and a borrower, are to be disbursed periodically as such construction work progresses. Such loans may include advances for the purchase price of the real property upon which such improvements are to be constructed. Any construction loan may be converted into a loan with permanent financing, and the term of the permanent financing shall be considered to begin at the end of the term allowed for construction.

(f) An association may lend funds without requiring security. No unsecured loan shall exceed the maximum amount authorized by regulation by the Commissioner of Banks.

(g) An association may invest in loans secured by a lien on unimproved real property.

(h)   An association may invest in loans secured by the cash surrender value of any life insurance policy on the life of the borrower. However, the amount of such loan shall in no event exceed ninety percent (90%) of the cash surrender value of such life insurance policy.

(i)   An association may invest in loans, obligations and advances of credit made for the payment of expenses of college or university education. Such loans may be secured, partly secured or unsecured, and the association may require a comaker or comakers, an insurance guarantee under a governmental student loan guarantee plan, or other protection against contingencies. The borrower shall certify to the association that the proceeds of the loan are to be used by a full-time student solely for the payment of expenses of college or university education or community college education.

(j)   An association may lend funds on any collateral deemed sufficient by the board of directors to properly secure loans. Loans made solely upon security of collateral consisting of stock or equity securities which are not listed on a national stock exchange or regularly quoted and offered for trade on an over-the-counter market, shall be considered loans without security.

(k)   An association may lend funds on the security of a mobile home subject to such rules and regulations governing such loans as may be promulgated by the Commissioner of Banks. (1981, c. 282, s. 3; 1983, c. 144, s. 19; 1987, c. 564, s. 14; 2001-193, s. 16.)

§ 54B-152. Real property encumbrances.

(a)   Real property is deemed unencumbered within the meaning of this Chapter unless the security instrument thereon establishes a first lien upon such real property or interest therein.

(b)   Notwithstanding the provisions of the immediately preceding subsection, real property is not deemed encumbered within the meaning of this Chapter merely by reason of the existence of:

(1)   An instrument reserving a right-of-way, sewer rights, or rights in wells; or

(2)   Building restrictions or other restrictive covenants; or

(3) A lease under which rents or profits are reserved by the owner; or

(4) Current taxes or assessments not yet payable; or

(5) Other encumbrances which, in accordance with sound lending practices in the locality, are not regarded as constituting defects in title to real property. (1981, c. 282, s. 3; 1999-179, s. 1.)

§ 54B-153. Prohibited security.

No association may accept its own capital stock or its own mutual capital certificates as security for any loan made by such association. (1981, c. 282, s. 3.)

§ 54B-154. Insider loans.

The Commissioner of Banks may promulgate rules and regulations no less stringent than the requirements of the appropriate federal regulatory authority, and as he deems necessary, to govern the making of loans to officers and directors, and their associates, and companies or other business entities controlled by them. (1981, c. 282, s. 3; 1983, c. 144, s. 20; 1989 (Reg. Sess., 1990), c. 806, s. 10; 2001-193, s. 16.)

§ 54B-155. Rule-making power of Commissioner of Banks.

The Commissioner of Banks shall, from time to time, promulgate such rules and regulations in respect to loans permitted to be made by State associations as may be reasonably necessary to assure that such loans are in keeping with sound lending practices and to promote the purposes of this Chapter; provided, that such rules and regulations shall not prohibit an association from making any loan which is a permitted loan for federal associations under federal regulatory authority. (1981, c. 282, s. 3; 2001-193, s. 16.)

§ 54B-156. Loan expenses and fees.

(a) Subject to the provisions of N.C.G.S. Chapter 24, an association may require borrowers to pay all reasonable expenses incurred by the association in connection with making, closing, disbursing, extending, adjusting or renewing loans. Such charges may be collected by the association from the borrower and paid to any persons, including any director, officer or employee of the association who may render services in connection with the loan, or such charges may be paid directly by the borrower.

(b) An association may require a borrower to pay a reasonable charge for late payments made during the course of repayment of a loan. Subject to the provisions of G.S. 24-10.1, such payments may be levied only upon such terms and conditions as shall be fixed by the association's board of directors and agreed to by the borrower in the loan contract. (1981, c. 282, s. 3; 1989 (Reg. Sess., 1990), c. 806, s. 16.)

§ 54B-157. Loans conditioned on certain transactions prohibited.

No association or service corporation thereof shall require as a condition of making a loan that the borrower contract with any specific person or organization for particular services. (1981, c. 282, s. 3.)

§ 54B-158. Insured or guaranteed loans.

An association may make insured or guaranteed loans in accordance with the provisions of G.S. 53C-5-3. (1981, c. 282, s. 3; 2012-56, s. 41.)

§ 54B-159. Purchase of loans.

An association may invest any funds on hand in the purchase of loans of a type which the association could make in accordance with the provisions of this Chapter. (1981, c. 282, s. 3.)

§ 54B-160. Participation in loans.

An association may invest in a participating interest in loans of a type which the association would be authorized to originate. (1981, c. 282, s. 3; 1981 (Reg. Sess., 1982), c. 1238, s. 15.)

§ 54B-161. Sale of loans.

An association may sell any loan, including any participating interest in a loan. (1981, c. 282, s. 3; 1981 (Reg. Sess., 1982), c. 1238, s. 16.)

§ 54B-162. Power to borrow money.

An association, in its certificate of incorporation or in its bylaws, may authorize the board of directors to borrow money and the board of directors may by resolution adopted by a vote of at least two thirds of the entire board duly recorded in the minutes may authorize the officers of the association to borrow money for the association on such terms and conditions as it may deem proper. (1981, c. 282, s. 3; 1981 (Reg. Sess., 1982), c. 1238, s. 17.)

§ 54B-163. Methods of loan repayment.

Subject to such rules and regulations as the Commissioner of Banks may prescribe, an association shall agree in writing with borrowers as to the method or plan by which an indebtedness shall be repaid. (1981, c. 282, s. 3; 2001-193, s. 16.)

§ 54B-164. Loans to one borrower.

(a) The aggregate amount of mortgage loans outstanding granted by an association to any one borrower shall not exceed ten percent (10%) of the net withdrawal value of such association's withdrawable accounts or an amount equal to the total net worth of such association, whichever amount is less.

(b)   Notwithstanding any other provision of law, in order to protect the public, including members, depositors, and stockholders of a State association, the Commissioner of Banks may establish limits on loans to any one borrower if he finds that a State association is operating with unsafe and unsound lending practices. The Commissioner of Banks shall promulgate rules and regulations to govern the establishment of the limits authorized by this section. (1981, c. 282, s. 3; 1985, c. 659, s. 14; 2001-193, s. 16.)

§ 54B-165. Professional services.

(a)   A State association or service corporation thereof must notify borrowers prior to the loan commitment of their right to select the attorney or law firm rendering legal services in connection with the loan, and the person or organization rendering insurance services in connection with the loan. Such persons or organizations must be approved by the association's board of directors, pursuant to such rules and regulations as the Commissioner of Banks may prescribe.

(b)   A State association or service corporation thereof may require borrowers to reimburse such association for legal services rendered to it by its own attorney only when the fee is limited to legal services required by the making of such loan. (1981, c. 282, s. 3; 2001-193, s. 16.)

§ 54B-166. Nonconforming investments.

Unless otherwise provided, every loan or other investment made in violation of this Chapter shall be due and payable according to its terms and the obligation thereof shall not be impaired; provided, that such violation consists only of the lending of an excessive sum on authorized security or of investing in an unauthorized investment. (1981, c. 282, s. 3.)

§ 54B-167. Scope of Article.

Nothing in this Article shall be construed to modify Chapter 24 of the General Statutes, or other applicable law, or to allow fees, charges, or interest beyond that permitted by Chapter 24 or other applicable law. (1981, c. 282, s. 3.)

§§ 54B-168 through 54B-179. Reserved for future codification purposes.

Article 8.

Other Investments.

§ 54B-180. Other investments.

In addition to the loans and investments permitted under Article 7 of this Chapter, the assets of a State association in excess of the demands of its members or customers may be invested subject to the approval of the board of directors only as described under the provisions of this Article. (1981, c. 282, s. 3.)

§ 54B-181. Business property of a State association.

A State association may invest in real property and equipment necessary for the conduct of its business and in real property to be held for its future use. Such association may invest in an office building or buildings, and appurtenances for the purpose of the transaction of such association's business or for rental. No such investment may be made without the prior written approval of the Commissioner of Banks if the total amount of such investments exceeds the association's net worth. (1981, c. 282, s. 3; 2001-193, s. 16.)

§ 54B-182. United States obligations.

A State association may invest in any obligation issued and fully guaranteed in principal and interest by the United States government or any instrumentality thereof. (1981, c. 282, s. 3.)

§ 54B-183. North Carolina obligations.

A State association may invest in any obligation issued and fully guaranteed in principal and interest by the State of North Carolina or any instrumentality thereof. (1981, c. 282, s. 3.)

§ 54B-184. Federal Home Loan Bank obligations.

A State association may invest in the stock of the Federal Home Loan Bank of which such association is a member, and in bonds or other evidences of indebtedness or obligation of any Federal Home Loan Bank. (1981, c. 282, s. 3.)

§ 54B-185. Deposits in banks.

A State association may invest in certificates of deposit, time insured deposits, savings accounts, or demand deposits of such banks as are approved by the board of directors of the association. (1981, c. 282, s. 3.)

§ 54B-186. Deposits in other associations.

A State association may invest in withdrawable accounts of any association as approved by the board of directors. (1981, c. 282, s. 3; 1981 (Reg. Sess., 1982), c. 1238, s. 18.)

§ 54B-187. Fannie Mae obligations.

A State association may invest in stock or other evidences of indebtedness or obligations of Fannie Mae, or any successor thereto. (1981, c. 282, s. 3; 2001-487, s. 14(d).)

§ 54B-188. Municipal and county obligations.

A State association may invest in bonds or other evidences of indebtedness which are direct general obligations of any county, city, town, village, school district, sanitation or park district, or other political subdivision or municipal corporation of this State; or in bonds or other evidences of indebtedness which are payable from revenues or earnings specifically pledged therefor, which are issued by the county or an adjoining county or a political subdivision or municipal corporation of a county in this State. (1981, c. 282, s. 3.)

§ 54B-189. Stock in education agency.

A State association may invest in stock or obligations of any corporation doing business in this State, or of any agency of this State or of the United States, where the principal business of such corporation or agency is to make loans for the financing of a college or university education, or education at a community college in this State. (1981, c. 282, s. 3; 1987, c. 564, s. 14.)

§ 54B-190. Industrial development corporation stock.

A State association may invest in stock or other evidence of indebtedness or obligations of business or industrial development corporations chartered by this State or by the United States. (1981, c. 282, s. 3.)

§ 54B-191. Urban renewal investment corporation stock.

A State association may invest in stock or other evidence of indebtedness or obligations of an urban renewal investment corporation chartered under the laws of this State or of the United States. (1981, c. 282, s. 3.)

§ 54B-192. Urban renewal projects.

(a) A State association may invest in the initial purchase and development, or the purchase or commitment to purchase after completion, of unimproved residential real property or improved residential real property for sale or rental, including projects for the reconstruction, rehabilitation or rebuilding of residential properties to meet the minimum standards of health and occupancy prescribed by appropriate local authorities, and the provision of accommodations for retail stores, shops and other community services which are reasonably incident to such housing projects. No such investment shall be made under the provisions of this section without the prior approval of the Commissioner of Banks. The Commissioner of Banks may approve such investment under the provisions of this section only when the association shows:

(1) That the association has adequate assets available for such an investment;

(2) That the amount of the proposed investment does not exceed ninety percent (90%) of the reasonable market value of the property or interest therein; and

(3) Reserved.

(4) That the proposed project is to be located in an area, including any contiguous area acquired incidentally thereto, determined by the Commissioner of Banks to be an urban renewal, redevelopment, blighted or conservation area, or any similar area provided for by the laws of this State or of the United States, or local ordinances for slum clearance, conservation, blighted area clearance, redevelopment, urban renewal or of a similar nature or purpose.

(b) Nothing herein contained shall prohibit a State association from developing or building on land acquired by it under any other provisions of this Chapter; nor shall a State association be prohibited from completing the construction of buildings pursuant to any construction loan contract where the borrower has failed to comply with the terms of such contract. (1981, c. 282, s. 3; 2001-193, s. 16.)

§ 54B-193. Loans on sufficient collateral; other investments.

(a) A State association may invest in loans secured by any collateral deemed sufficient by the board of directors to properly secure loans; however, if the collateral consists of stock or equity securities of any kind, the stock or securities must be listed on a national stock exchange or regularly quoted and offered for trade on an over-the-counter market.

(b) Subject to such limitations as the Commissioner of Banks may prescribe by regulation, a State association may invest in any investment deemed appropriate by its board of directors. (1981, c. 282, s. 3; 1981 (Reg. Sess., 1982), c. 1238, s. 19; 2001-193, s. 16.)

§ 54B-194. Service corporations.

(a) Any association or group of associations whose principal offices are located within this State, may establish service corporations under the provisions of Chapter 55 for corporate organization, provided that the Commissioner of Banks receives copies of the proposed articles of incorporation and bylaws for approval, prior to filing them with the Secretary of State. Any such association may also invest in the capital stock, obligations or other securities of existing service corporations.

(b) No State association may make any investment in service corporations if its aggregate investment would exceed ten percent (10%) of its total assets.

(c) Service corporations shall be subject to audit and examination by the Commissioner of Banks, and the cost of examination shall be paid by the service corporation.

(d) The permitted activities of a service corporation shall be described in the rules and regulations as promulgated by the Commissioner of Banks. In addition, a service corporation may engage in those activities which are approved for service corporations owned solely by federal associations who have their principal offices in this State, unless such activities are prohibited by the Commissioner of Banks.

(e) The location of the principal and branch offices of a service corporation must be approved by the Commissioner of Banks. (1981, c. 282, s. 3; 1981 (Reg. Sess., 1982), c. 1238, s. 20; 1989 (Reg. Sess., 1990), c. 806, s. 11; 2001-193, s. 16.)

§ 54B-195. Any loan or investment permitted for federal associations.

Subject to such limitations and restrictions as the Commissioner of Banks may prescribe through rules and regulations, any State association is authorized and permitted to make any loan or investment, or engage in any activity, which may be permitted for federal associations whose principal offices are located within this State. Every loan or investment made by a State association prior to the enactment of this Chapter shall for all purposes be considered to have been permitted loans or investments if federal associations were authorized to make such loans or investments at the time they were made by the State association. (1981, c. 282, s. 3; 1983, c. 144, s. 21; 1989 (Reg. Sess., 1990), c. 806, s. 12; 2001-193, s. 16.)

§ 54B-196. Reserved for future codification purposes.

§ 54B-197. Effect of change in law or regulation.

Any loan or investment made by a State association which was in compliance with the law or regulations in effect at the time such loan or investment was made will remain a legal loan or investment even though the power to make such loans or investments in the future is amended or revoked. (1981, c. 282, s. 3.)

§§ 54B-198 through 54B-209. Reserved for future codification purposes.

Article 9.

Liquidity Fund.

§ 54B-210. Components of liquidity fund.

(a) Every State association shall establish and maintain a regulatory capital account in an amount and in such funds and investments that comply with the requirements of the appropriate federal regulatory authorities.

(b) The failure of a State association to maintain the required level and type of regulatory capital may be grounds for supervisory action by the Commissioner of Banks.

(c) The Commissioner of Banks may adopt rules to implement this section. (1981, c. 282, s. 3; 1981 (Reg. Sess., 1982), c. 1238, s. 21; 1983, c. 144, s. 22; 1989, c. 76, s. 10; 1989 (Reg. Sess., 1990), c. 806, s. 13; 2001-193, s. 16.)

§ 54B-211. Renewal of liquidity fund.

If the liquidity fund falls below the amount required by the Commission, the association shall make no new real property loans until the required level has been attained. The refinancing, recasting or renewal of loans previously made and loans made as a result of foreclosure sales under instruments held by the association shall not be considered as new loans, within the meaning of this section. (1981, c. 282, s. 3.)

§§ 54B-212 through 54B-215. Reserved for future codification purposes.

Article 10.

General Reserve.

§ 54B-216. General reserve.

(a) Every State association shall establish and maintain general valuation allowances and specific loss reserves in compliance with the requirements of the appropriate federal regulatory authorities.

(b) The failure of a State association to maintain the required level of general valuation allowances or specific loss reserves may be grounds for supervisory action by the Commissioner of Banks.

(c) The Commissioner of Banks may adopt rules to implement this section.

(d) to (f) Repealed by Session Laws 1989, c. 76, s. 11. (1981, c. 282, s. 3; 1981 (Reg. Sess., 1982), c. 1238, s. 2; 1989, c. 76, s. 11; 1989 (Reg. Sess., 1990), c. 806, s. 14; 2001-193, s. 16.)

§§ 54B-217 through 54B-220. Reserved for future codification purposes.

Article 11.

Foreign Associations.

§§ 54B-221 through 54B-235. Repealed by Session Laws 1983 (Regular Session, 1984), c. 1087, s. 6, effective July 5, 1984.

Article 12.

Mutual Deposit Guaranty Associations.

§ 54B-236. Definitions.

The term "institution" as used in this Article shall mean savings and loan associations organized or operated under the provisions of this Chapter, or credit unions organized or operated under the provisions of Articles 14A to 14L of Chapter 54 of the General Statutes, or any institution that is eligible for insurance by the Federal Deposit Insurance Corporation or the National Credit

Union Administration. (1981, c. 282, s. 3; 1983, c. 144, s. 23; 1985, c. 659, s. 15; 1989 (Reg. Sess., 1990), c. 806, s. 15.)

§ 54B-237. Organization of a mutual deposit guaranty association.

(a) Any number of institutions, not less than 25, may become incorporated as a mutual deposit guaranty association without capital stock subject to the limitations prescribed in this Article. A mutual deposit guaranty association shall be governed by a board of directors or board of trustees of which a majority shall be representatives of the public and shall not be employees or directors of any insured member institution or have an interest in any insured member institution other than as a result of being a depositor or borrower.

(b) Articles of incorporation of a guaranty association shall be filed in the office of the Secretary of State. The Secretary of State shall, upon receipt of such articles, transmit a copy of them to the Secretary of Commerce and shall not record them until authorized to do so by the Secretary of Commerce. (1981, c. 282, s. 3; 1983, c. 719, s. 2; 1989, c. 751, s. 9(c); 1991 (Reg. Sess., 1992), c. 959, s. 7.)

§ 54B-238. Examination and certification by Secretary of Commerce.

(a) Upon receipt from the Secretary of State of a copy of the articles of incorporation of a proposed guaranty association, the Secretary of Commerce shall at once examine all the facts connected with the formation of the proposed corporation. If the articles of incorporation are correct in form and substance and the examination shows that such corporation, if formed, would be entitled to commence the business of a guaranty association, the Secretary of Commerce shall so certify to the Secretary of State.

(b) The Secretary of Commerce may refuse to make such certification if upon examination he has reason to believe the proposed corporation is to be formed for any business other than assuring the liquidity of member institutions and guaranteeing deposits therein, if upon examination he has reason to believe that the character and general fitness of the incorporators are not such as to command the confidence of the general public or if the best interests of the public will not be promoted by its establishment. (1981, c. 282, s. 3; 1983, c. 719, s. 2; 1989, c. 751, s. 8(3); 1991 (Reg. Sess., 1992), c. 959, s. 8.)

§ 54B-239. Recordation of articles of incorporation.

Upon receipt of the certification provided for in G.S. 54B-238, the Secretary of State shall record the articles of incorporation of such guaranty association and furnish a certified copy thereof to the incorporators and to the Secretary of Commerce. Upon such recordation, such association shall be deemed a corporation. All papers thereafter filed in the office of the Secretary of State relating to such corporation shall be recorded as provided by law and a certified copy forwarded to the Secretary of Commerce. (1981, c. 282, s. 3; 1983, c. 719, s. 2; 1989, c. 751, s. 9(c); 1991 (Reg. Sess., 1992), c. 959, s. 9.)

§ 54B-240. Proposed amendments submitted to Secretary of Commerce.

Any proposed amendments to the articles of incorporation of a mutual deposit guaranty association shall be filed in the office of the Secretary of State, who shall forward a copy thereof to the Secretary of Commerce, and shall not record the amendments until authorized to do so by certification of the Secretary of Commerce. (1981, c. 282, s. 3; 1983, c. 719, s. 2; 1989, c. 751, s. 8(4); 1991 (Reg. Sess., 1992), c. 959, s. 10.)

§ 54B-241. Examination and certification of amendments.

(a) Upon receipt from the Secretary of State of a copy of proposed amendments to the articles of incorporation of a mutual deposit guaranty association, the Secretary of Commerce shall at once examine the proposed amendments to determine their effect on the operation of the guaranty association.

(b) In the event the proposed amendments are correct in form and substance and the examination shows that if adopted they would not change the character or principal business of the guaranty association, the Secretary of Commerce shall so certify to the Secretary of State.

(c) The Secretary of Commerce may refuse to make certification if upon examination he has reason to believe that the proposed amendments would change the character of the business of the guaranty association or that the best interests of the public will not be promoted by their adoption. (1981, c. 282, s. 3; 1983, c. 719, s. 2; 1989, c. 751, s. 8(5); 1991 (Reg. Sess., 1992), c. 959, s. 11.)

§ 54B-242. Recordation of amendments.

Upon receipt of the certification provided for in G.S. 54B-241, the Secretary of State shall record the amendments to the articles of incorporation and furnish a certified copy thereof to the mutual deposit guaranty association and to the Secretary of Commerce. (1981, c. 282, s. 3; 1983, c. 719, s. 2; 1989, c. 751, s. 9(c); 1991 (Reg. Sess., 1992), c. 959, s. 12.)

§ 54B-243. Reserve for losses.

A mutual deposit guaranty association shall maintain at all times an amount of funds equal to no less than one percent (1%) of its insured liability to cover losses of its members. These funds may include cash, investments, and reinsurance. (1981, c. 282, s. 3.)

§ 54B-244. Purposes and powers of mutual deposit guaranty associations.

(a) The purposes of a mutual deposit guaranty association incorporated in accordance with the provisions of this Article are to:

(1) Assure the liquidity of a member institution;

(2) Guarantee the withdrawable accounts, shares of deposits of member institutions;

(3) Serve, when appointed, as receiver of a member institution.

(b) A mutual deposit guaranty association incorporated in accordance with the provisions of this Article may:

(1) Lend money to a member institution for the purpose of assuring its liquidity and withdrawable accounts, shares or deposits therein;

(2) Purchase any assets owned by a member institution for the purpose of assuring its liquidity and withdrawable accounts, shares or deposits therein;

(3) Invest any of its funds in:

a. Bonds or interest-bearing obligations of the United States or for which the faith and credit of the United States are pledged for the payment of principal and interest;

b. Bonds or interest-bearing obligations of this State;

c. Farm loans issued under the Federal Farm Loan Act and amendments thereto;

d. Notes, debentures, and bonds of a federal home loan bank issued under the Federal Home Loan Bank Act and any amendments thereto;

e. Bonds or other securities issued under the Home Owners' Loan Act of 1933 and any amendments thereto;

f. Securities acceptable to the United States to secure government deposits in national banks;

g. Deposits in any financial institution that is subject to examination and supervision by the United States or by this State;

h. Bonds or other evidences of indebtedness of counties and municipalities of the State of North Carolina, provided, that said bonds or other evidences of indebtedness of the counties and municipalities shall have a rating by Moody's Investors Services, Inc., of not less than AA, and a rating by the North Carolina Municipal Council, Inc., of not less than 90 points out of 100 points;

i. Stock in banking institutions licensed to do business in this State;

j. Securities and other investments authorized as liquid investments for any financial institution that is subject to examination and supervision by the United States or by this State;

k. Notes, bonds, debentures or securities rated in one of the four highest grades by a nationally recognized investment rating service.

l. Stock in banking institutions not licensed to do business in this State provided such investment is made in conjunction with any merger or other fundamental change approved by the Commissioner of Banks under the provisions of G.S. 54B-44.

(4) Issue its capital notes or debentures to member institutions, provided the holders of these capital notes or debentures shall not be individually responsible for any debts, contracts, or engagements of the guaranty association issuing the notes or debentures;

(5) Borrow money;

(6) Exercise any corporate power or powers not inconsistent with, and which may be necessary or convenient to, the accomplishment of its purposes of assuring liquidity of member institutions and guaranteeing withdrawable accounts, shares or deposits therein;

(7) Serve as receiver of a member institution;

(8) Make or cause to be made examinations or audits or member institutions. (1981, c. 282, s. 3; 1983, c. 144, s. 24; 2001-193, s. 16.)

§ 54B-245. Filing of semiannual financial reports; fees.

Each mutual deposit guaranty association shall on the 30th day of June and the 31st day of December of each year, or within 40 days thereafter, file with the Secretary of Commerce a report for the preceding half year, showing its financial condition at the end thereof. Such reports shall be in such form and contain such information as may be prescribed by the Secretary of Commerce. Each guaranty association doing business in this State shall pay to the Secretary of Commerce, at the time of filing each semiannual report required by this section, the sum of five dollars ($5.00). All such fees shall be paid into the

State treasury to the credit of the general fund. (1981, c. 282, s. 3; 1983, c. 719, s. 2; 1989, c. 751, s. 9(c); 1991 (Reg. Sess., 1992), c. 959, s. 13.)

§ 54B-246. Supervision by Secretary of Commerce.

(a) In addition to any and all other powers, duties and functions vested in the Secretary of Commerce under the provisions of this Article, and for the protection of member institutions and the general public, the Secretary of Commerce shall have general control and supervision over all mutual deposit guaranty associations doing business in this State. Mutual deposit guaranty associations shall be subject to the control and supervision of the Secretary of Commerce as to their conduct, organization, management, business practices, reserve requirements and their financial and fiscal matters. The grant of general control and supervision over mutual deposit guaranty associations to the Secretary of Commerce by this Article shall in no way be deemed to affect the existing powers, duties and responsibilities of the Credit Union Commission, the Commissioner of Banks, or the State Banking Commission except for the removal herein of general control and supervision over mutual deposit guaranty associations from the Administrator of the Savings Institutions Division to the Secretary of Commerce.

(b) The Secretary of Commerce shall have the right, and is hereby empowered to issue rules and regulations whenever he deems it necessary for the administration of this Article as well as rules and regulations with respect to:

(1) Types of financial records to be maintained by mutual deposit guaranty associations;

(2) Retention periods of various financial records;

(3) Internal control procedures of mutual deposit guaranty associations;

(4) Conduct and management of mutual deposit guaranty associations;

(5) Additional reports which may be required by the Secretary of Commerce.

It shall be the duty of the board of directors or board of trustees of the mutual deposit guaranty association to put into effect and to carry out such rules and regulations.

(c) At least once each year the Secretary of Commerce shall make or cause to be made an examination into the affairs of each mutual deposit guaranty association doing business in this State. The Administrator of the Credit Union Division of this State, in his capacity as supervisor of state-chartered credit unions, if he deems it necessary, may designate agents to participate in such examination. The Commissioner of Banks, in his capacity as supervisor of State chartered savings and loan associations, may designate agents to participate in such examination. The expenses of such yearly examination shall be paid by the mutual deposit guaranty association so examined. (1981, c. 282, s. 3; 1983, c. 719, s. 2; 1989, c. 76, s. 23; c. 751, s. 8(6); 1991 (Reg. Sess., 1992), c. 959, s. 14; 2001-193, ss. 13, 16.)

§ 54B-247. Special examinations.

Whenever the Secretary of Commerce deems it necessary, he may make or cause to be made a special examination or audit of any mutual deposit guaranty association doing business in this State, in addition to the regular examination provided for by this Article. The expenses of such a special examination or audit shall be paid by the mutual deposit guaranty association so examined. (1981, c. 282, s. 3; 1983, c. 719, s. 2; 1989, c. 751, s. 8(7); 1991 (Reg. Sess., 1992), c. 959, s. 15.)

§ 54B-248. Right to enter and to conduct investigations.

The Secretary of Commerce or any examiner appointed by him shall have access to and may compel the production of all books, papers, securities, moneys, and other property of a mutual deposit guaranty association under examination by him. He may administer oaths to and examine the officers and agents of such association as to its affairs. (1981, c. 282, s. 3; 1983, c. 719, s. 2; 1989, c. 751, s. 8(8); 1991 (Reg. Sess., 1992), c. 959, s. 16.)

§ 54B-249. Removal of officers or employees.

The Secretary of Commerce shall have the right, and is hereby empowered, to require the board of directors or board of trustees of any guaranty association to immediately remove from office any officer, director, trustee or employee of any mutual deposit guaranty association doing business in this State, who shall be found by the Secretary of Commerce to be dishonest, incompetent, or reckless in the management of the affairs of the mutual deposit guaranty association, or in violation of the lawful orders, rules and regulations issued by the Secretary of Commerce, or who violates any of the laws set forth in Chapter 54B of the General Statutes. (1981, c. 282, s. 3; 1983, c. 719, s. 2; 1989, c. 751, s. 8(9); 1991 (Reg. Sess., 1992), c. 959, s. 17.)

§§ 54B-250 through 54B-260. Reserved for future codification purposes.

Article 13.

Savings and Loan Holding Companies.

§ 54B-261. Savings and loan holding companies.

(a) Notwithstanding any other provision of law, any stock association may simultaneously with its incorporation or conversion to a stock association provide for its ownership by a savings and loan holding company. In the case of a conversion, members of the converting association shall have the right to purchase capital stock of the holding company in lieu of capital stock of the converted association in accordance with G.S. 54B-33(c)(6).

(a1) Notwithstanding any other provision of law, any stock association may reorganize its ownership, to provide for ownership by a savings and loan holding company, upon adoption of a plan of reorganization by a favorable vote of not less than two-thirds of the members of the board of directors of the association and approval of such plan of reorganization by the holders of not less than a majority of the issued and outstanding shares of stock of the association. The plan of reorganization shall provide that (i) the resulting ownership shall be vested in a North Carolina corporation, (ii) all stockholders of the stock association shall have the right to exchange shares, (iii) the exchange of stock shall not be subject to State or federal income taxation, (iv) stockholders not wishing to exchange shares shall be entitled to appraisal rights as provided under Article 13 of Chapter 55 of the General Statutes and (v) the plan of reorganization is fair and equitable to all stockholders.

(a2)   Notwithstanding any other provision of law, a mutual association may reorganize its ownership to provide for ownership by a savings and loan holding company upon adoption of a plan of reorganization by a favorable vote of not less than two-thirds of the members of the board of directors of the association and approval of the plan of reorganization by a majority of the voting members of the association. The plan of reorganization shall provide that (i) the resulting ownership shall be vested in a North Carolina corporation, (ii) the resulting ownership of one or more subsidiary associations shall be evidenced by stock shares, (iii) the substantial portion of the assets and all of the insured deposits and part or all of the other liabilities shall be transferred to one or more subsidiary associations, (iv) the reorganization shall not be subject to State or federal income taxation, and (v) the plan of reorganization is fair and equitable to all members of the association. The Commissioner of Banks shall promulgate rules regarding the formation of the subsidiary associations and the holding company, including the rights of members, levels of investment in the holding company subsidiaries, and stock sales.

(b)   Repealed by Session Laws 1983, c. 144, s. 8.

(c)   A savings and loan holding company may invest in any investment authorized by its Board of Directors, except as limited by regulations promulgated by the Commissioner of Banks pursuant to this Article.

(d)   Any entity which controls a state stock association, or acquires control of a state stock association, is a savings and loan holding company. (1981, c. 282, s. 3; 1983, c. 144, s. 8; 1983 (Reg. Sess., 1984), c. 1087, ss. 4, 5; 1985, c. 659, s. 16; 1989, c. 76, s. 12; 1989 (Reg. Sess., 1990), c. 806, s. 21; 2001-193, s. 16; 2011-347, s. 3.)

§ 54B-262. Supervision of savings and loan holding companies.

Savings and loan holding companies shall be under the supervision of the Commissioner of Banks. The Commissioner of Banks shall exercise all powers and responsibilities with respect to savings and loan holding companies which he exercises with respect to associations. (1981, c. 282, s. 3; 2001-193, s. 16.)

§ 54B-263. Reserved for future codification purposes.

§ 54B-264. Reserved for future codification purposes.

Article 14.

Savings and Loan Interstate Branches.

§ 54B-265. Title.

This Article shall be known and may be cited as the North Carolina Savings and Loan Interstate Branch Act. (1993, c. 191, s. 2.)

§ 54B-266. Definitions.

As used in this Article, unless the context clearly requires otherwise, the following definitions apply:

(1) Repealed by Session Laws 2004-203, s. 35(a), effective August 17, 2004.

(2) "Association" means a savings and loan association and includes a State association or a federal association unless limited by use of the words "State" or "federal".

(3) "Branch" means a full-service office of an association through which it renders a savings and loan service other than its principal office. An association may engage in any authorized function or service through an authorized branch office.

(4) "Commission" means the State Banking Commission.

(5) "Home state" means (i) as to a state association, the state which granted the association its charter, and (ii) as to a federal association, the state in which the association has its principal office.

(6) "Out-of-state association" means an association chartered by any state other than this State and whose principal office is not within this State.

(7) "State association" means an association chartered under the laws of this State.

(8) "Supervisor" means the state association supervisor or equivalent state official having primary regulatory authority over an out-of-state association. (1993, c. 191, s. 2; 2001-193, ss. 16, 17; 2004-203, s. 35(a).)

§ 54B-267. Establishment of branches by out-of-state associations.

Any out-of-state association that meets the requirements of this Article may establish a branch within North Carolina either by (i) de novo entry; (ii) the purchase of an existing branch; (iii) the purchase of all or substantially all of the assets of a State association located in North Carolina; or (iv) merger or consolidation. (1993, c. 191, s. 2.)

§ 54B-268. Application requirements.

(a) Any out-of-state association desiring to establish a branch office under this Article shall file with the Commissioner of Banks a written application meeting the following requirements:

(1) The out-of-state association shall agree to comply with all the applicable rules and regulations, and informational filing requirements contained in the laws and rules of this State that would apply to a State association engaging in an equivalent form of transaction. Additionally, the Commissioner of Banks shall apply the same standards of approval to the application of the out-of-state association as would apply to an application by a State association for an equivalent form of transaction.

(2) The out-of-state association shall provide the Commissioner of Banks, in the manner prescribed by the Commissioner of Banks, with such additional information as the Commissioner of Banks deems necessary, to fully evaluate the application.

(3) The out-of-state association shall pay an application fee established by the Commissioner of Banks pursuant to G.S. 54B-9.

(4) The out-of-state association shall not commence operations of the branch office until it has received the written approval of the Commissioner of Banks.

(b) The Commissioner of Banks shall act on the application within 90 days of receipt of the completed application. (1993, c. 191, s. 2; 2001-193, s. 16.)

§ 54B-269. Conditions for approval.

No application by an out-of-state association received under this Article may be finally approved by the Commissioner of Banks unless:

(1) The Commissioner of Banks has received in writing approval of the proposed transaction from the supervisor of the out-of-state association;

(2) The supervisor of the out-of-state association agrees in writing to share with the Commissioner of Banks examination reports prepared by the supervisor and any other information deemed necessary by the Commissioner of Banks regarding the out-of-state association;

(3) The out-of-state association agrees in writing to make available to the Commissioner of Banks all information that may be required to effectively examine the association;

(4) The out-of-state association agrees in writing that so long as it maintains a branch in North Carolina, it will meet the conditions set forth in this Article and comply with all applicable North Carolina laws and any rules issued thereunder, as well as any orders or directives issued to the association by the Commissioner of Banks;

(5) The home state of the out-of-state association permits associations chartered under the laws of this State to establish branches within its border; and

(6) The out-of-state association designates and files with the Office of the Secretary of State a document appointing an agent in this State to receive service of judicial process. (1993, c. 191, s. 2; 2001-193, s. 16.)

§ 54B-270. Special conditions.

(a) The Commissioner of Banks may require an out-of-state association to designate one of its branches in North Carolina as a "headquarters branch" and may, by rule, require that reports, books, and records required of associations doing business under this Article be available at the designated headquarters branch.

(b) Once an out-of-state association has established at least one branch in North Carolina pursuant to this Article, subsequent applications to establish additional branches shall be considered on the same basis as an application of a State association to establish an additional branch pursuant to G.S. 54B-22.

(c) If an out-of-state association establishes a branch or branches by merger with or purchase from an association located in this State, and the out-of-state association and the association located in this State are both owned by the same holding company, any conditions, limitations, or restrictions placed on the holding company, pursuant to Articles 3A and 13 of this Chapter, shall continue to apply to both the acquiring out-of-state association and its holding company. (1993, c. 191, s. 2; 2001-193, s. 16.)

§ 54B-271. Powers.

An out-of-state association that establishes a branch in North Carolina may engage in all the activities authorized by North Carolina law for a State association except to the extent that such activities have been expressly prohibited by the state supervisor of the out-of-state association or the laws of the out-of-state association's home state. (1993, c. 191, s. 2.)

§ 54B-272. Establishment of out-of-state branches by state associations.

With the prior consent of the Commissioner of Banks, any association chartered under the laws of North Carolina may establish a branch in any other state in accordance with the laws of such other state. (1993, c. 191, s. 2; 2001-193, s. 16.)

§ 54B-273. Regulatory and supervisory oversight.

(a) The Commissioner of Banks may enter into such agreements as necessary regarding the scope, timing, coordination, and frequency of examinations and other supervisory matters, including the sharing of information gathered in such examinations, with other supervisors and federal association regulators. This authority applies to both out-of-state associations and their holding companies.

(b) The Commissioner of Banks may require periodic reports on the financial condition of any out-of-state association or its holding company that maintains a branch within North Carolina and may from time to time require from any such out-of-state associations other reports under oath in such scope and detail as the Commissioner of Banks may reasonably determine to be necessary for the purpose of assuring continuing compliance with the provisions of this Article.

(c) The Commissioner of Banks may, if necessary, conduct full-scope, on-site examinations of any branch established pursuant to this Article.

(d) Out-of-state associations shall be assessed and required to pay supervisory and examination fees in accordance with G.S. 54B-57 and the rules issued thereunder. (1993, c. 191, s. 2; 2001-193, s. 16.)

§ 54B-274. Enforcement.

(a) Any enforcement authority available to the Commissioner of Banks for use against a State association may, subject to the provisions of Chapter 150B of the General Statutes, be used against a branch established under this Article and against the out-of-state association or its parent holding company establishing such branch.

(b) The Commissioner of Banks may suspend or revoke the authority of an out-of-state association to establish or maintain a branch in North Carolina upon a finding of fact or condition or circumstance that is grounds for denial of an application to establish and maintain a branch under this Article.

(c) The Commissioner of Banks may enforce the provisions of this Article through an action in any court of North Carolina or any other state or any court of the United States as provided in G.S. 54B-64, 54B-65, 54B-66, and 54B-68 for the purpose of obtaining an appropriate remedy for violation of any provisions of this Article.

(d) The Commissioner of Banks may enter into joint actions with other supervisors or federal association regulators, or both, having concurrent jurisdiction over any out-of-state association that has a branch in North Carolina or over any State association that has a branch in another state, or may take such action independently to carry out the Commissioner of Banks' responsibilities under this Article and assure compliance with the provisions of this Article and the applicable association laws of this State. (1993, c. 191, s. 2; 2001-193, s. 16.)

§ 54B-275. Branch closings.

An out-of-state association that is subject to an order or written agreement revoking its authority to establish or maintain a branch in North Carolina and any State association that is subject to an order or written agreement revoking its authority to establish or maintain a branch in another state shall wind up the business of that branch in an orderly manner that protects the depositors, customers, and creditors of the branch, and that complies with all North Carolina laws and all other applicable laws regarding the closing of the branch. (1993, c. 191, s. 2.)

§ 54B-276. Rules.

The Commission may adopt rules as necessary to carry out the provisions of this Article. (1993, c. 191, s. 2.)

§ 54B-277. Appeal of Commissioner of Banks' decision.

Any aggrieved party in a proceeding under this Article may, within 30 days after final decision of the Commissioner of Banks, appeal such decision to the Commission. The Commission, within 30 days of receipt of the notice of appeal, shall approve, disapprove, or modify the Commissioner of Banks' decision. Failure of the Commission to act within 30 days of receipt of notice of appeal shall constitute a final decision of the Commission approving the decision of the Commissioner of Banks. Notwithstanding any other provision of law, any aggrieved party to a decision of the Commission shall be entitled to an appeal pursuant to G.S. 54B-16. (1993, c. 191, s. 2; 2001-193, s. 16.)

§ 54B-278. Severability.

If any provision of this Article or the application of such provision to any persons or circumstances is found invalid, the remainder of this Article and its application to persons or circumstances other than those as to which it is held invalid, shall not be affected. (1993, c. 191, s. 2.)

Chapter 54C.

Savings Banks.

Article 1.

General Provisions.

§ 54C-1. Title.

This Chapter shall be known and may be cited as "Savings Banks." (1991, c. 680, s. 1.)

§ 54C-2. Purpose.

The purposes of this Chapter are:

(1) To provide for the safe and sound conduct of the business of savings banks, the conservation of their assets, and the maintenance of public confidence in savings banks

(2) To provide for the protection of the interests of customers and members.

(3) To provide the opportunity for savings banks to remain competitive with each other and with other depository institutions existing under other laws of this and other states and the United States.

(4) To provide for an increase in the savings base of the State and local control of the means of finance and accumulation of capital.

(5) To provide the opportunity for the management of savings banks to exercise prudent business judgment in conducting the affairs of savings banks to the extent compatible with the purposes recited in this section.

(6) To provide adequate rulemaking power and administrative discretion so that the regulation and supervision of savings banks are readily responsive to changes in local economic conditions and depository institution practices. (1991, c. 680, s. 1.)

§ 54C-3. Applicability of Chapter.

This Chapter, unless the context otherwise specifies, shall apply to all State savings banks. (1991, c. 680, s. 1.)

§ 54C-4. Definitions and application of terms.

(a) Except with respect to this Chapter and Chapter 54B, the term "savings and loan association" when used in the General Statutes shall include savings banks chartered under this Chapter.

(b) Unless the context otherwise requires, the following definitions apply in this Chapter:

(1) Repealed by Session Laws 2001-193, s. 7, effective July 1, 2001.

(2) Affiliate. - Any person or corporation that controls, is controlled by, or is under common control with a savings institution.

(3) Associate. - Any person's relationship with (i) any corporation or organization, other than the applicant or a majority-owned subsidiary of the applicant, of which the person is an officer or partner or is, directly or indirectly, the beneficial owner of ten percent (10%) or more of any class of equity securities, (ii) any trust or other estate in which the person has a substantial beneficial interest or as to which the person serves as trustee or in a similar fiduciary capacity, and (iii) any relative or spouse who lives in the same house as that person, or any relative of that person's spouse who lives in the same house as that person, or who is a director or officer of the applicant or any of its parents or subsidiaries.

(4) Association. - A savings and loan association as defined by G.S. 54B-4(b)(5).

(5) Branch office. - An office of a savings bank, other than its principal office, that renders savings institution services.

(6) Capital stock. - Securities that represent ownership of a stock savings bank.

(7) Certificate of incorporation or charter. - The document that represents the corporate existence of a State savings bank.

(8) Commission. - The State Banking Commission.

(8a) Commissioner. - The Commissioner of Banks authorized pursuant to Article 2 of Chapter 53C of the General Statutes.

(9) Conflict of interest. - A matter before the board of directors in which one or more of the directors, officers, or employees has a direct or indirect financial interest in its outcome.

(10) Control. - The power, directly or indirectly, to direct the management or policies of a savings bank or to vote twenty-five percent (25%) or more of any class of voting securities for a savings bank.

(11) Depository institution. - A person, firm, or corporation engaged in the business of receiving, soliciting, or accepting money or its equivalent on deposit, or of lending money or its equivalent, or of both.

(12) Disinterested directors. - Those directors who have absolutely no direct or indirect financial interest in the matter before them.

(13) Dividends on stock. - The earnings of a savings bank paid out to holders of capital stock in a stock savings bank.

(14) Division. - The Savings Institutions Division.

(15) Examination and investigation. - A supervisory inspection of a savings bank or proposed savings bank that may include inspection of every relevant piece of information including subsidiary or affiliated businesses.

(16) Immediate family. - One's spouse, father, mother, children, brothers, sisters, and grandchildren; and the father, mother, brothers, and sisters of one's spouse; and the spouse of one's child, brother, or sister.

(17) Insurance of deposit accounts. - Insurance on a savings bank's deposit accounts when the beneficiary is the holder of the insured account.

(18) Loan production office. - An office of a savings bank other than the principal or branch offices whose activities are limited to the generation of loans.

(19) Members. - Deposit account holders and borrowers in a State mutual savings bank.

(20) Mutual savings bank. - A savings bank owned by members of the savings bank and organized under this Chapter.

(21) Net worth. - A savings bank's total assets less total liabilities as defined by generally accepted accounting principles plus unallocated, general loan loss reserves.

(22) Original incorporators. - One or more natural persons who are the organizers of a State savings bank responsible for the business of a proposed savings bank from the filing of the application to the Commission's final decision on the application.

(23) Plan of conversion. - A detailed outline of the procedure of the conversion of a savings institution from one to another regulatory authority, from one to another form of ownership, or from one to another charter.

(24) Principal office. - The office that houses the headquarters of a savings bank.

(25) Proposed savings bank. - An entity in organizational procedures before the Commission's final decision on its charter application.

(26) Registered agent. - The person named in the certificate of incorporation upon whom service of legal process is deemed binding upon the savings bank.

(27) Savings bank. - A State savings bank or a federal savings bank, unless limited by use of the words "State" or "federal".

(28) Savings institution. - Either an association or a savings bank.

(29) Service corporation. - A corporation operating under Article 7 of this Chapter that engages in activities determined by the rules of the Administrator to be incidental to the conduct of a depository institution business as provided in this Chapter, or engages in activities that further or facilitate the corporate purposes of a savings bank, or furnishes services to a savings bank or subsidiaries of a savings bank, the voting stock of which is owned directly or indirectly by one or more savings institutions.

(30) State savings bank. - A depository institution organized and operated under this Chapter; or a corporation organized under federal law and so converted as to be operated under this Chapter.

(31) Stock savings bank. - A savings bank owned by holders of capital stock and organized under this Chapter.

(32) Voluntary dissolution. - The dissolution and liquidation of a savings bank initiated by its ownership. (1991, c. 680, s. 1; 1991 (Reg. Sess., 1992), c. 829, s. 4; 2001-193, ss. 7, 8, 17; 2012-56, s. 42.)

§ 54C-5. Reserved for future codification purposes.

Article 2.

Incorporation and Organization.

§ 54C-6. Hearings.

Any hearing required to be held by this Chapter shall be conducted in accordance with Article 3A of Chapter 150B of the General Statutes. (1991, c. 680, s. 1.)

§ 54C-7. Application of Chapter on business corporations.

All law relating to private corporations, and particularly the North Carolina Business Corporation Act, Chapter 55 of the General Statutes, that is not inconsistent with this Chapter or with the proper business of depository institutions is applicable to all State savings banks. (1991, c. 680, s. 1.)

§ 54C-8. Scope and prohibitions; existing charters; injunctions.

(a)   Nothing in this Chapter shall be construed to invalidate any charter that was valid before the enactment of this Chapter. Any savings banks so chartered on October 1, 1991, may continue operation in accordance with the Chapter under which it was chartered. However, after October 1, 1991, no depository institution may be qualified as a savings bank except in accordance with this Chapter.

(b)   Except as provided in subsection (a) of this section, no person, corporation, company, or savings bank, except one incorporated and licensed in accordance with this Chapter or federal law to operate a savings bank, shall operate as a savings bank. Unless so authorized as a State or federal savings bank and engaged in transacting a depository institution business, no person, corporation, company, or savings bank domiciled and doing business in this State shall:

(1)   Use in its name the term "savings bank" or words of similar import or connotation that lead the public reasonably to believe that the business so conducted is that of a savings bank; or

(2)   Use any sign, or circulate or use any letterhead, billhead, circular, or paper whatsoever, or advertise or communicate in any manner that would lead the public reasonably to believe that it is conducting the business of a savings bank.

(c)   Upon application by the Commissioner of Banks or by any savings bank, a court of competent jurisdiction may issue an injunction to restrain any person or entity from violating or from continuing to violate subsection (b) of this section. (1991, c. 680, s. 1; 1997-241, s. 1; 2001-193, s. 16.)

§ 54C-9. Application to organize a savings bank.

(a)   The original incorporators, a majority of whom shall be domiciled in this State, may organize and establish a savings bank in order to promote the purposes of this Chapter, subject to approval as provided in this Chapter. The original incorporators shall file with the Commissioner of Banks a preliminary application to organize a State savings bank in the form to be prescribed by the Commissioner of Banks, together with the proper nonrefundable application fee.

(b)   The Commissioner of Banks shall receive the application to organize a State savings bank not less than 60 days before the scheduled consideration of the application by the Commission. The application shall contain the following:

(1)   The original of the certificate of incorporation, which shall be signed by the original incorporators, or a majority of them, and shall be properly acknowledged by a person duly authorized by this State to take proof or acknowledgment of deeds; and two conformed copies;

(2) The names and addresses of the incorporators; and the names and addresses of the initial members of the board of directors;

(3) Statements of the anticipated receipts, expenditures, earnings, and financial condition of the savings bank for its first three years of operation, or any longer period as the Commissioner of Banks may require;

(4) A showing satisfactory to the Commission that:

a. The public convenience and advantage will be served by the establishment of the proposed savings bank;

b. There is a reasonable demand and necessity in the community that will be served by the establishment of the proposed savings bank;

c. The proposed savings bank will have a reasonable probability of sustaining profitable and beneficial operations within a reasonable time in the community in which the proposed savings bank intends to locate;

d. The proposed savings bank, if established, will promote healthy and effective competition in the community in the delivery to the public of savings institution services;

(5) The proposed bylaws; and

(6) Statements, exhibits, maps, and other data that may be prescribed or requested by the Commissioner of Banks, which data shall be sufficiently detailed and comprehensive so as to enable the Commissioner of Banks to pass upon the criteria set forth in this Article.

(c) The application shall be signed by the original incorporators, or a majority of them, and shall be properly acknowledged by a person duly authorized by this State to take proof and acknowledgment of deeds. (1991, c. 680, s. 1; 1991 (Reg. Sess., 1992), c. 829, s. 5; 2001-193, s. 16.)

§ 54C-10. Certificate of incorporation.

(a) The certificate of incorporation of a proposed mutual savings bank shall set forth the following:

(1) The name of the savings bank, which shall not so closely resemble the name of an existing depository institution doing business under the laws of this State as to be likely to mislead the public.

(2) The county and city or town where its principal office is to be located in this State; and the name of its registered agent and the address of its registered office, including county and city or town, and street and number.

(3) The period of duration, which may be perpetual. When the certificate of incorporation fails to state the period of duration, it is considered perpetual.

(4) The purposes for which the savings bank is organized that are limited to purposes permitted under the laws of this State for savings banks.

(5) The amount of the entrance fee per deposit account based upon the amount pledged.

(6) The minimum amount on deposit in deposit accounts before it shall commence business.

(7) Any provision not inconsistent with this Chapter and the proper operation of a savings bank, which the incorporators shall set forth in the certificate of incorporation for the regulation of the internal affairs of the savings bank.

(8) The number of directors, which shall not be less than seven, constituting the initial board of directors, which may be classified in the certificate of incorporation, and the name and address of each person who is to serve as a director until the first meeting of members, or until a successor is elected and qualified.

(9) The names and addresses of the incorporators.

(b) The certificate of incorporation of a proposed stock savings bank shall set forth the following:

(1) The name of the savings bank, which shall not so closely resemble the name of an existing depository institution doing business under the laws of this State as to be likely to mislead the public.

(2) The county and city or town where its principal office is to be located in this State; and the name of its registered agent and the address of its registered office, including county and city or town, and street and number.

(3) The period of duration, which may be perpetual. When the certificate of incorporation fails to state the period of duration, it is considered perpetual.

(4) The purposes for which the savings bank is organized, which shall be limited to purposes permitted under the laws of this State for savings banks.

(5) With respect to the shares of stock which the savings bank shall have authority to issue:

a. If the stock is to have a par value, the number of the shares of stock and the par value of each.

b. If the stock is to be without par value, the number of the shares of stock.

c. If the stock is to be of both kinds mentioned in sub-subdivisions a. and b. of this subdivision, particulars in accordance with those sub-subdivisions.

d. If the stock is to be divided into classes, or into series within a class of preferred or special shares of stock, the certificate of incorporation shall also set forth a designation of each class, with a designation of each series within a class, and a statement of the preferences, limitations, and relative rights of the stock of each class or series.

(6) The minimum amount of consideration to be received for its shares of stock before it shall commence business.

(7) A statement as to whether stockholders have preemptive rights to acquire additional or treasury shares of the savings bank.

(8) Any provision not inconsistent with this Chapter or the proper operation of a savings bank, which the incorporators shall set forth in the certificate of incorporation for the regulation of the internal affairs of the savings bank.

(9) The number of directors, which shall not be less than seven, constituting the initial board of directors, which may be classified in accordance with the certificate of incorporation, and the name and address of each person who is to

serve as a director until the first meeting of the stockholders, or until a successor is elected and qualified.

(10)　The names and addresses of the incorporators. (1991, c. 680, s. 1.)

§ 54C-11. Commissioner of Banks to consider application.

Upon receipt of an application to organize and establish a savings bank, the Commissioner of Banks shall examine or cause to be examined all the relevant facts connected with the formation of the proposed savings bank. If it appears to the Commissioner of Banks that the proposed savings bank has complied with all the requirements set forth in this Chapter and the rules for the formation of a savings bank and is otherwise lawfully entitled to be organized and established as a savings bank, the Commissioner of Banks shall present the application to the Commission for its consideration. (1991, c. 680, s. 1; 2001-193, s. 16.)

§ 54C-12. Criteria to be met before the Commissioner of Banks may recommend approval of an application.

(a)　The Commissioner of Banks may recommend approval of an application to form a mutual savings bank only when all of the following criteria are met:

(1)　The proposed savings bank has an operational expense fund, from which to pay organizational and incorporation expenses, in an amount determined by the Commissioner of Banks to be sufficient for the safe and proper operation of the savings bank, but in no event less than seventy-five thousand dollars ($75,000). The moneys remaining in the expense fund shall be held by the savings bank for at least one year from its date of licensing. No portion of the fund shall be released to an incorporator or director who contributed to it, nor to any other contributor, nor to any other person, and no dividends shall be accrued or paid on the funds without the prior approval of the Commissioner of Banks.

(2)　The proposed savings bank has pledges for deposit accounts in an amount to be determined by the Commissioner of Banks to be sufficient for the safe and proper operation of the savings bank, but in no event less than four million dollars ($4,000,000).

(3) All entrance fees for deposit accounts of the proposed savings bank have been made with legal tender of the United States.

(4) The name of the proposed savings bank will not mislead the public and is not the same as an existing depository institution or so similar to the name of an existing depository institution as to mislead the public.

(5) The character, general fitness, and responsibility of the incorporators and the initial board of directors of the proposed savings bank, a majority of whom shall be residents of North Carolina, will command the confidence of the community in which the proposed savings bank intends to locate.

(6) There is reasonable demand and necessity in the community that will be served by the establishment of the proposed savings bank.

(7) The public convenience and advantage will be served by the establishment of the proposed savings bank.

(8) The proposed savings bank will have a reasonable probability of sustaining profitable and beneficial operations in the community.

(9) The proposed savings bank, if established, will promote healthy and effective competition in the community in the delivery to the public of savings institution services.

(b) The Commissioner of Banks may recommend approval of an application to form a stock savings bank only when all of the following criteria are met:

(1) The proposed savings bank has prepared a plan to solicit subscriptions for capital stock in an amount determined by the Commissioner of Banks to be sufficient for the safe and proper operation of the savings bank, but in no event less than three million dollars ($3,000,000).

(2) The name of the proposed savings bank will not mislead the public and is not the same as an existing depository institution or so similar to the name of an existing depository institution as to mislead the public; and contains the wording "corporation," "incorporated," "limited," "company," or an abbreviation of one of these words or other words sufficient to distinguish stock savings banks from mutual savings banks.

(3) The character, general fitness, and responsibility of the incorporators, initial board of directors, and initial stockholders of the proposed savings bank will command the confidence of the community in which the proposed savings bank intends to locate.

(4) All subscriptions for capital stock of the proposed savings bank have been purchased with legal tender of the United States.

(5) There is a reasonable demand and necessity in the community that will be served by the establishment of the proposed savings bank.

(6) The public convenience and advantage will be served by the establishment of the proposed savings bank.

(7) The proposed savings bank will have a reasonable probability of sustaining profitable and beneficial operations in the community.

(8) The proposed savings bank, if established, will promote healthy and effective competition in the community in the delivery to the public of savings institution services.

(c) The minimum amount of pledges for deposit accounts or subscriptions for capital stock may be adjusted if the Commissioner of Banks determines that a greater requirement is necessary or that a smaller requirement will provide a sufficient capital base. The Commissioner of Banks' findings and recommendations to the Commission shall be based upon due consideration of (i) the population of the proposed trade area, (ii) the total deposits of the depository institutions operating in the proposed trade area, (iii) the economic conditions of and projections for the proposed trade area, (iv) the business experience and reputation of the proposed management, (v) the business experience and reputation of the proposed incorporators and directors, and (vi) the projected deposit growth, capitalization, and profitability of the proposed savings bank. (1991, c. 680, s. 1; 2001-193, s. 16.)

§ 54C-13. Commission to review findings and recommendations of Commissioner of Banks.

(a)   If the Commissioner of Banks does not have the completed application within 120 days of the filing of the preliminary application, the application shall be returned to the applicants.

(b)   When the Commissioner of Banks has completed the examination and investigation of the facts relevant to the establishment of the proposed savings bank, the Commissioner of Banks shall present the findings and recommendations to the Commission at a public hearing. The Commission shall approve or reject an application within 180 days of the submission of the preliminary application.

(c)   Not less than 45 days before the public hearing held for the consideration of the application to establish a savings bank, the incorporators shall cause to be published a notice in a newspaper of general circulation in the area to be served by the proposed savings bank. The notice shall contain:

(1)   A statement that the application has been filed with the Commissioner of Banks;

(2)   The name of the community where the principal office of the proposed savings bank intends to locate;

(3)   A statement that a public hearing shall be held to consider the application; and

(4)   A statement that any interested or affected party may file a written statement either favoring or protesting the creation of the proposed savings bank. The statement shall be filed with the Commissioner of Banks within 30 days of the date of publication.

(d)   The Commission, at the public hearing, shall consider the findings and recommendations of the Commissioner of Banks and shall hear oral testimony that the Commissioner of Banks may wish to give or be called upon to give, and shall also receive information and hear testimony from the original incorporators of the proposed savings bank and from any and all other interested or affected parties. The Commission shall hear only testimony and receive only information that is relevant to the consideration of the application and the operation of the proposed savings bank. (1991, c. 680, s. 1; 2001-193, s. 16.)

§ 54C-14. Grounds for approval or denial of application.

(a)   After consideration of the findings, recommendations, and any oral testimony of the Commissioner of Banks, and the consideration of any other information and evidence, either written or oral, as has come before it at the public hearing, the Commission shall approve or disapprove the application within 30 days after the public hearing. The Commission shall approve the application if it finds that the certificate of incorporation is in compliance with G.S. 54C-10 and that there is compliance with all the criteria set out in G.S. 54C-12, the remainder of this Chapter, rules, and the General Statutes.

(b)   If the Commission approves the application, the Commissioner of Banks shall notify the Secretary of State with a certificate of approval, accompanied by the original of the certificate of incorporation and the two conformed copies.

(c)   Upon receipt of the certificate of approval, the original of the certificate of incorporation, and the two conformed copies and upon the payment by the newly chartered savings bank of the appropriate organization tax and fees, the Secretary of State shall file the certificate of incorporation in accordance with G.S. 55-1-20. The Secretary of State shall certify, under official seal, the two conformed copies of the certificate of incorporation, one of which shall be forwarded immediately to the original incorporators or their representatives, the other of which shall be forwarded to the office of the Commissioner of Banks for filing. Upon the recordation of the certificate of incorporation by the Secretary of State, the savings bank is a body politic and corporate under the name stated in the certificate, and may begin the savings bank business when duly licensed by the Commissioner of Banks.

(d)   The certificate of incorporation, or a copy, duly certified by the Secretary of State, by the register of deeds of the county where the savings bank is located, or by the Commissioner of Banks, under their respective seals, is evidence in all courts and places, and is, in all judicial proceedings, deemed prima facie evidence of the complete organization and incorporation of the savings bank purporting thereby to have been established.

(e)   After approval of the application, the Commissioner of Banks shall supervise and monitor the organization process. The Commissioner of Banks shall ensure that sufficient pledges for deposit accounts or subscriptions for capital stock as well as insurance of deposit accounts have been secured by the organizers. (1991, c. 680, s. 1; 2001-193, s. 16.)

§ 54C-15. Final decision.

The Commission shall present the Commissioner of Banks with a final decision that is in accordance with Chapter 150B of the General Statutes. (1991, c. 680, s. 1; 2001-193, s. 16.)

§ 54C-16. Appeal.

The final decision of the Commission may be appealed in accordance with Chapter 150B of the General Statutes. (1991, c. 680, s. 1.)

§ 54C-17. Insurance of accounts required.

A State savings bank shall obtain and maintain insurance on all members' and customers' deposit accounts from an insurance corporation created by an act of Congress. Before the licensing of a savings bank, a certificate of incorporation duly recorded under G.S. 54C-14(c), is deemed to be sufficient certification to the insuring corporation that the savings bank is a legal corporate entity. The insurance shall be obtained within the time limit prescribed in G.S. 54C-19. Subject to the rules of the Commissioner of Banks, a State savings bank may obtain or participate in efforts to obtain insurance of deposits that is in excess of the amount eligible for federal insurance of accounts. This insurance is known as "excess insurance". (1991, c. 680, s. 1; 2001-193, s. 16.)

§ 54C-18. Repealed by Session Laws 1999-179, s. 2.

§ 54C-19. Time allowed to commence business.

A newly chartered savings bank shall commence business within one year after the date upon which its corporate existence began. A savings bank that does not commence business within this time, shall forfeit its corporate existence, unless the Commissioner of Banks, before the expiration of the one year period, approves an extension of the time within which the association may commence business, upon a written request stating the reasons for the request. Upon forfeiture, the certificate of incorporation shall expire, and any and all action taken in connection with the incorporation and chartering of the savings bank, with the exception of fees paid to the Division, shall become null and void. The Commissioner of Banks shall determine if a savings bank has failed to commence business within one year, without extension as provided in this section, and shall notify the Secretary of State and the register of deeds in the county in which the savings bank is located that the certificate of incorporation has expired. (1991, c. 680, s. 1; 2001-193, s. 16.)

§ 54C-20. Licensing.

A newly chartered savings bank is entitled to a license to operate upon payment to the Division of the appropriate license fee as prescribed by the Commissioner of Banks, when it shows to the satisfaction of the Commissioner of Banks evidence of capable, efficient, and equitable management, that the organization of the savings bank has been conducted lawfully and is complete, and when it passes a final inspection by the Commissioner of Banks or the Commissioner of Banks' representative preceding the opening of its doors for business. (1991, c. 680, s. 1; 2001-193, s. 16.)

§ 54C-21. Amendments to certificate of incorporation.

(a) An amendment to the certificate of incorporation of a State savings bank shall be made at any annual or special meeting of the savings bank, held in accordance with G.S. 54C-106 and G.S. 54C-107, by a majority of votes or shares cast by members or stockholders present in person or by proxy at the meeting. Any amendment shall be certified by the appropriate corporate official, submitted to the Commissioner of Banks for approval or rejection, and if approved, then certified by the Commissioner of Banks and recorded as provided in G.S. 54C-14 for certificates of incorporation.

(b) Notwithstanding subsection (a) of this section, a State savings bank may change its registered office or its registered agent, or both, in accordance with G.S. 55D-31. The savings bank shall file a copy of the statement or certificate certified by the Secretary of State in the office of the Commissioner of Banks. (1991, c. 680, s. 1; 2001-193, s. 16; 2001-358, s. 47(h); 2001-387, s. 173; 2001-413, s. 6.)

§ 54C-22. List of stockholders to be maintained.

A stock savings bank organized and operated under this Chapter shall, at all times, keep a current list of the names of all its stockholders. Whenever called upon by the Commissioner of Banks, a stock savings bank shall file in the office of the Commissioner of Banks a correct list of all its stockholders, the resident address of each, the number of shares of stock held by each, and the dates of issue. (1991, c. 680, s. 1; 2001-193, s. 16.)

§ 54C-23. Branch offices.

(a) A State savings bank may apply to the Commissioner of Banks for permission to establish a branch office. The application shall be in the form prescribed by the Commissioner of Banks and shall be accompanied by the proper branch application fee. The Commissioner of Banks shall approve or deny branch applications within 120 days of filing.

(b) The Commissioner of Banks shall approve a branch application when all of the following criteria are met:

(1) The applicant has gross assets of at least ten million dollars ($10,000,000).

(2) The applicant has evidenced financial responsibility.

(3) The applicant has a net worth equal to or exceeding the amount required by the insurer of deposit accounts.

(4) The applicant has an acceptable internal control system that includes certain basic internal control requirements essential to the protection of assets and the promotion of operational efficiency regardless of the size of the applicant.

(c) Upon receipt of a branch application, the Commissioner of Banks shall examine or cause to be examined all the relevant facts connected with the establishment of the proposed branch office. If it appears to the satisfaction of the Commissioner of Banks that the applicant has complied with all the requirements set forth in this section and the regulations for the establishment of a branch office and that the savings bank is otherwise lawfully entitled to establish the branch office, then the Commissioner of Banks shall approve the branch application.

(d) Not more than 10 days following the filing of the branch application with the Commissioner of Banks, the applicant shall cause a notice to be published in a newspaper of general circulation in the area to be served by the proposed branch office. The notice shall contain:

(1) A statement that the branch application has been filed with the Commissioner of Banks;

(2) The proposed address of the branch office, including city or town and street; and

(3) A statement that any interested or affected party may file a written statement with the Commissioner of Banks, within 30 days of the date of the publication of the notice, protesting the establishment of the proposed branch office and requesting a hearing before the Commissioner of Banks on the application.

(e) Any interested or affected party may file a written statement with the Commissioner of Banks within 30 days of the date of initial publication of the branch application notice, protesting the establishment of the proposed branch office and requesting a hearing before the Commissioner of Banks on the application. If a hearing is held on the branch application, the Commissioner of Banks shall receive information and hear testimony only from the applicant and from any interested or affected party that is relevant to the branch application and the operation of the proposed branch office. The Commissioner of Banks shall issue the final decision on the branch application within 30 days following the hearing. The final decision shall be in accordance with Chapter 150B of the General Statutes.

(f) If a hearing is not held on the branch application, the Commissioner of Banks shall issue the final decision within 120 days of the filing of the application. The final decision shall be in accordance with Chapter 150B of the General Statutes.

(g) A party to a branch application may appeal the final decision of the Commissioner of Banks to the Commission at any time after the final decision, but not later than 30 days after a written copy of the final decision is served upon the party and the party's attorney of record by personal service or by certified mail. Failure to file an appeal within the time stated shall operate as a waiver of the right of the party to review by the Commission and by a court of competent jurisdiction in accordance with Chapter 150B of the General Statutes, relating to judicial review. (1991, c. 680, s. 1; 2001-193, s. 16.)

§ 54C-24. Request to change location of a branch or principal office.

The board of directors of a State savings bank may change the location of a branch office or the principal office of the savings bank with the prior written approval of the Commissioner of Banks. The Commissioner of Banks may request, and the savings bank shall provide, any information that the Commissioner of Banks determines is necessary to evaluate the request. (1991, c. 680, s. 1; 2001-193, s. 16.)

§ 54C-25. Approval revoked; branch office.

The Commission may, for good cause and after a hearing, order the closing of a branch office. The order shall be made in writing to the savings bank and shall fix a reasonable time after which the savings bank shall close the branch office. (1991, c. 680, s. 1.)

§ 54C-26. Branch offices closed.

The Board of a State savings bank may discontinue the operation of a branch office upon giving at least 90 days prior written notice to the Commissioner of Banks and depositors, the notice to include the date upon which the branch office shall be closed. (1991, c. 680, s. 1; 1991 (Reg. Sess., 1992), c. 829, s. 6; 2001-193, s. 16.)

§ 54C-27. Loan production office.

A State savings bank may open or close a loan production office with the prior written approval of the Commissioner of Banks. The Commissioner of Banks may request, and the savings bank shall provide, any information that the Commissioner of Banks determines is necessary to evaluate the request. (1991, c. 680, s. 1; 2001-193, s. 16.)

§ 54C-28. Reserved for future codification purposes.

§ 54C-29. Reserved for future codification purposes.

Article 3.

Corporate Changes.

§ 54C-30. Conversion to savings bank.

(a)   An association or State or national bank, upon a majority vote of its board of directors, may apply to the Commissioner of Banks for permission to convert to a State savings bank and for certification of appropriate amendments to its certificate of incorporation to effect the change. Upon receipt of an application to convert to a State savings bank, the Commissioner of Banks shall examine all facts connected with the conversion. The depository institution applying for permission to convert shall pay all the expenses and cost of the examination.

(b)   The converting depository institution shall submit a plan of conversion as a part of the application to the Commissioner of Banks. The Commissioner of Banks may approve it with or without amendment. If the Commissioner of Banks approves the plan, then the plan shall be submitted to the members or stockholders as provided in subsection (c) of this section. If the Commissioner of Banks refuses to approve the plan, the objections shall be stated in writing and the converting depository institution shall be given an opportunity to amend the plan to obviate the objections or to appeal the Commissioner of Banks' decision to the Commission.

(c) After lawful notice to the members or stockholders of the converting depository institution and full and fair disclosure, the substance of the plan shall be approved by a majority of the votes or shares present, in person or by proxy. Following the vote of the members or stockholders, the results of the vote certified by an appropriate officer of the converting depository institution shall be filed with the Commissioner of Banks. The Commissioner of Banks shall then either approve or disapprove the requested conversion to a State savings bank. After approval of the conversion, the Commissioner of Banks shall supervise and monitor the conversion process and shall ensure that the conversion is conducted lawfully and under the approved plan of conversion. (1991, c. 680, s. 1; 1991 (Reg. Sess., 1992), c. 829, s. 7; 2001-193, s. 16.)

§ 54C-31. Conversion from State to federal charter.

A State savings bank, stock or mutual, organized and operated under this Chapter, may convert to a federal charter in accordance with the laws and regulations of the United States and with the same force and effect as though originally incorporated under these laws. The procedure to effect this conversion is as follows:

(1) The savings bank shall submit a plan of conversion to the Commissioner of Banks, who may approve the plan, with or without amendment, or refuse to approve the plan. If the Commissioner of Banks approves the plan, then the plan shall be submitted to the members or stockholders as provided in the subdivision (2) of this section. If the Commissioner of Banks refuses to approve the plan, the objections shall be stated in writing and the converting savings bank shall be given an opportunity to amend the plan to obviate the objections or to appeal the Commissioner of Banks' decision to the Commission.

(2) A meeting of the members or stockholders shall be held upon not less than 15 days' notice to each member or stockholder. Notice of the meeting may be mailed to each member or stockholder, postage prepaid, to the last known address, or the board of directors may cause notice of the meeting to be published, once a week for two weeks preceding the meeting, in a newspaper of

general circulation in the county where the savings bank has its principal office. It is regarded as sufficient notice of the purpose of the meeting if the notice contains substantially the following statement: "The purpose of this meeting is to consider the conversion of this State chartered savings bank to a federal charter, under the laws of the United States." An appropriate officer of the savings bank shall make proof by affidavit at the meeting of due service of the notice or call for the meeting.

(3) At the meeting of the members or stockholders of the savings bank, the members or stockholders may, by affirmative vote of a majority of votes or shares present, in person or by proxy, resolve to convert the savings bank to a federal charter. A copy of the minutes of the meeting of the members or stockholders certified by an appropriate officer of the savings bank shall be filed in the office of the Commissioner of Banks. The certified copy when so filed is prima facie evidence of the holding and the action of the meeting.

(4) Within a reasonable time after the receipt of a certified copy of the minutes, the Commissioner of Banks shall either approve or disapprove the proceedings of the meeting for compliance with the procedure set forth in this section. If the Commissioner of Banks approves the proceedings, the Commissioner of Banks shall issue a certificate of approval of the conversion. The savings bank shall record the certificate in the office of the Secretary of State. If the Commissioner of Banks disapproves the proceedings, the Commissioner of Banks shall provide a written explanation of the disapproval and notify the savings bank of the disapproval. The savings bank may appeal a disapproval to the Commission.

(5) The savings bank shall file an application, in the manner prescribed or authorized by the laws and regulations of the United States, to consummate the conversion to a federal charter. A copy of the charter or authorization issued to the savings bank by the appropriate federal regulatory authority shall be filed with the Commissioner of Banks. Upon filing with the Commissioner of Banks, the savings bank shall cease to be a State savings bank and shall be a federal depository institution.

(6) Whenever any savings bank converts to a federal charter it shall cease to be a savings bank under the laws of this State, except that its corporate existence is deemed to be extended for the purpose of prosecuting or defending suits by or against it and of enabling it to close its business affairs as a State savings bank and to dispose of and convey its property. At the time when the conversion becomes effective all the property of the State savings bank

including all its rights, title, and interest in and to all property of whatever kind, whether real, personal or mixed, and things in action, and every right, privilege, interest, and asset of any conceivable value or benefit then existing, belonging or pertaining to it, or which would inure to it, shall immediately by act of law and without any conveyance or transfer, and without any further act or deed, be vested in and become the property of the federal depository institution, which shall have, hold and enjoy the same in its own right as fully and to the same extent as the same was possessed, held, and enjoyed by the savings bank; and the federal depository institution as of the effective time of the conversion shall succeed to all the rights, obligations, and relations of the State savings bank. (1991, c. 680, s. 1; 2001-193, s. 16.)

§ 54C-32. Simultaneous charter and ownership conversion.

(a) In the event of a State charter to federal charter conversion, when the form of ownership will also simultaneously be changed from stock to mutual, or from mutual to stock, the conversion shall proceed initially as if it involves only a charter conversion, under G.S. 54C-31. After the savings bank becomes a federal depository institution, then the federal regulatory authority shall govern the continuing conversion of the form of ownership of the newly converted depository institution.

(b) In the event of a federal charter to State charter conversion, when the form of ownership will also simultaneously be changed from stock to mutual or from mutual to stock, the conversion shall proceed initially as if it involves only a charter conversion under G.S. 54C-30. After the federal depository institution becomes a State savings bank, G.S. 54C-33 or G.S. 54C-34 shall govern the continuing conversion of the form of ownership of the newly converted savings bank.

(c) This section shall not apply to any simultaneous charter and ownership conversion accomplished in conjunction with a merger under G.S. 54C-39. (1991, c. 680, s. 1.)

§ 54C-33. Conversion of mutual to stock savings bank.

(a) A mutual savings bank may convert from mutual to the stock form of ownership as provided in this section.

(b) A mutual savings bank may apply to the Commissioner of Banks for permission to convert to a stock savings bank and for certification of appropriate amendments to the savings bank's certificate of incorporation. Upon receipt of an application to convert from mutual to stock form the Commissioner of Banks shall examine all facts connected with the requested conversion. The savings bank applying for permission to convert shall pay all expenses and cost of the examination, monitoring, and supervision.

(c) The savings bank shall submit a plan of conversion as a part of the application to the Commissioner of Banks. The Commissioner of Banks may approve it with or without amendment, if it appears that:

(1) After conversion the savings bank will be in sound financial condition and will be soundly managed;

(2) The conversion will not impair the capital of the savings bank nor adversely affect the savings bank's operations;

(3) The conversion will be fair and equitable to the members of the savings bank and no person whether member, employee, or otherwise, will receive any inequitable gain or advantage by reason of the conversion;

(4) The savings bank services provided to the public by the savings bank will not be adversely affected by the conversion;

(5) The substance of the plan has been approved by a vote of two-thirds of the board of directors of the savings bank;

(6) All shares of stock issued in connection with the conversion are offered first to the members of the savings bank; except that any one or more tax qualified employee stock benefit plans may first purchase in the aggregate not more than ten percent (10%) of the total offering of shares;

(7) All stock shall be offered to members of the savings bank and others in prescribed amounts and otherwise under a formula and procedure that is fair and equitable and will be fairly disclosed to all interested persons; and

(8) The plan provides a statement as to whether stockholders shall have preemptive rights to acquire additional or treasury shares of the savings bank.

If the Commissioner of Banks approves the plan, then the plan shall be submitted to the members as provided in subsection (d) of this section. If the Commissioner of Banks refuses to approve the plan, the Commissioner of Banks shall state the objections in writing and give the converting savings bank an opportunity to amend the plan to obviate the objections or to appeal the Commissioner of Banks' decision to the Commission.

(d) After lawful notice to the members of the savings bank and full and fair disclosure, the substance of the plan shall be approved by a majority of the total votes that members of the savings bank are eligible and entitled to cast. The vote by the members may be in person or by proxy. Following the vote of the members, the results of the vote certified by an appropriate officer of the savings bank shall be filed with the Commissioner of Banks. The Commissioner of Banks shall then either approve or disapprove the requested conversion. After approval of the conversion, the Commissioner of Banks shall supervise and monitor the conversion process and shall ensure that the conversion is conducted lawfully and under the savings bank's approved plan of conversion.

(e) Any rules that the Commissioner of Banks may adopt to govern conversions shall equal or exceed the requirements for conversion, if any, imposed by the federal insurer of deposit accounts. (1991, c. 680, s. 1; 1991 (Reg. Sess., 1992), c. 829, s. 8; 2001-193, s. 16.)

§ 54C-34. Conversion of stock savings bank to mutual savings bank.

A stock savings bank organized and operating under this Chapter may, subject to the approval of the Commissioner of Banks, convert to a mutual savings bank under this section. Any rules that the Commissioner of Banks may adopt governing the conversion of stock savings banks to mutual savings banks shall include requirements that:

(1) The conversion neither impair the capital of the converting savings bank nor adversely affect its operations;

(2) The conversion shall be fair and equitable to all stockholders of the converting savings bank;

(3) The public shall not be adversely affected by the conversion;

(4) Conversion of a savings bank shall be accomplished only under a plan approved by the Commissioner of Banks. The plan shall have been approved by an affirmative vote of two-thirds of the members of the board of directors of the converting savings bank, after a full and fair disclosure to the stockholders, by an affirmative vote of a majority of the total votes that stockholders of the savings bank are eligible and entitled to cast; and

(5) The plan of conversion provides that:

a. Deposit accounts be issued in connection with the conversion to the stockholders of the converting savings bank;

b. A uniform date be fixed for the determination of the stockholders to whom, and the amount to each stockholder of which, deposit accounts shall be made available; and

c. Deposit accounts so made available to stockholders be based upon a fair and equitable formula approved by the Commissioner of Banks and fully and fairly disclosed to the stockholders of the converting savings bank. (1991, c. 680, s. 1; 2001-193, s. 16.)

§ 54C-35. Merger of like savings banks.

Any two or more mutual savings banks or any two or more stock savings banks organized and operating, may merge or consolidate into a single savings bank. The procedure to effect the merger is as follows:

(1) The directors, or a majority of them, of the savings banks that desire to merge may, at separate meetings, enter into a written agreement of merger signed by them and under the corporate seals of the respective savings banks specifying each savings bank to be merged and the savings bank that is to receive into itself the merging savings bank or banks, and prescribing the terms and conditions of the merger and the mode of carrying it into effect. The merger agreement may provide other provisions with respect to the merger as appear necessary or desirable, or as the Commissioner of Banks may require.

(2) The merger agreement together with copies of the minutes of the meetings of the respective boards of directors verified by the secretaries of the respective savings banks shall be submitted to the Commissioner of Banks, who shall cause a careful investigation and examination to be made of the affairs of the savings banks proposing to merge, including a determination of their respective assets and liabilities. Each savings bank that is investigated and examined shall pay the cost and expense for the examination. If, as a result of the investigation, the Commissioner of Banks concludes that the members or stockholders of each of the savings banks proposing to merge will be benefited by the merger, the Commissioner of Banks shall, in writing, approve the merger. If the Commissioner of Banks deems that the proposed merger will not be in the interest of all members or stockholders of the savings banks so merging, the Commissioner of Banks shall, in writing, disapprove the merger. If the Commissioner of Banks approves the merger agreement, then it shall be submitted, within 45 days after notice to the savings banks of the approval, to the members or stockholders of each savings bank, as provided in subdivision (3) of this section. The savings bank may appeal the disapproval of the merger to the Commission.

(3) A special meeting of the members or stockholders of each of the savings banks shall be held separately upon notice of not less than 20 days to members or stockholders of each savings bank. The notice of meeting shall specify the time, place, and purpose of such meeting. Notice shall be given to members of each mutual savings bank in accordance with the methods specified in its charter and bylaws and by one or more of the following methods: (i) personal service or (ii) postage prepaid mail to the last address of each member appearing upon the records of the savings bank. Provided; however, with respect to a merger of two mutual savings banks, as an alternative to the methods of notice specified above, the mutual savings bank which is to be the surviving savings bank of the proposed merger may provide the notice of meeting by publication of notice at least once a week for four consecutive weeks in one or more newspapers in general circulation in the county or counties in which the savings bank has its principal and any branch offices. Notice shall be given to stockholders of each stock-owned savings bank in accordance with the method specified for a meeting of stockholders in its charter and bylaws. The secretary or other officer of each savings bank shall make proof by certification at such meeting of the due service of the notice or call for said meeting.

(4) At separate meetings of the members or stockholders of the respective savings banks, the members or stockholders may adopt, by an affirmative vote of a majority of the votes or shares present, in person or by proxy, a resolution

to merge into a single savings bank upon the terms of the merger agreement as shall have been agreed upon by the directors of the respective savings banks and as approved by the Commissioner of Banks. Upon the adoption of the resolution, a copy of the minutes of the proceedings of the meetings of the members or stockholders of the respective savings banks, certified by an appropriate officer of the merging savings banks, shall be filed in the office of the Commissioner of Banks. Within 15 days after the receipt of a certified copy of the minutes of the meetings, the Commissioner of Banks shall either approve or disapprove the proceedings for compliance with this section. If the Commissioner of Banks approves the proceedings, the Commissioner of Banks shall issue a certificate of approval of the merger. The certificate shall be filed and recorded in the office of the Secretary of State. When the certificate is so filed, the merger agreement shall take effect according to its terms and is binding upon all the members or stockholders of the savings banks merging, and it is deemed to be the act of merger of the constituent savings banks under the laws of this State, and the certificate or certified copy thereof is evidence of the agreement and act of merger of the savings banks and the observance and performance of all acts and conditions necessary to have been observed and performed precedent to the merger. Within 60 days after its receipt from the Secretary of State, the certified copy of the certificate shall be filed with the register of deeds of the county or counties in which the respective savings banks so merged have recorded their original certificates of incorporation. Failure to so file shall subject the savings bank to only a penalty of one hundred dollars ($100.00) to be collected by the Secretary of State. If the Commissioner of Banks disapproves the proceedings, the Commissioner of Banks shall issue a written statement of the reasons for the disapproval and notify the savings banks to that effect. The savings banks may appeal the disapproval to the Commission.

(5) Upon the merger of any savings bank, as above provided, into another:

a. Its corporate existence is merged into that of the receiving savings bank; and all its right, title, interest in and to all property of whatsoever kind, whether real, personal or mixed, and things in action, and every right, privilege, interest or asset of any conceivable value or benefit then existing belonging or pertaining to it, or which would inure to it under an unmerged existence, shall immediately by act of law and without any conveyance or transfer, and without any further act or deed, be vested in and become the property of the receiving savings bank, which shall have, hold, and enjoy the same in its own right as fully and to the same extent as if the same were possessed, held, or enjoyed by the savings banks so merged; and the receiving savings bank shall absorb fully and completely the savings bank or banks so merged.

b. Its rights, liabilities, obligations, and relations to any person shall remain unchanged and the savings bank into which it has been merged shall, by the merger, succeed to all the relations, obligations, and liabilities as though it had itself assumed or incurred the same. No obligation or liability of a member, customer, or stockholder in a savings bank that is a party to the merger shall be affected by the merger, but obligations and liabilities shall continue as they existed before the merger, unless otherwise provided in the merger agreement.

c. A pending action or other judicial proceeding to which a savings bank that is so merged is a party, is not deemed to have abated or to have discontinued by reason of the merger, but may be prosecuted to final judgment, order, or decree in the same manner as if the merger had not been made; or the receiving savings bank may be substituted as a party to the action or proceeding, and any judgment, order, or decree may be rendered for or against it that might have been rendered for or against the other savings bank if the merger had not occurred.

(6) Notwithstanding any other provision of this section, the Commissioner of Banks may waive any or all of the foregoing requirements upon finding that waiver would be in the best interest of the members or stockholders of the merging savings banks. (1991, c. 680, s. 1; 1995, c. 479, s. 5; 2001-193, s. 16.)

§ 54C-36. Simultaneous conversion/merger.

(a) The Commissioner of Banks shall not approve any application for the conversion of a savings bank from mutual to stock form and its simultaneous (i) merger into a stock-owned savings institution or bank or (ii) acquisition by an operating financial institution holding company except as authorized in subsection (b) of this section. As used in this section, "simultaneous conversion/merger" shall mean a transaction in which the members of a mutual savings bank proposing to convert to stock form are offered the opportunity to purchase (i) stock in the savings institution or bank into which it will be merged or (ii) stock in the holding company by which it will be acquired.

(b) The Commissioner of Banks shall approve a plan of simultaneous conversion/merger only if:

(1) The transaction is proposed to address supervisory concerns of the Commissioner of Banks as to the safety and soundness of the mutual savings bank; or

(2) The mutual savings bank:

a. Operates in a local market area in which long-term trends make reasonable growth, continued profitability, and safe and sound operation appear unlikely;

b. Furnishes evidence concerning its asset size, capital to assets ratio, and other factors, which may include a cost/benefit analysis, satisfactory to the Commissioner of Banks that a simultaneous conversion/merger is more likely than remaining independent, merging with a mutual institution, converting to stock ownership, or other alternatives available to the savings bank to result in deposit, credit, and other financial services being provided within the local community safely and soundly on a long-term basis; and

c. Furnishes evidence satisfactory to the Commissioner of Banks that no director, officer, or other person associated with the parties to the proposed transaction will receive benefits as a result of the simultaneous conversion/merger which in the aggregate exceed those permitted under the federal regulations governing similar transactions.

(c) The Commissioner of Banks may adopt rules to govern simultaneous conversion/mergers, which rules shall contain restrictions or limitations which equal or exceed the limitations or restrictions contained in the rules of federal regulatory agencies governing similar transactions. No plan of a simultaneous conversion/merger shall be approved by the Commissioner of Banks unless it includes notification by first class mail to the members of the savings bank to be acquired explaining the plan including economic benefits or incentives to be received by officers and directors of the association, if any. Shares of stock in the acquiring entity purchased at a discount or otherwise by members of the savings bank as part of the simultaneous conversion/merger shall be without limitation on subsequent sales by such members: provided, however, rules adopted by the Commissioner of Banks may place limitations of the sale of such stock purchased by officers and directors of the savings bank. (1991, c. 680, s. 1; 1995, c. 479, s. 6; 2001-193, s. 16.)

§ 54C-37. Merger of mutual and stock savings banks.

Any two or more savings banks, when one or more is mutually owned and one or more is stock owned, may merge to form either a mutual or stock savings bank in separate conversion-merger proceedings or in simultaneous conversion-merger proceedings. (1991, c. 680, s. 1.)

§ 54C-38. Simultaneous merger and conversion.

Any combination of associations and State savings banks may merge to form either an association or a State savings bank. (1991, c. 680, s. 1.)

§ 54C-39. Merger of federal charters with State savings banks.

Any two or more depository institutions, when one or more is a State savings bank and one or more is a federal depository institution operating in North Carolina, may merge under either a State savings bank charter or a federal charter. (1991, c. 680, s. 1.)

§ 54C-40. Merger of savings banks with banks and associations.

(a) A State savings bank, upon a majority vote of its board of directors, may apply to the Commissioner of Banks for permission to merge with any bank, as defined in G.S. 53C-1-4(4), or any association, as defined in G.S. 54B-4.

(b) The State savings bank shall submit a plan of merger as a part of the application to the Commissioner of Banks. The Commissioner of Banks may recommend approval of the plan of merger with or without amendment.

If the Commissioner of Banks approves the plan, then the plan shall be submitted to the stockholders or members as provided in subsection (c) of this section. If the Commissioner of Banks refuses to approve the plan, the Commissioner of Banks shall state the objections in writing and give the merging savings bank an opportunity to amend the plan to obviate the objections or to appeal the Commissioner of Banks' decision to the Commission.

(c)   After lawful notice to the stockholders or members of the savings bank and full and fair disclosure, the substance of the plan shall be approved by a majority of the total votes that stockholders or members of the savings bank are eligible and entitled to cast. The vote by the stockholders or members may be in person or by proxy. Following the vote of the stockholders or members, the results of the vote certified by an appropriate officer of the savings bank shall be filed with the Commissioner of Banks. The Commissioner of Banks shall then either approve or disapprove the requested merger.

(d)   A merger between a mutual savings bank and a mutual savings and loan association shall be conducted in accordance with the provisions of G.S. 54C-35. (1991, c. 680, s. 1; 1995, c. 479, s. 7; 2001-193, s. 16; 2012-56, s. 43.)

§ 54C-41. Voluntary dissolution by directors.

A State savings bank may be voluntarily dissolved by a majority vote of the board of directors when substantially all of the assets have been sold for the purpose of terminating the business of the savings bank or as provided in G.S. 55-14-01 and when a certificate of dissolution is recorded in the manner required by this Chapter for the recording of certificates of incorporation. (1991, c. 680, s. 1.)

§ 54C-42. Voluntary dissolution by stockholders or members.

At any annual or special meeting called for the purpose of dissolution, a savings bank may, by an affirmative vote, in person or by proxy, of at least two-thirds of the total number of shares or votes that all members or stockholders of the association are entitled to cast, resolve to dissolve and liquidate the savings bank and adopt a plan of voluntary dissolution. Upon adoption of the resolution and plan of voluntary dissolution, the members or stockholders shall proceed to elect not more than three liquidators who shall post bond as required by the Commissioner of Banks. The liquidators shall have full power to execute the plan; and the procedure thereafter shall be as follows:

(1) A copy of the resolution, certified by an appropriate officer of the savings bank, together with the minutes of the meeting of members or stockholders, the plan of liquidation, and an itemized statement of the savings bank's assets and liabilities, sworn to by a majority of its board of directors, shall be filed with the Commissioner of Banks. The minutes of the meeting of members or stockholders shall be certified by an appropriate officer of the association, and shall set forth the notice given, the time of mailing thereof, the vote on the resolution, the total number of shares or votes that all members of the savings bank were entitled to cast thereon, and the names of the liquidators elected.

(2) If the Commissioner of Banks finds that the proceedings are in accordance with this Chapter, and that the plan of liquidation is not unfair to any person affected, the Commissioner of Banks shall attach a certificate of approval to the plan and shall forward one copy to the liquidators and one copy to the savings bank's federal deposit account insurance corporation. Once the Commissioner of Banks has approved the resolution and the plan of liquidation, it shall thereafter be unlawful for the savings bank to accept any additional deposit accounts or additions to deposit accounts or make any additional loans, but all its income and receipts in excess of actual expenses of liquidation of the savings bank shall be applied to the discharge of its liabilities.

(3) The liquidating savings bank shall pay a reasonable compensation, subject to the approval of the Commissioner of Banks, to the appointed liquidator.

(4) The plan becomes effective upon the recording of the Commissioner of Banks' certificate of approval in the manner required by this Chapter for the recording of the certificate of incorporation.

(5) The liquidation of the savings bank is subject to the supervision and examination of the Commissioner of Banks. (1991, c. 680, s. 1; 2001-193, s. 16.)

§ 54C-43. Reports of voluntary dissolution.

Upon completion of liquidation, the liquidator shall file with the Commissioner of Banks a final report and accounting of the liquidation. The Commissioner of Banks' approval of the report shall operate as a complete and final discharge of the liquidator, the board of directors, and each member or stockholder in connection with the liquidation of the savings bank. Upon approval of the report, the Commissioner of Banks shall issue a certificate of dissolution of the savings bank and shall record same in the manner required by this Chapter for the recording of certificates of incorporation. The dissolution is effective upon the recording of the certificates of incorporation. (1991, c. 680, s. 1; 2001-193, s. 16.)

§ 54C-44. Stock dividends.

No dividend on stock shall be paid unless the savings bank has the prior written approval of the Commissioner of Banks, except as provided in any rules that the Commissioner of Banks may adopt. (1991, c. 680, s. 1; 2001-193, s. 16.)

§ 54C-45. Supervisory mergers, consolidations, conversions, and combination mergers and conversions.

Notwithstanding any other provision of this Chapter, in order to protect the public, including members, depositors, and stockholders of a State savings bank, the Commissioner of Banks, upon making a finding that a State savings bank is unable to operate in a safe and sound manner, may authorize or require a short form merger, consolidation, conversion, or combination merger and conversion of the State savings bank, or any other transaction, as to which the finding is made. (1991, c. 680, s. 1; 2001-193, s. 16.)

§ 54C-46. Interim savings banks.

(a) Article 2 of this Chapter shall not apply to applications for permission to organize an interim State savings bank so long as the application is approved by the Commissioner of Banks.

(b) Preliminary approval of an application for permission to organize an interim State savings bank is conditional upon the Commissioner of Banks' approval of an application to merge the interim savings bank and an existing stock savings bank or on the Commissioner of Banks' approval of any other transaction. (1991, c. 680, s. 1; 2001-193, s. 16.)

§ 54C-47. Conversion to bank.

(a) A State savings bank, upon a majority vote of its board of directors, may apply to the Commissioner of Banks for permission to convert to a bank, as defined under G.S. 53C-1-4(4), or to a national bank or other form of depository institution and for certification of appropriate amendments to its certificate of incorporation to effect the change. Upon receipt of an application to so convert, the Commissioner of Banks shall examine all facts connected with the conversion, including receipt of approval of the converting institution's plan of conversion by other federal or state regulatory agencies having jurisdiction over the institution upon completion of its conversion. The depository institution applying for permission to convert shall pay all the expenses and costs of examination.

(b) The converting depository institution shall submit a plan of conversion as a part of the application to the Commissioner of Banks. The Commissioner of Banks may approve it with or without amendment. If the Commissioner of Banks approves the plan, then the plan shall be submitted to the members or stockholders as provided in subsection (c) of this section. If the Commissioner of Banks refuses to approve the plan, the Commissioner of Banks' objections shall be stated in writing and the converting depository institution shall be given an opportunity to amend its plan to obviate the objections or to appeal the Commissioner of Banks' decision to the Commission.

(c) After lawful notice to the members or stockholders of the converting depository institution and full and fair disclosure, the substance of the plan shall be approved by the members or the shareholders at a duly called and properly convened meeting of the members or shareholders. Following the meeting of the members or shareholders, the results of the vote certified by an appropriate officer of the converting depository institution shall be filed with the Commissioner of Banks. The Commissioner of Banks shall then either approve or disapprove the requested conversion to a bank, national bank, or other form of depository institution. After approval of the conversion, the Commissioner of Banks shall supervise and monitor the conversion process and shall ensure that the conversion is conducted lawfully and under the approved plan of conversion. (1993, c. 163, s. 6; 2001-193, s. 16; 2012-56, s. 44.)

§§ 54C-48 through 54C-51. Reserved for future codification purposes.

Article 4.

Supervision.

§ 54C-52. Supervision.

(a) The Commissioner of Banks shall perform the duties and exercise the powers as to savings banks organized or operated under this Chapter, except as otherwise provided herein.

(b) The Commission may review, approve, disapprove, or modify any action taken by the Commissioner of Banks in the exercise of the powers, duties, and functions granted to the Commissioner of Banks by this Chapter. (1991, c. 680, s. 1; 2001-193, s. 16.)

§ 54C-53. Power of Commissioner of Banks to adopt rules and definitions; reproduction of records.

(a) The Commissioner of Banks shall adopt rules, definitions, and forms as may be necessary for the supervision and regulation of savings banks and for the protection of the public investing in savings banks.

(b) Without limiting the generality of subsection (a) of this section, the Commissioner of Banks may adopt rules, definitions, and forms with respect to the following:

(1) Reserve requirements;

(2) Stock ownership and dividends;

(3) Stock transfers;

(4) Original incorporators, stockholders, directors, officers, and employees of a savings bank;

(5) Bylaws;

(6) The operation of savings banks;

(7) Deposit accounts, bonus plans, and contracts for savings programs;

(8) Loans and loan expenses;

(9) Investments and resource management;

(10) Forms of proxies, holders of proxies, and proxy solicitations;

(11) Types of financial records to be maintained by savings banks;

(12) Retention periods of various financial records;

(13) Internal control procedures of savings banks;

(14) Conduct and management of savings banks;

(15) Chartering and branching;

(16) Liquidations, dissolutions, and receiverships;

(17) Mergers, consolidations, conversions, and combination mergers and conversions;

(18) Interim savings banks;

(19) Reports that may be required by the Commissioner of Banks;

(20) Conflicts of interest;

(21) Service corporations; and

(22) Subsidiary savings banks and holding companies, including the rights of members, levels of investment in the subsidiaries, and stock sales.

(c) A savings bank may cause any or all of its records to be recorded, copied, or reproduced by any photographic, photostatic, or miniature photographic process that correctly, accurately, permanently copies, reproduces, or forms a medium for copying or reproducing the original record on a film or other durable material.

(d) A photographic, photostatic, or miniature photographic copy or reproduction is deemed to be an original record in all courts and administrative agencies for the purpose of its admissibility in evidence. A facsimile, exemplification or certified copy of any photographic copy or reproduction is deemed to be a facsimile, exemplification, or certified copy of the original record for all purposes.

(e) This section, with reference to the retention and disposition of records, shall apply to any federal savings bank operating in North Carolina unless in conflict with regulations prescribed by its federal regulatory authority. (1991, c. 680, s. 1; 2001-193, s. 16.)

§ 54C-54. Examinations by Commissioner of Banks; report.

(a) It is the Commissioner of Banks' duty, if at any time the Commissioner of Banks deems it prudent, to examine and investigate everything relating to the business of a State savings bank or a holding company thereof, and to appoint a suitable and competent person to make the investigation. The investigator shall file with the Commissioner of Banks a full report of the findings in the case, including any violation of law or any unauthorized or unsafe practices of the savings bank disclosed by the examination.

(b) The Commissioner of Banks shall furnish a copy of the report to the savings bank examined and may, upon request, furnish a copy of, or excerpts from, the report to the insurer of accounts.

(c) No savings bank may willfully delay or willfully obstruct an examination in any fashion. A person failing to comply with this subsection is guilty of a Class 1 misdemeanor.

(d) No person who possesses or controls any books, accounts, or papers of any State savings bank shall refuse to exhibit same to the Commissioner of Banks or the Commissioner of Banks' agent on demand, or shall knowingly or willingly make any false statement in regard to the same. A person failing to comply with this subsection is guilty of a Class 1 misdemeanor. (1991, c. 680, s. 1; 1993, c. 539, ss. 435, 436; 1994, Ex. Sess., c. 24, s. 14(c); 2001-193, s. 16.)

§ 54C-55. Supervision and examination fees authorized; use of funds collected under Chapter.

(a)   Every State savings bank, including savings banks in process of voluntary liquidation, or a holding company thereof, shall pay into the office of the Commissioner of Banks each July a supervisory fee. Examination fees shall be paid promptly upon an association's receipt of the examination billing. The Commissioner of Banks, subject to the advice and consent of the Commission, shall, on or before June 1 of each year:

(1)   Determine and fix the scale of supervisory and examination fees to be assessed and collected during the next fiscal year; and

(2)   Determine and fix the amount of the fee and set the fee collection schedule for the fees to be assessed to and collected from applicants to defray the cost of processing their charter, branch, merger, conversion, holding company acquisition, and name change applications.

(b)   All funds and revenue collected by the Division under this section and all other sections of this Chapter that authorize the collection of fees and other funds shall be deposited with the State Treasurer and expended under the terms of the Executive Budget Act, solely to defray expenses incurred by the office of the Commissioner of Banks in carrying out its supervisory and auditing functions.

(c)   Notwithstanding subsections (a) and (b) of this section, whenever the Commissioner of Banks under G.S. 54C-54 appoints a suitable and competent person, other than a person employed by the Commissioner of Banks' office, to make an examination and investigation of the business of a State savings bank, the savings bank shall pay all costs and expenses relative to the examination and investigation. (1991, c. 680, s. 1; 1998-215, s. 38(b); 2001-193, s. 16.)

§ 54C-56. Prolonged audit, examination, or revaluation; payment of costs.

(a) If, in the opinion of the Commissioner of Banks, an examination conducted under G.S. 54C-55 fails to disclose the complete financial condition of a savings bank, the Commissioner of Banks may in order to ascertain its complete financial condition:

(1) Make an extended audit or examination of the savings bank or cause an audit or examination to be made by an independent auditor; and

(2) Make an extended revaluation of any of the assets or liabilities of the savings bank or cause an independent appraiser to make a revaluation.

(b) The Commissioner of Banks shall collect from the savings bank a reasonable sum for actual or necessary expenses of an audit, examination, or revaluation. (1991, c. 680, s. 1; 2001-193, s. 16.)

§ 54C-57. Commissioner of Banks to have right of access to books and records of the savings bank; right to issue subpoenas, administer oaths, examine witnesses.

(a) The Commissioner of Banks and the Commissioner of Banks' agents:

(1) Shall have free access to all books and records of a savings bank, or a service corporation or holding company thereof, that relate to its business, and the books and records kept by an officer, agent, or employee relating to or upon which any record is kept;

(2) May subpoena witnesses and administer oaths or affirmations in the examination of any director, officer, agent, or employee of a savings bank, or a service corporation or holding company thereof or of any other person in relation to its affairs, transactions, and conditions;

(3) May require the production of records, books, papers, contracts, and other documents; and

(4) May order that improper entries be corrected on the books and records of a savings bank.

(b) The Commissioner of Banks may issue subpoenas duces tecum.

(c)   If a person fails to comply with a subpoena so issued or a party or witness refuses to testify on any matters, a court of competent jurisdiction, on the application of the Commissioner of Banks, shall compel compliance by proceedings for contempt as in the case of disobedience of the requirements of a subpoena issued from the court or a refusal to testify in the court. (1991, c. 680, s. 1; 2001-193, s. 16.)

§ 54C-58. Test appraisals of collateral for loans; expense paid.

(a)   The Commissioner of Banks may direct the making of test appraisals of real estate and other collateral securing loans made by savings banks doing business in this State, employ competent appraisers, or prescribe a list from which competent appraisers may be selected, for the making of these appraisals by the Commissioner of Banks, and any and all other acts incident to the making of test appraisals.

(b)   In lieu of causing an appraisal to be made, the Commissioner of Banks may accept an appraisal caused to be made by the insurer of accounts.

(c)   The expense and cost of test appraisals made under this section shall be defrayed by the savings bank subjected to the test appraisals, and each savings bank doing business in this State shall pay all reasonable costs and expenses of the test appraisals when it is directed. (1991, c. 680, s. 1; 2001-193, s. 16.)

§ 54C-59. Relationship of savings banks with the Savings Institutions Division.

(a)   Except as provided by subsection (b) of this section, a savings bank or any director, officer, employee, or representative thereof shall not grant or give to any employee of the Savings Institutions Division or to their spouses, any loan or gratuity, directly or indirectly.

(b)   No employee of the Savings Institutions Division shall:

(1) Hold an office or position in any State savings bank or exercise any right to vote on any State savings bank matter by reason of being a member of the savings bank;

(2) Be interested, directly or indirectly, in any savings bank organized under the laws of this State; or

(3) Undertake any indebtedness as a borrower, directly or indirectly, or act as endorser, surety, or guarantor, or sell or otherwise dispose of any loan or investment to any savings bank organized under the laws of this State.

(c) Notwithstanding subsection (b) of this section, any employee of the Savings Institutions Division may be a deposit account holder and receive earnings on a deposit account.

(d) Any employee of the Savings Institutions Division shall dispose of any right or interest in a savings bank, held either directly or indirectly, that is prohibited under subsection (b) of this section, within 60 days after the date of the employee's appointment or employment. If any employee of the Division is indebted as borrower, directly or indirectly, or is an endorser, surety, or guarantor on a note, at the time of appointment or employment, the employee may continue in that capacity until the loan is paid off.

(e) If any employee of the Savings Institutions Division has a loan or other note acquired by a State savings bank through the secondary market, the employee may continue with the debt until the loan or note is paid off. (1991, c. 680, s. 1; 2001-193, s. 9.)

§ 54C-60. Confidential information.

(a) The following records or information of the Commission, the Commissioner of Banks, or the agent of either shall be confidential and shall not be disclosed:

(1) Information obtained or compiled in preparation of or anticipation of, or during an examination, audit, or investigation of any association;

(2) Information reflecting the specific collateral given by a named borrower, the specific amount of stock owned by a named stockholder, any stockholder list

supplied to the Commissioner of Banks under G.S. 54C-22, or specific deposit accounts held by a named member or customer;

(3) Information obtained, prepared, or compiled during or as a result of an examination, audit, or investigation of any savings bank by an agency of the United States, if the records would be confidential under federal law or regulation;

(4) Information and reports submitted by savings banks to federal regulatory agencies, if the records or information would be confidential under federal law or regulation;

(5) Information and records regarding complaints from the public received by the Division that concern savings banks when the complaint would or could result in an investigation, except to the management of those savings banks; and

(6) Any other letters, reports, memoranda, recordings, charts or other documents or records that would disclose any information of which disclosure is prohibited in this subsection.

(b) A court of competent jurisdiction may order the disclosure of specific information.

(c) The information contained in an application is deemed to be public information. Disclosure shall not extend to the financial statement of the incorporators nor to any further information deemed by the Commissioner of Banks to be confidential.

(d) Nothing in this section shall prevent the exchange of information relating to savings banks and the business thereof with the representatives of the agencies of this State, other states, or of the United States, or with reserve or insuring agencies for savings banks. The private business and affairs of an individual or company shall not be disclosed by any person employed by the Division, any member of the Commission, or by any person with whom information is exchanged under the authority of this subsection.

(e) An official or employee of this State violating this section is liable to any person injured by disclosure of the confidential information for all damages sustained thereby. Penalties provided are not exclusive of other penalties. (1991, c. 680, s. 1; 2001-193, s. 16.)

§ 54C-60.1. Confidential records.

(a) As used in this section:

(1) "Compliance review committee" means:

a. An audit, loan review, or compliance committee appointed by the board of directors of a savings bank or any other person to the extent the person acts at the direction of or reports to a compliance review committee; and

b. Whose functions are to audit, evaluate, report, or determine compliance with any of the following:

1. Loan underwriting standards;

2. Asset quality;

3. Financial reporting to federal or State regulatory agencies;

4. Adherence to the savings bank's investment, lending, accounting, ethical, and financial standards; or

5. Compliance with federal or State statutory requirements.

(2) "Compliance review documents" means documents prepared for or created by a compliance review committee.

(3) "Loan review committee" means a person or group of persons who, on behalf of a savings bank, reviews assets, including loans held by the savings bank, for the purpose of assessing the credit quality of the loans or the loan application process, compliance with the savings bank's investment and loan policies, and compliance with applicable laws and regulations.

(4) "Person" means an individual, group of individuals, board, committee, partnership, firm, association, corporation, or other entity.

(b) Savings banks chartered under the laws of North Carolina or of the United States shall maintain complete records of compliance review documents, and the documents shall be available for examination by any federal or State savings bank regulatory agency having supervisory jurisdiction. Notwithstanding Chapter 132 of the General Statutes, compliance review documents in the custody of a savings bank or regulatory agency are confidential, are not open for public inspection, and are not discoverable or admissible in evidence in a civil action against a savings bank, its directors, officers, or employees, unless the court finds that the interests of justice require that the documents be discoverable or admissible in evidence. (1995, c. 408, s. 3.)

§ 54C-61. Annual license fees.

A state savings bank shall pay an annual license fee set by the Commissioner of Banks, subject to the advice and consent of the Commission. The license fee shall be used to defray the expenses incurred by the Division in supervising State savings banks. The Commissioner of Banks may license each State savings bank upon receipt of the license fee and filing of an application in the form prescribed by the Commissioner of Banks. (1991, c. 680, s. 1; 2001-193, s. 16.)

§ 54C-62. Statement filed by savings bank; fees.

A State savings bank shall file in the office of the Commissioner of Banks, on or before the first day of February in each year, in the form prescribed by the Commissioner of Banks, a statement of the business standing and financial condition of the savings bank on the preceding 31st day of December, signed and sworn to by the secretary or other officer duly authorized by the board of directors of the savings bank before a notary public. The statement shall be accompanied by a filing fee set by the Commissioner of Banks, subject to the advice and consent of the Commission. The filing fees shall be used to defray the expenses incurred by the Division in supervising State savings banks. (1991, c. 680, s. 1; 1993, c. 163, s. 3; 2001-193, s. 16.)

§ 54C-63. Statement examined, approved, and published.

It is the duty of the Commissioner of Banks to receive and thoroughly examine each annual statement required by G.S. 54C-62, and if made in compliance with the requirements thereof, each State savings bank shall at its own expense, publish an abstract of the same in a newspaper having general circulation within each market area of the savings bank as selected by the managing officer. (1991, c. 680, s. 1; 1991 (Reg. Sess., 1992), c. 829, s. 9; 1993, c. 163, s. 4; 2001-193, s. 16.)

§ 54C-64. Prohibited practices.

A person who engages in any of the following acts or practices is guilty of a Class 1 misdemeanor:

(1) Defamation: Making, publishing, disseminating, or circulating, directly or indirectly, or aiding, abetting, or encouraging the making, publishing, disseminating, or circulating of any oral, written, or printed statement that is false regarding the financial condition of any savings bank.

(2) False information and advertising: Making, publishing, disseminating, circulating, or otherwise placing before the public in any publication, media, notice, pamphlet, letter, poster, or any other way, an advertisement, announcement, or statement containing any assertion, representation, or statement with respect to the savings bank business or with respect to any person in the conduct of the savings bank business that is untrue, deceptive, or misleading.

(3) Repealed by Session Laws 1997-241, s. 2. (1991, c. 680, s. 1; 1993, c. 539, s. 437; 1994, Ex. Sess., c. 24, s. 14(c); 1993 (Reg. Sess., 1994), c. 767, s. 22; 1997-241, s. 2.)

§§ 54C-65 through 54C-75. Reserved for future codification purposes.

Article 5.

Enforcement.

§ 54C-76. Cease and desist orders.

(a) If a person or savings bank is engaging in, or has engaged in, any unsafe or unsound practice or unfair and discriminatory practice in conducting the savings bank's business, or of any other law, rule, order, or condition imposed in writing by the Commissioner of Banks, the Commissioner of Banks may issue a notice of charges to the person or association. A notice of charges shall specify the acts alleged to sustain a cease and desist order, and state the time and place at which a hearing shall be held. A hearing before the Commission on the charges shall be held no earlier than seven days, and no later than 15 days after issuance of the notice. The charged institution is entitled to a further extension of seven days upon filing a request with the Commissioner of Banks. The Commissioner of Banks may also issue a notice of charges if there are reasonable grounds to believe that a person or savings bank is about to engage in any unsafe or unsound business practice, or any violation of this Chapter, or any other law, rule, or order. If, by a preponderance of the evidence, it is shown that any person or savings bank is engaged in, or has been engaged in, or is about to engage in, any unsafe or unsound business practice, or unfair and discriminatory practice or any violation of this Chapter, or any other law, rule, or order, a cease and desist order shall be issued. The Commission may issue a temporary cease and desist order to be effective for 15 days and which may be extended once for a period of 15 days.

(b) If a person or State savings bank is engaging in, has engaged in, or is about to engage in any unsafe or unsound practice in conducting the savings bank's business, or any violation of this Chapter or of any other law, rule, order, or condition imposed in writing by the Commissioner of Banks, and the Commissioner of Banks has determined that immediate corrective action is required, the Commissioner of Banks may issue a temporary cease and desist order. A temporary cease and desist order is effective immediately upon issuance for a period of 15 days, and may be extended once for a period of 15 days. The order shall state its duration on its face and the words, "Temporary Cease and Desist Order." A hearing before the Commission shall be held within the time that the order remains effective, at which time a temporary order may be dissolved or made permanent. (1991, c. 680, s. 1; 2001-193, s. 16.)

§ 54C-77. Civil penalties; State savings banks.

(a)   Except as otherwise provided in this Article, a savings bank that is found to have violated this Article may be ordered to pay a civil penalty of up to twenty thousand dollars ($20,000). A savings bank that is found to have violated or failed to comply with any cease and desist order issued under the authority of this Article may be ordered to pay a civil penalty of up to twenty thousand dollars ($20,000) for each day that the violation or failure to comply continues.

The clear proceeds of civil penalties provided for in this section shall be remitted to the Civil Penalty and Forfeiture Fund in accordance with G.S. 115C-457.2.

(b)   To enforce this section, the Commissioner of Banks may assess the penalty, appear in a court of competent jurisdiction, and move the court to order payment of the penalty. Before the assessment of the penalty, the Commissioner of Banks shall hold a hearing, which shall comply with Article 3A of Chapter 150B of the General Statutes.

(c)   If the Commissioner of Banks determines that, as a result of a violation of this Article or of a failure to comply with any cease and desist order issued under the authority of this Article, a situation exists requiring immediate corrective action, the Commissioner of Banks may impose the civil penalty in this section on the savings bank without a prior hearing, and the penalty is effective as of the date of notice to the association. Imposition of the penalty may be directly appealed to the Wake County Superior Court.

(d)   Nothing in this section shall prevent anyone damaged by a State savings bank from bringing a separate cause of action in a court of competent jurisdiction. (1991, c. 680, s. 1; 1998-215, s. 38(a); 2001-193, s. 16.)

§ 54C-78. Civil penalties; directors, officers, and employees.

(a)   A person, whether a director, officer, or employee, who is found to have violated this Article, whether willfully or as a result of gross negligence, gross incompetency, or recklessness, may be ordered to pay a civil penalty of up to five thousand dollars ($5,000) per violation. A person who is found to have violated or failed to comply with any cease and desist order issued under the authority of this Article, may be ordered to pay a civil penalty of up to five thousand dollars ($5,000) per violation for each day that the violation or failure to comply continues. The clear proceeds of civil penalties provided for in this subsection shall be remitted to the Civil Penalty and Forfeiture Fund in accordance with G.S. 115C-457.2.

(b) To enforce this section, the Commissioner of Banks may assess the penalty, appear in a court of competent jurisdiction, and move the court to order payment of the penalty. Before the assessment of the penalty, the Commissioner of Banks shall hold a hearing, which shall comply with Article 3A of Chapter 150B of the General Statutes.

(c) Whenever the Commissioner of Banks determines that an emergency exists that requires immediate corrective action, the Commissioner of Banks, either before or after instituting any other action or proceeding authorized by this Article, may request the Attorney General to institute a civil action in a court of competent jurisdiction, in the name of the State upon the relation of the Commissioner of Banks seeking injunctive relief to restrain or enjoin the violation or threatened violation of this Article and for any other and further relief as the court may deem proper. Instituting an action for injunctive relief shall not relieve any party to the proceedings from any civil or criminal penalty prescribed for violation of this Article.

(d) Nothing in this section shall prevent anyone damaged by a director, officer, or employee of a State savings bank from bringing a separate cause of action in a court of competent jurisdiction. (1991, c. 680, s. 1; 1991 (Reg. Sess., 1992), c. 829, s. 10; 1998-215, s. 39; 2001-193, s. 16.)

§ 54C-79. Criminal penalties.

(a) This section shall in no event extend to persons who are found to have acted only with gross negligence, simple negligence, recklessness, or incompetence.

(b) In addition to any of the other penalties or remedies provided by this Article, the following are deemed to be Class 1 misdemeanors:

(1) The willful or knowing violation of this Article by any employee of the Division.

(2) The willful or knowing violation of a cease and desist order that has become final in that no further administrative or judicial appeal is available.

(c) In addition to any of the other penalties or remedies provided by this Article, the willful omission, making, or concurrence in making or publishing a written report, exhibit, or entry in a financial statement on the books of the association, which contains a material statement known to be false is deemed to be a Class 1 misdemeanor. For purposes of this section, "material" shall mean "so substantial and important as to influence a reasonable and prudent businessman or investor."

(d) The Commissioner of Banks may enforce this section in a court of competent jurisdiction. (1991, c. 680, s. 1; 1993, c. 539, s. 438; 1994, Ex. Sess., c. 24, s. 14(c); 2001-193, s. 16.)

§ 54C-80. Primary jurisdiction.

Whenever an agency of the United States government defers to the Commissioner of Banks, or notifies the Commissioner of Banks of pending action against a savings bank chartered by this State, or fails to exercise its authority over any State or federally chartered savings bank doing business in this State, the Commissioner of Banks may exercise jurisdiction over the savings bank. (1991, c. 680, s. 1; 2001-193, s. 16.)

§ 54C-81. Supervisory control.

(a) Whenever the Commissioner of Banks determines that a savings bank is conducting its business in an unsafe or unsound manner or in any fashion that threatens the financial integrity or sound operation of the savings bank, the Commissioner of Banks may serve a notice of charges on the savings bank, requiring it to show cause why it should not be placed under supervisory control. The notice of charges shall specify the grounds for supervisory control, and set the time and place for a hearing. A hearing before the Commission shall be held within 15 days after issuance of the notice of charges, and shall comply with Article 3A of Chapter 150B of the General Statutes.

(b) If, after the hearing provided in subsection (a) of this section, the Commission determines that supervisory control of the savings bank is necessary to protect the savings bank's members, customers, stockholders, or creditors, or the general public, the Commissioner of Banks shall issue an order taking supervisory control of the savings bank. An appeal may be filed in the Wake County Superior Court.

(c)   If the order taking supervisory control becomes final, the Commissioner of Banks may appoint an agent to supervise and monitor the operations of the savings bank during the period of supervisory control. During the period of supervisory control, the savings bank shall act in accordance with any instructions and directions as may be given by the Commissioner of Banks, directly or through a supervisory agent, and shall not act or fail to act except when to do so would violate an outstanding cease and desist order.

(d)   Within 180 days of the date the order taking supervisory control becomes final, the Commissioner of Banks shall issue an order approving a plan for the termination of supervisory control. The plan may provide for:

(1)   The issuance by the savings bank of capital stock;

(2)   The appointment of one or more officers, one or more directors, or one or more officers and directors;

(3)   The reorganization, merger, or consolidation of the savings bank; and

(4)   The dissolution and liquidation of the savings bank.

The order approving the plan shall not take effect for 30 days during which time period an appeal may be filed in the Wake County Superior Court.

(e)   The costs incident to this proceeding shall be paid by the savings bank, provided the costs are found to be reasonable.

(f)   For the purposes of this section, an order is deemed final if:

(1)   No appeal is filed within the specific time allowed for the appeal, or

(2)   After all judicial appeals are exhausted. (1991, c. 680, s. 1; 2001-193, s. 16.)

§ 54C-82. Removal of directors, officers, and employees.

(a)   If, in the Commissioner of Banks' opinion, one or more directors, officers, or employees of a savings bank has participated in or consented to any violation of this Chapter, or any other law, rule, or order, or any unsafe or unsound business practice in the operation of any savings bank; or any insider loan not specifically authorized by or under this Chapter; or any repeated violation of or failure to comply with any savings bank's bylaws, the Commissioner of Banks may serve a written notice of charges upon the director, officer, and employee in question, and the savings bank, stating the Commissioner of Banks' intent to remove the director, officer, or employee. The notice shall specify the conduct and place for the hearing before the Commission to be held. A hearing shall be held no earlier than 15 days and no later than 30 days after the notice of charges is served, and it shall comply with Article 3A of Chapter 150B of the General Statutes. If, after the hearing, the Commission determines that the charges asserted have been proven by a preponderance of the evidence, the Commissioner of Banks may issue an order removing the director, officer, or employee in question. The order is effective upon issuance and may include the entire board of directors or all of the officers of the savings bank.

(b)   If it is determined that a director, officer, or employee of a savings bank has knowingly participated in or consented to any violation of this Chapter, or any other law, rule, or order, or engaged in any unsafe or unsound business practice in the operation of any savings bank, or any repeated violation of or failure to comply with any savings bank's bylaws, and that as a result, a situation exists requiring immediate corrective action, the Commissioner of Banks may issue an order temporarily removing the person pending a hearing. The order shall state its duration on its face and the words, "Temporary Order of Removal," and is effective upon issuance, for a period of 15 days, and may be extended once for a period of 15 days. A hearing shall be held within 10 days of the expiration of a temporary order, or any extension thereof, at which time a temporary order may be dissolved or converted to a permanent order.

(c)   Any removal under subsections (a) or (b) of this section is effective in all respects as if the removal had been made by the board of directors and the members or the stockholders of the savings bank in question.

(d)   Without the prior written approval of the Commissioner of Banks, no director, officer, or employee permanently removed under this section shall be eligible to be elected, reelected, or appointed to any position as a director, officer, or employee of that savings bank, nor shall that director, officer, or employee be eligible to be elected to or retain a position as a director, officer, or employee of any other State savings bank. (1991, c. 680, s. 1; 2001-193, s. 16.)

§ 54C-83. Involuntary liquidation.

(a) The Commissioner of Banks, with prior approval of the Commission, may take custody of the books, records, and assets of every kind and character of any savings bank organized and operated under this Chapter for any of the purposes enumerated in this section, if it reasonably appears from examinations or from reports made to the Commissioner of Banks that:

(1) The directors, officers, or liquidators have neglected, failed, or refused to take action that the Commissioner of Banks may deem necessary for the protection of the savings bank or have impeded or obstructed an examination;

(2) The net worth of the savings bank is impaired to the extent that the realizable value of its assets is insufficient to pay in full its creditors and holders of deposit accounts;

(3) The business of the savings bank is being conducted in a fraudulent, illegal, or unsafe manner, or that the savings bank is in an unsafe or unsound condition to transact business; for purposes of this subdivision, any savings bank that, except as authorized in writing by the Commissioner of Banks, fails to make full payment of any withdrawal when due is in an unsafe or unsound condition to transact business, notwithstanding the certificate of incorporation or the statutes or regulations with respect to payment of withdrawals in event a savings bank does not pay all withdrawals in full;

(4) The officers, directors, or employees have assumed duties or performed acts in excess of those authorized by statute or regulation or charter, or without supplying the required bond;

(5) The savings bank has experienced a substantial dissipation of assets or earnings due to any violation or violation of statute or regulation, or due to any unsafe or unsound practice or practices;

(6) The savings bank is insolvent, or is in imminent danger of insolvency or has suspended its ordinary business transactions due to insufficient funds; or

(7) The savings bank is unable to continue operations.

(b) Unless the Commissioner of Banks finds that an emergency exists that may result in loss to members, deposit account holders, stockholders, or creditors, and that requires that the Commissioner of Banks take custody immediately, the Commissioner of Banks shall first give written notice to the directors and officers specifying the conditions criticized and allowing a reasonable time in which corrections may be made before a receiver shall be appointed as outlined in subsection (d) of this section.

(c) The purposes for which the Commissioner of Banks may take custody of a savings bank include examination or further examination, conservation of its assets, restoration of impaired capital, and the making of any reasonable or equitable adjustment deemed necessary by the Commissioner of Banks under any plan of reorganization.

(d) If the Commissioner of Banks, after taking custody of a savings bank, finds that one or more of the reasons for having taken custody continue to exist through the period of custody, with little or no likelihood of amelioration of the situation, then the Commissioner of Banks shall appoint as receiver or coreceiver any qualified person, firm, or corporation for the purpose of liquidation of the savings bank, which receiver shall furnish bond in form, amount, and with surety as the Commissioner of Banks may require. The Commissioner of Banks may appoint the association's deposit account insurance corporation or its nominee as the receiver, and the insuring corporation shall be permitted to serve without posting bond.

(e) In the event the Commissioner of Banks appoints a receiver for a savings bank, the Commissioner of Banks shall mail a certified copy of the appointment order by certified mail to the address of the savings bank as it appears on the records of the Division, and to any previous receiver or other legal custodian of the savings bank, and to any court or other authority to which the previous receiver or other legal custodian is subject. Notice of the appointment may be published in a newspaper of general circulation in the county where the savings bank has its principal office.

(f) Whenever a receiver for a savings bank is appointed under subsection (d) of this section, the savings bank may within 30 days thereafter bring an action in the Superior Court of Wake County, for an order requiring the Commissioner of Banks to remove the receiver.

(g)   The duly appointed and qualified receiver shall take possession promptly of the savings bank for which the receiver has been so appointed, in accordance with the terms of the appointment, by service of a certified copy of the Commissioner of Banks' appointment order upon the savings bank at its principal office through the officer or employee who is present and appears to be in charge. Immediately upon taking possession of the savings bank, the receiver shall take possession and title to books, records, and assets of every description of the savings bank. The receiver, by operation of law and without any conveyance or other instrument, act or deed, shall succeed to all the rights, titles, powers, and privileges of the savings bank, its members or stockholders, holders of deposit accounts, its officers and directors or any of them; and to the titles to the books, records, and assets of every description of any previous receiver or other legal custodian of the savings bank. The members, stockholders, holders of deposit accounts, officers or directors, or any of them, shall not thereafter, except as expressly provided in this section have or exercise any rights, powers or privileges or act in connection with any assets or property of any nature of the savings bank in receivership. The Commissioner of Banks, with the approval of the Commission, may at any time, direct the receiver to return the savings bank to its previous or a newly constituted management. The Commissioner of Banks may provide for a meeting or meetings of the members or stockholders for any purpose, including the election of directors or an increase in the number of directors, or both, or the election of an entire new board of directors; and may provide for a meeting or meetings of the directors for any purpose including the filling of vacancies on the board, the removal of officers and the election of new officers, or for any of these purposes. Any meeting of members or stockholders, or of directors, shall be supervised or conducted by a representative of the Commissioner of Banks.

(h)   A duly appointed and qualified receiver may:

(1)   Demand, sue for, collect, receive and take into possession all the goods and chattels, rights and credits, moneys and effects, lands and tenements, books, papers, chooses in action, bills, notes and property of every description of the savings bank;

(2)   Foreclose mortgages, deeds of trust, and other liens executed to the savings bank to the extent the savings bank would have had this right;

(3)   Institute suits for the recovery of any estate, property, damages, or demands existing in favor of the savings bank, and shall, upon the receiver's

own application, be substituted as party plaintiff in the place of the savings bank in any suit or proceeding pending at the time of the receiver's appointment;

(4) Sell, convey, and assign all the property rights and interests owned by the savings bank;

(5) Appoint agents;

(6) Examine and investigate papers and persons, and pass on claims as provided in the regulations as prescribed by the Commissioner of Banks;

(7) Make and carry out agreements with the insuring corporation or with any other financial institution for the payment or assumption of the savings bank's liabilities, in whole or in part, and to sell, convey, transfer, pledge, or assign assets as security or otherwise and to make guarantees in connection therewith; and

(8) Perform all other acts that might be done by the employees, officers, and directors.

These powers shall be continued in effect until liquidation and dissolution or until return of the savings bank to its prior or newly constituted management.

(i) A receiver may, at any time during the receivership and before final liquidation, be removed and a replacement appointed by the Commissioner of Banks.

(j) The Commissioner of Banks may determine that the liquidation proceedings should be discontinued. The Commissioner of Banks shall then remove the receiver and restore all the rights, powers, and privileges of its members and stockholders, customers, employees, officers, and directors, or restore these rights, powers, and privileges to its members, stockholders, and customers, and grant these rights, powers, and privileges to a newly constituted management, all as of the time of the restoration of the savings bank to its management unless another time for the restoration is specified by the Commissioner of Banks. The return of a savings bank to its management or to a newly constituted management from the possession of a receiver shall, by operation of law and without any conveyance or other instrument, act or deed, vest in the savings bank the title to all property held by the receiver in the capacity as receiver for the savings bank.

(k)   A receiver may also be appointed under the authority of G.S. 1-502. No judge or court, however, shall appoint a receiver for any State savings bank unless five days' advance notice of the motion, petition, or application for appointment of a receiver has been given to the savings bank and to the Commissioner of Banks.

(l)   Following the appointment of a receiver, the Commissioner of Banks may request the Attorney General to institute an action in the name of the Commissioner of Banks in the superior court against the savings bank for the orderly liquidation and dissolution of the association, and for an injunction to restrain the officers, directors, and employees from continuing the operation of the savings bank.

(m)   Claims against the State association in receivership shall have the following order of priority for payment:

(1)   Costs, expenses, and debts of the savings bank incurred on or after the date of the appointment of the receiver, including compensation for the receiver.

(2)   Claims of holders of special purpose or thrift accounts.

(3)   Claims of holders of deposit accounts.

(4)   Claims of general creditors.

(5)   Claims of stockholders of a stock savings bank.

(6)   All remaining assets to members and stockholders in an amount proportionate to their holdings as of the date of the appointment of the receiver.

(n)   All claims of each class described within subsection (m) of this section shall be paid in full so long as sufficient assets remain. Members of the class for which the receiver cannot make payment in full because assets will be depleted during payment to that class shall be paid an amount proportionate to their total claims.

(o)   The Commissioner of Banks may direct the payment of claims for which no provision is made in this section, and may direct the payment of claims within a class.

(p) When all assets of the savings bank have been fully liquidated, and all claims and expenses have been paid or settled, and the receiver has recommended a final distribution, the dissolution of the savings bank in receivership shall be accomplished in the following manner:

(1) The receiver shall file with the Commissioner of Banks a detailed report, in a form to be prescribed by the Commissioner of Banks, of the receiver's acts and proposed final distribution, and dissolution.

(2) Upon the Commissioner of Banks' approval of the final report of the receiver, the receiver shall provide notice and thereafter shall make the final distribution, in any manner as the Commissioner of Banks may direct.

(3) When a final distribution has been made except as to any unclaimed funds, the receiver shall deposit the unclaimed funds with the Commissioner of Banks and shall deliver to the Commissioner of Banks all books and records of the dissolved association.

(4) Upon completion of the foregoing procedure, and upon the joint petition of the Commissioner of Banks and receiver to the superior court, the court may find that the savings bank should be dissolved, and following publication of notice of dissolution as the court may direct, the court may enter a decree of final resolution and the savings bank shall therefore be dissolved.

(5) Upon final dissolution of the savings bank in receivership or at any time as the receiver shall be otherwise relieved of duties, the Commissioner of Banks shall cause an audit to be conducted, during which the receiver shall be available to assist. The accounts of the receiver shall then be ruled upon by the Commissioner of Banks and Commission and if approved, the receiver shall thereupon be given a final and complete discharge and release. (1991, c. 680, s. 1; 2001-193, s. 16.)

§ 54C-84. Judicial review.

A person or State savings bank against whom a cease and desist order is issued or a fine is imposed may have the order or fine reviewed by a court of competent jurisdiction. Except as otherwise provided, an appeal may be made only within 30 days of the issuance of the order or the imposition of the fine, whichever is later. (1991, c. 680, s. 1.)

§ 54C-85. Indemnity.

No person who is fined or penalized for a violation of any criminal provision of this Article shall be reimbursed or indemnified in any fashion by the savings bank for the fine or penalty. (1991, c. 680, s. 1.)

§ 54C-86. Cumulative penalties.

All penalties, fines, and remedies provided by this Article are cumulative. (1991, c. 680, s. 1.)

§ 54C-87. Emergency limitations.

The Commissioner of Banks, with the approval of the Governor, may impose a limitation upon the amounts withdrawable or payable from deposit accounts of savings banks during any specifically defined period when the limitation is in the public interest and welfare. (1991, c. 680, s. 1; 2001-193, s. 16.)

§§ 54C-88 through 54C-99. Reserved for future codification purposes.

Article 6.

Corporate Administration.

§ 54C-100. Membership of a mutual association.

The membership of a mutual State savings bank shall consist of:

(1)   Those who hold deposit accounts in a savings bank, and

(2) Those who borrow funds and those who become obligated on a loan from the savings bank, for as long as the loan remains unpaid and the borrower remains liable to the savings bank for the payment of the loan.

A person, as a matter of right or in a trust or other fiduciary capacity, or any partnership, association, corporation, political subdivision, or public or governmental unit or entity may become a member of a mutual savings bank. Members shall be possessed of voting rights and any other rights as are provided by a savings bank's certificate of incorporation and bylaws as approved by the Commissioner of Banks. Members are the owners of a mutual savings bank. (1991, c. 680, s. 1; 2001-193, s. 16.)

§ 54C-101. Directors.

(a) The directors of a mutual savings bank shall be elected by the members at an annual meeting, held under G.S. 54C-106, for any terms as the bylaws of the savings bank may provide. Director's terms may be classified in the certificate of incorporation. Voting for directors by deposit account holders shall be weighted according to the total amount of deposit accounts held by the members, subject to any maximum number of votes per member which a savings bank may choose to prescribe in its bylaws. Voting rights for borrowers shall be fully prescribed in a detailed manner in the bylaws of the savings bank.

(b) The directors of a stock savings bank shall be elected by the stockholders at an annual meeting, held under G.S. 54C-106, for any terms as the bylaws of the savings bank may provide. Director's terms may be classified in the certificate of incorporation.

(c) A director of a State savings bank shall have a significant ownership interest in the State savings bank.

(d) A State savings bank shall have no less than five directors. (1991, c. 680, s. 1.)

§ 54C-102. Bylaws.

The bylaws and any amendments shall be certified by the appropriate corporate official and submitted to the Commissioner of Banks for approval before they may become effective. (1991, c. 680, s. 1; 2001-193, s. 16.)

§ 54C 103. Duties and liabilities of officers and directors to their associations.

Officers and directors of a State savings bank shall act in a fiduciary capacity towards the savings bank and its members or stockholders. They shall discharge duties of their respective positions in good faith, and with that diligence and care which ordinarily prudent persons would exercise under similar circumstances in like positions. (1991, c. 680, s. 1.)

§ 54C-104. Conflicts of interest.

Each director, officer, and employee of a State savings bank has a fundamental duty to avoid placing himself in a position which creates, or which leads to or could lead to a conflict of interest or appearance of a conflict of interest having adverse effects on the interests of members, customers, or stockholders of the savings bank, soundness of the savings bank, and the purposes of this Chapter. (1991, c. 680, s. 1.)

§ 54C-105. Voting rights.

Voting rights in the affairs of a State savings bank may be exercised by members and stockholders by voting either in person or by proxy. (1991, c. 680, s. 1.)

§ 54C-106. Annual meetings notice required.

(a)   A savings bank shall hold an annual meeting of its members or stockholders. The annual meeting shall be held at a time and place as shall be provided in the bylaws or determined by the board of directors.

(b) The board of directors of a mutual savings bank shall cause to be published once a week for two weeks preceding such meeting, in a newspaper of general circulation in the county where such savings bank has its principal office, a notice of the meeting, signed by the savings bank's secretary, and stating the time and place where it is to be held. In addition to the foregoing notice, a savings bank shall disseminate additional notice of any annual meeting by notice made available to all members entering the premises of any office or branch of the savings bank in the regular course of business by posting therein, in full view of the public and its members, one or more conspicuous signs or placards announcing the pending meeting, the time, date and place of the meeting and the availability of additional information. Printed matter shall be freely available to the members containing any information as may be prescribed in rules issued by the Commissioner of Banks. The additional notice shall be given at any time within the period of 60 days before and 14 days before the meeting and shall continue through the time of the meeting.

(c) The board of directors of a stock savings bank shall cause a written or printed notice, signed by the savings bank's secretary and stating the time and place of the annual meeting, to be delivered not less than 10 days nor more than 50 days before the date of the meeting, either personally or by mail to each stockholder of record entitled to vote at the meeting. If mailed, the notice is deemed to be delivered when deposited in the United States postal service addressed to the stockholder at the address as it appears on the records of the corporation, with postage thereon prepaid. (1991, c. 680, s. 1; 2001-193, s. 16.)

§ 54C-107. Special meetings; notice required.

(a) Special meetings of members or stockholders of a savings bank may be called by the president or the board of directors or by any other officers or persons as may be provided for in the charter or bylaws of the savings bank.

(b) Notice of any special meeting of members or stockholders shall be given in the same manner as provided for annual meetings under G.S. 54C-106. (1991, c. 680, s. 1.)

§ 54C-108. Quorum.

Unless otherwise provided in the savings bank's charter or bylaws, 50 holders of deposit accounts in a mutual savings bank or 50 stockholders or a majority of shares eligible to vote in a stock savings bank, present in person or represented by proxy, shall constitute a quorum at any annual or special meeting. (1991, c. 680, s. 1.)

§ 54C-109. Bonding.

(a)   A savings bank shall maintain a blanket indemnity bond of at least a minimum amount as prescribed by the Commissioner of Banks.

(b)   A savings bank that employs collection agents, who for any reason are not covered by the bond required in this section, shall provide for the bonding of each agent in an amount equal to at least twice the average monthly collections of the agent. The agents shall be required to make settlement with the association at least once monthly. No coverage by bond will be required of any agent that is a bank or an association insured by the Federal Deposit Insurance Corporation. The amount and form of the bonds and the sufficiency of the surety thereon shall be approved by the board of directors and the Commissioner of Banks before it is valid. A bond shall provide that its cancellation, either by the surety or by the insured, shall not become effective unless and until 30 days' notice in writing shall have been given to the Commissioner of Banks. (1991, c. 680, s. 1; 2001-193, s. 16.)

§§ 54C-110 through 54C-120. Reserved for future codification purposes.

Article 7.

Loans and Investments.

§ 54C-121. Loans.

(a)   A savings bank may loan funds as follows:

(1) On the security of deposit accounts, but no loan shall exceed the withdrawal value of the pledged deposit account.

(2) On the security of real property:

a. Of a value, determined in accordance with this Chapter and any appraisal rules as the Commissioner of Banks may adopt sufficient to provide good and ample security for the loan;

b. With a fee simple title or a leasehold title of no less duration than 10 years beyond the maturity of the loan;

c. With the title established by any evidence of title as is consistent with sound lending practices; and

d. With the security interest in such real estate evidenced by an appropriate written instrument and the loan evidenced by a note, bond, or similar written instrument. A loan on the security of the whole of the beneficial interest in a land trust satisfies the requirements of this sub-subdivision if the title to the land is held by a corporate trustee and if the real estate held in the land trust meets the other requirements of this subdivision.

(3) For the purpose of repair, improvement, rehabilitation, furnishing, or equipment of real estate.

(4) For the purpose of financing or refinancing an existing ownership interest, in certificates of stock, certificates of beneficial interest, or other evidence of an ownership interest in, and a proprietary lease from, a corporation, trust or partnership formed for the purpose of the cooperative ownership of real estate, secured by the assignment or transfer of the certificates or other evidence of ownership of the borrower.

(5) For the purchase of loans that, at the time of purchase, the savings bank could make in accordance with this Chapter.

(6) For the purchase of installment contracts for the sale of real estate, and title thereto that is subject to the contract, but in each instance only if the savings bank, at the time of purchase, could make a mortgage loan of the same amount and for the same length of time on the security of the real estate.

(7) For the purchase of loans guaranteed or insured, wholly or in part, by the United States or any of its instrumentalities.

(8) For secured or unsecured financing for business, corporate, personal, family, or household purposes, or for secured or unsecured loans for agricultural or commercial purposes, subject to any rules as the Commissioner of Banks may adopt.

(9) For the purpose of mobile home financing.

(10) For loans secured by no more that ninety percent (90%) of the cash surrender value of any life insurance policy.

(11) For loans on any collateral that would be a legal investment if made by the savings bank under this Chapter.

(b) Notwithstanding any provision of this Chapter to the contrary, a savings bank may make any loan that the savings bank could make if it were incorporated and operating as a federal association or as a State or national bank. (1991, c. 680, s. 1; 2001-193, s. 16.)

§ 54C-122. Lending procedures.

(a) The board of directors shall establish procedures by which loans are to be considered, approved, and made by the savings bank.

(b) All actions on loan applications to the savings bank shall be reported to the board of directors at its next meeting.

(c) Subject to any rules as the Commissioner of Banks deems appropriate, a savings bank may lend funds on any collateral deemed sufficient by the board of directors to properly secure loans. Loans made solely upon security of collateral consisting of stock or equity securities that are not listed on a national stock exchange or regularly quoted and offered for trade on an over-the-counter market are considered loans without security.

(d) A savings bank may lend funds without requiring security. No unsecured loan shall exceed the maximum amount authorized by rules of the Commissioner of Banks.

(e) A savings bank may make insured or guaranteed loans in accordance with G.S. 53C-5-3.

(f) A savings bank may invest any funds on hand in the purchase of loans of a type that the savings bank could make in accordance with this Chapter.

(g) A savings bank may invest in a participating interest in loans of a type that the savings bank could make in accordance with this Chapter.

(h) A savings bank may sell any loan, including any participating interest in a loan. (1991, c. 680, s. 1; 2001-193, s. 16; 2012-56, s. 45.)

§ 54C-123. Prohibited security.

No savings bank may accept its own capital stock or its own mutual capital certificates as security for any loan made by the savings bank. (1991, c. 680, s. 1.)

§ 54C-124. Loans conditioned on certain transactions prohibited.

(a) No savings bank or service corporation thereof shall require, as a condition of making a loan, that the borrower contract with any specific person or organization for particular services.

(b) A savings bank or service corporation thereof shall notify borrowers before the loan commitment of their right to select the attorney or law firm rendering legal services in connection with the loan, and the person or organization rendering insurance services in connection with the loan. These persons or organizations shall be approved by the savings bank's board of directors, under any rules as the Commissioner of Banks may prescribe.

(c) A savings bank or service corporation thereof may require borrowers to reimburse the savings bank for legal services rendered to it by its own attorney only when the fee is limited to legal services required by the making of the loan. (1991, c. 680, s. 1; 2001-193, s. 16.)

§ 54C-125. Loan expenses and fees.

(a) Subject to Chapter 24 of the General Statutes, a savings bank may require borrowers to pay all reasonable expenses incurred by the savings bank in connection with making, closing, disbursing, extending, adjusting, or renewing loans. The charges may be collected by the savings bank from the borrower and paid to any persons, including any director, officer, or employee of the savings bank who may render services in connection with the loan, or the charges may be paid directly by the borrower.

(b) A savings bank may require a borrower to pay a reasonable charge for late payments made during the course of repayment of a loan. Subject to G.S. 24-10.1, the payments may be levied only upon the terms and conditions that are fixed by the savings bank's board of directors and agreed to by the borrower in the loan contract.

(c) Nothing in this Article shall be construed to modify Chapter 24 of the General Statutes, or other applicable law, or to allow fees, charges, or interest beyond that permitted by Chapter 24 of the General Statutes or other applicable law. (1991, c. 680, s. 1.)

§ 54C-126. Methods of loan repayment.

Subject to any rules as the Commissioner of Banks may prescribe, a savings bank shall agree in writing with borrowers as to the method or plan by which an indebtedness shall be repaid. (1991, c. 680, s. 1; 2001-193, s. 16.)

§ 54C-127. Insider loans.

The Commissioner of Banks may adopt rules no less stringent than the requirements of the appropriate federal regulatory authority to govern the making of loans to officers and directors, and their associates, and companies or other business entities controlled by them. (1991, c. 680, s. 1; 2001-193, s. 16.)

§ 54C-128. Rulemaking power of Commissioner of Banks.

Any rule that the Commissioner of Banks may adopt in respect to loans permitted to be made by State savings banks as may be reasonably necessary to assure that the loans are in keeping with sound lending practices and to promote the purposes of this Chapter shall not prohibit a savings bank from making any loan that is a permitted loan for federal savings banks under federal regulatory authority. (1991, c. 680, s. 1; 2001-193, s. 16.)

§ 54C-129. Nonconforming loans and investments.

Unless otherwise provided, every loan or other investment made in violation of this Chapter is due and payable according to its terms and the obligation thereof is not impaired; provided, that the violation consists only of the lending of an excessive sum on authorized security or of investing in an unauthorized investment. (1991, c. 680, s. 1.)

§ 54C-130. Limitation on loans to one borrower.

(a) The total loans and extensions of credit, both direct and indirect, by a savings bank to any person, other than a municipal corporation for money borrowed, outstanding at one time and not fully secured, as determined in a manner consistent with subsection (b) of this section, by collateral having a market value at least equal to the amount of the loan or extension of credit shall not exceed fifteen percent (15%) of the net worth of the savings bank. The total liabilities of a firm shall include the liabilities of the members of the firm.

(b) The total loans and extensions of credit, both direct and indirect, by a savings bank to any person outstanding at one time and fully secured by readily marketable collateral having a market value, as determined by reliable and continuously available price quotations, at least equal to the amount of the funds outstanding shall not exceed ten percent (10%) of the net worth of the savings bank. This limitation shall be separate from and in addition to the limitation contained in subsection (a) of this section.

(c) For purposes of this section, the term "person" is deemed to include an individual or a corporation, partnership, trust, association, joint venture, pool, syndicate, sole proprietorship, unincorporated organization, or any other form of entity not specifically listed in this subsection. Loans or extensions of credit to one person include loans made to other persons when the proceeds of the loans or extensions of credit are to be used for the direct benefit of the first person or when the persons are engaged in a common enterprise.

(d) The limitations of this section shall not apply to loans or obligations to the extent that they are secured or covered by guarantees or by commitments or agreements to take over or purchase the same, made by any federal reserve bank or by the United States or any instrumentality of the United States, including any corporation wholly owned directly or indirectly by the United States.

(e) The limitations of this section shall not apply to loans or obligations made for the following:

(1) For any purpose otherwise permitted by this Chapter, not to exceed five hundred thousand dollars ($500,000);

(2) To develop domestic residential housing units, not to exceed the lesser of thirty million dollars ($30,000,000) or thirty percent (30%) of the savings bank's net worth if the purchase price of each single family dwelling unit which is financed under this provision does not exceed five hundred thousand dollars ($500,000) and the loans or obligations made under this provision do not, in the aggregate, exceed one hundred fifty percent (150%) of the savings bank's net worth; or

(3) Loans to one borrower to finance the sale of real property acquired in satisfaction of debts previously contracted in good faith, not to exceed fifty percent (50%) of the savings bank's net worth. (1991, c. 680, s. 1.)

§ 54C-131. Investment in banking premises.

A savings bank may invest in real property and equipment and in leasehold improvements to rented facilities necessary for the conduct of its business and in real property to be held for its future use. A savings bank may invest in office buildings and appurtenances for the purpose of the transaction of the savings bank's business. This investment may not be made without the prior written approval of the Commissioner of Banks if the total amount of these investments exceeds fifty percent (50%) of the savings bank's net worth. Facilities, furniture, and fixtures leased for the purpose set forth in this section are not included in this limitation. (1991, c. 680, s. 1; 2001-193, s. 16.)

§ 54C-132. United States obligations.

A savings bank may invest in any obligation issued and fully guaranteed in principal and interest by the United States government or any instrumentality of the United States. (1991, c. 680, s. 1.)

§ 54C-133. North Carolina obligations.

A savings bank may invest in any obligation issued and fully guaranteed in principal and interest by the State or any instrumentality of the State. (1991, c. 680, s. 1.)

§ 54C-134. Federal Home Loan Bank obligations.

A savings bank may invest in the stock of the Federal Home Loan Bank of which the association is a member, and in bonds or other evidences of indebtedness or obligation of any Federal Home Loan Bank. (1991, c. 680, s. 1.)

§ 54C-135. Deposits in depository institutions.

A savings bank may invest in certificates of deposit, time-insured deposits, savings accounts, demand deposits, or withdrawable accounts of any banks, associations, or savings banks as are approved by the board of directors of the savings bank. (1991, c. 680, s. 1.)

§ 54C-136. Federal government-sponsored enterprise obligations.

A savings bank may invest in stock or other evidences of indebtedness or obligations of Fannie Mae, the Federal Home Loan Mortgage Corporation, or any other federal government sponsored enterprise, or any successor thereto. (1991, c. 680, s. 1; 2001-487, s. 14(e).)

§ 54C-137. Municipal and county obligations.

A savings bank may invest in bonds or other evidences of indebtedness that are direct general obligations of any county, city, town, village, school district, sanitation, or park district, or other political subdivision or municipal corporation of this State; or in bonds or other evidences of indebtedness that are payable from revenues or earnings specifically pledged therefor, which are issued by a county or a political subdivision or municipal corporation of a county in this State. (1991, c. 680, s. 1.)

§ 54C-138. Stock in education agency.

A savings bank may invest in stock or obligations of any corporation doing business in this State, or of any agency of this State or of the United States, where the principal business of the corporation or agency is to make loans for the financing of a college or university education, or education at an industrial education center, technical institute, or community college. (1991, c. 680, s. 1.)

§ 54C-139. Industrial development corporation stock.

A savings bank may invest in stock or other evidence of indebtedness or obligations of business or industrial development corporations chartered by this State or by the United States. (1991, c. 680, s. 1.)

§ 54C-140. Urban renewal investment corporation stock.

A savings bank may invest in stock or other evidence of indebtedness or obligations of an urban renewal investment corporation chartered under the laws of this State or of the United States. (1991, c. 680, s. 1.)

§ 54C-141. Limitations on investment in stocks and securities.

(a) No savings bank shall make an investment in the capital stock of any other State or federal depository institution that represents more than five percent (5%) of the capital stock of that depository institution.

(b) No savings bank shall invest in stock of other than investment grade. No savings bank shall invest in the aggregate more than fifty percent (50%) of its net worth in the stocks of other corporations, firms, partnerships, or companies, unless the stock is purchased to protect the savings bank from loss. Of this amount, no more than two and one-half percent (2 1/2%) of the savings bank's net worth may be invested in the stock or securities of any one issuer. This limitation shall not apply to stock or ownership interests in corporations, firms, partnerships, or companies that are subsidiaries of the savings bank. The term "invest" is deemed to include operating a business entity acquired by the savings bank, provided, however, that no savings bank shall make any investment resulting in operations that are not closely related to the savings bank business without the prior written approval of the Commissioner of Banks. Any stocks owned or hereafter acquired in excess of the limitations imposed in this section shall be disposed of at public or private sale within six months after the date of acquiring the same, and if not so disposed of they shall be charged to the profit and loss account, and no longer carried on the books as an asset. The limit of time in which the stocks are disposed of or charged off the books of the savings bank may be extended by the Commissioner of Banks if the Commissioner of Banks determines it is in the best interest of the savings bank that the extension be granted.

(c) This limitation shall not apply with respect to obligations of the government of the United States or its agencies, or to other obligations guaranteed by the United States, North Carolina, or any other state, or of a city, town, township, county, school district, or other political subdivision of this State. (1991, c. 680, s. 1; 2001-193, s. 16.)

§ 54C-142. Suspension of investment and loan limitation.

The board of directors of any savings bank may, by resolution duly passed at a meeting of the board, request the Commissioner of Banks to suspend temporarily the limitations on loans and investments as they may apply to any particular loan or investment in excess of the limitations of G.S. 54C-130 and G.S. 54C-141 that the savings bank desires to make. Upon receipt of a duly certified copy of the resolution, the Commissioner of Banks may suspend the limitations on loans and investments insofar as they would apply to the loan or investment that the savings bank desires to make, as long as every loan or investment is amply secured and is for a period not longer than 36 months. (1991, c. 680, s. 1; 2001-193, s. 16.)

§ 54C-143. Commercial lending.

A savings bank may lend and invest in commercial loans in an aggregate amount that either (i) does not exceed fifteen percent (15%) of its total assets; or (ii) equals a percentage of its total assets greater than fifteen percent (15%), if approved by the Commissioner of Banks upon written request of the savings bank. In considering a request for an increased limit, the Commissioner of Banks shall take into consideration the commercial lending expertise of the management and the overall risk profile of the savings bank making the request. For the purposes of this section, "commercial loan" means a loan for business, commercial, corporate, or agricultural purposes. (1991, c. 680, s. 1; 1999-179, s. 3; 2001-193, s. 16.)

§ 54C-144. Service corporations.

(a) A savings bank or group of savings banks or associations may establish service corporations under Chapter 55 of the General Statutes, provided that the Commissioner of Banks receives copies of the proposed articles of incorporation and bylaws for approval, before filing them with the Secretary of State. A savings bank may also invest in the capital stock, obligations, or other securities of existing service corporations.

(b) No savings bank may make any investment in service corporations if its aggregate investment would exceed ten percent (10%) of its total assets.

(c) A service corporation is subject to audit and examination by the Commissioner of Banks, and the service corporation shall pay the cost of examination.

(d) The permitted activities of a service corporation shall be described in the rules adopted by the Commissioner of Banks.

(e) The location of the principal and branch offices of a service corporation shall be approved by the Commissioner of Banks. (1991, c. 680, s. 1; 2001-193, s. 16.)

§ 54C-145. Parity in loans or investments.

Subject to any limitations and restrictions as the Commissioner of Banks may prescribe through rules, a savings bank may make any loan or investment, or engage in any activity, which may be permitted under State law for banks or under the laws of the United States for federal associations or national banks whose principal offices are located within this State. (1991, c. 680, s. 1; 2001-193, s. 16.)

§ 54C-146. Certain powers granted to State savings banks.

(a) In addition to the powers granted under this Chapter, but subject to any rules that the Commissioner of Banks may prescribe, a savings bank incorporated or operated under this Chapter may:

(1) Establish off the premises of any principal office or branch a customer communications terminal, point of sale terminal, automated teller machine, automated or other direct or remote information processing device or machine, whether manned or unmanned, through or by means of which funds or information relating to any financial service or transaction rendered to the public is stored and transmitted, instantaneously or otherwise to or from a savings bank terminal or terminals controlled or used by or with other parties. The establishment and use of a device or machine is not deemed to constitute a branch office, and the capital requirements and standards for approval of a branch office as set forth in the statutes and regulations are not applicable to the

establishment of any off-premises terminal, device or machine. Savings banks may, through mutual consent, share on-premises, unmanned, automated teller machines and cash dispensers.

(2) Issue credit cards, extend credit in connection therewith, and otherwise engage in or participate in credit card operations.

(3) Act as a trustee, executor, administrator, guardian, or in any other fiduciary capacity.

(4) Become a member of a clearing house association and pledge assets required for its qualification.

(5) a. Mutual capital certificates may be issued by State-chartered savings banks and sold directly to subscribers or through underwriters, and the certificates shall constitute part of the general reserve and net worth of the issuing savings bank. The Commissioner of Banks, in the rules relating to the issuance and sale of mutual capital certificates, shall provide that the certificates:

1. Are subordinate to all savings accounts, savings certificates, and debt obligations;

2. Constitute a claim in liquidation on the general reserves, surplus and undivided profits of the savings bank remaining after the payment of all savings accounts, savings certificates, and debt obligations;

3. Are entitled to the payment of dividends; and

4. May have a fixed or variable dividend rate.

b. The Commissioner of Banks shall provide in the rules for charging losses to the mutual capital, reserves, and other net worth accounts.

(b) To the extent that the Commissioner of Banks may authorize by rules, a savings bank may issue notes, bonds, debentures, or other obligations or securities. (1991, c. 680, s. 1; 2001-193, s. 16.)

§§ 54C-147 through 54C-160. Reserved for future codification purposes.

Article 8.

Operations.

§ 54C-161. Generally accepted accounting principles.

A savings bank shall maintain its books and records in accordance with generally accepted accounting principles. (1991, c. 680, s. 1.)

§ 54C-162. Liquidity.

A savings bank shall maintain cash and readily marketable investments in an amount that may be established in the rules of the Commissioner of Banks, but the requirement shall not be less than ten percent (10%) of the assets of the savings bank. Upon receipt of a duly certified copy of the resolution by the board of directors of any savings bank requesting a temporary suspension, the Commissioner of Banks may suspend the liquidity requirement for a period not longer than six months. (1991, c. 680, s. 1; 2001-193, s. 16.)

§ 54C-163. Net worth requirement.

A savings bank shall maintain net worth in an amount that may be established in the rules of the Commissioner of Banks, but the requirement shall not be less than five percent (5%) of the assets of the savings bank. Upon receipt of a duly certified copy of a resolution by the board of directors of any savings bank requesting a temporary suspension, the Commissioner of Banks may suspend the net worth requirement for a period not longer than six months. (1991, c. 680, s. 1; 2001-193, s. 16.)

§ 54C-164. Deposit accounts.

(a) A savings bank may raise capital through the solicitation of deposits from any person, natural or corporate, except as restricted or limited by law, or by any rules that the Commissioner of Banks may prescribe.

(b) A savings bank may receive deposits of funds upon any terms as the contract of deposit shall provide subject to withdrawals or to be paid upon checks of the depositor. (1991, c. 680, s. 1; 2001-193, s. 18.)

§ 54C-165. Joint accounts.

(a) Any two or more persons may open or hold a withdrawable account or accounts. The withdrawable account and any balance of the account is held by them as joint tenants, with or without right of survivorship, as the contract shall provide. The account may also be held under G.S. 41-2.1 and have incidents set forth in that section, but if the account is held under G.S. 41-2.1, the contract shall set forth that fact as well. Unless the persons establishing the account have agreed with the savings bank that withdrawals require more than one signature, payment by the savings bank to, or on the order of, any persons holding an account authorized by this section is a total discharge of the savings bank's obligation as to the amount so paid. Funds in a joint account established with the right of survivorship shall belong to the surviving joint tenant or tenants upon the death of a joint tenant, and the funds are subject only to the personal representative's right of collection as set forth in G.S. 28A-15-10(a)(3), or as provided in G.S. 41-2.1 if the account is established under that section. Payment by the savings bank of funds in the joint account to a surviving joint tenant or tenants shall terminate the personal representative's authority under G.S. 28A-15-10(a)(3) to collect against the savings bank for the funds so paid, but the personal representative's authority to collect the funds from the surviving joint tenant or tenants is not terminated. A pledge of the account by a holder shall, unless otherwise specifically agreed upon, be a valid pledge and transfer of the account, or of the amount so pledged, and shall not operate to sever or terminate the joint ownership of all or any part of the account. Persons establishing an account under this section shall sign a statement showing their election of the right of survivorship in the account, and containing language set forth in a conspicuous manner and substantially similar to the following:

"SAVINGS BANK (or name of institution) JOINT ACCOUNT

WITH RIGHT OF SURVIVORSHIP

G.S. 54C-165

We understand that by establishing a joint account under G.S. 54C-165 that:

1. The savings bank (or name of institution) may pay the money in the account to, or on the order of, any person named in the account unless we have agreed with the savings bank that withdrawals require more than one signature; and

2. Upon the death of one joint owner the money remaining in the account will belong to the surviving joint owners and will not pass by inheritance to the heirs of the deceased joint owner or be controlled by the deceased joint owner's will.

We DO elect to create the right of survivorship in this account.

_____

_____ "

(a1) This section is not deemed exclusive. Deposit accounts not conforming to this section are governed by other applicable law as appropriate.

(b) This section does not repeal or modify any law relating to estate taxes. This section regulates and protects the savings bank in its relationships with the joint owners of deposit accounts.

(c) No addition to the account nor any withdrawal or payment shall affect the nature of the account as a joint account or affect the right of any tenant to terminate the account. (1991, c. 680, s. 1; 1998-69, s. 18.)

§ 54C-166: Repealed by Session Laws 2011-236, s. 3, effective October 1, 2011.

§ 54C-166.1. Payable on Death (POD) accounts.

(a) If any natural person or natural persons establishing a deposit account shall execute a written agreement with the savings bank containing a statement that it is executed pursuant to the provisions of this section and providing for the account to be held in the name of the natural person or natural persons as owner or owners for one or more beneficiaries, the account and any balance thereof shall be held as a Payable on Death account. The account shall have the following incidents:

(1) Any owner during the owner's lifetime may change any designated beneficiary by a written direction to the savings bank.

(2) If there are two or more owners of a Payable on Death account, the owners shall own the account as joint tenants with right of survivorship and, except as otherwise provided in this section, the account shall have the incidents set forth in G.S. 54C-165.

(3) Any owner may withdraw funds by writing checks or otherwise, as set forth in the account contract, and receive payment in cash or check payable to the owner's personal order.

(4) If the beneficiary or beneficiaries are natural persons, there may be one or more beneficiaries and the following shall apply:

a. If only one beneficiary is living and of legal age at the death of the last surviving owner, the beneficiary shall be the owner of the account, and payment by the savings bank to such owner shall be a total discharge of the savings bank's obligation as to the amount paid. If two or more beneficiaries are living at the death of the last surviving owner, they shall be owners of the account as joint tenants with right of survivorship as provided in G.S. 54C-165, and payment by the savings bank to the owners or any of the owners shall be a total discharge of the savings bank's obligation as to the amount paid.

b. If only one beneficiary is living and that beneficiary is not of legal age at the death of the last surviving owner, the savings bank shall transfer the funds in the account to the general guardian or guardian of the estate, if any, of the minor beneficiary. If no guardian of the minor beneficiary has been appointed, the savings bank shall hold the funds in a similar interest bearing account in the name of the minor until the minor reaches the age of majority or until a duly appointed guardian withdraws the funds.

(5)   If the beneficiary is an entity other than a natural person, there shall be only one beneficiary.

(6)   If one or more owners survive the last surviving beneficiary who was a natural person, or if a beneficiary who is an entity other than a natural person should cease to exist before the death of the owner, the account shall become an individual account of the owner, or a joint account with right of survivorship of the owners, and shall have the legal incidents of an individual account in a case of a single owner or a joint account with right of survivorship, as provided in G.S. 54C-165, in the case of multiple owners.

(7)   Prior to the death of the last surviving owner, no beneficiary shall have any ownership interest in a Payable on Death account. Funds in a Payable on Death account established pursuant to this subsection shall belong to the beneficiary or beneficiaries upon the death of the last surviving owner, and the funds shall be subject only to the personal representative's right of collection as set forth in G.S. 28A-15-10(a)(1). Payment by the savings bank of funds in the Payable on Death account to the beneficiary or beneficiaries shall terminate the personal representative's authority under G.S. 28A-15-10(a)(1) to collect against the savings bank for the funds so paid, but the personal representative's authority to collect such funds from the beneficiary or beneficiaries is not terminated.

The natural person or natural persons establishing an account under this subsection shall sign a statement containing language set forth in a conspicuous manner and substantially similar to the language set out below; the language may be on a signature card or in an explanation of the account that is set out in a separate document whose receipt is acknowledged by the person or persons establishing the account:

"SAVINGS BANK (or name of institution)

PAYABLE ON DEATH ACCOUNT

G.S. 54C-166.1

I (or we) understand that by establishing a Payable on Death account under the provisions of North Carolina General Statute 54C-166.1 that:

1. During my (or our) lifetime I (or we), individually or jointly, may withdraw the money in the account.

2. By written direction to the savings bank (or name of institution) I (or we), individually or jointly, may change the beneficiary or beneficiaries.

3. Upon my (or our) death the money remaining in the account will belong to the beneficiary or beneficiaries, and the money will not be inherited by my (or our) heirs or be controlled by will.

_____

_____ "

(b) This section shall not be deemed exclusive. Deposit accounts not conforming to this section shall be governed by other applicable provisions of the General Statutes or the common law, as appropriate.

(c) No addition to such accounts, nor any withdrawal, payment, or change of beneficiary, shall affect the nature of such accounts as Payable on Death accounts or affect the right of any owner to terminate the account.

(d) This section does not repeal or modify any provisions of laws relating to estate taxes. (1991, c. 680, s. 1; 1998-69, s. 19; 2001-267, s. 4; 2001-487, s. 61(b); 2011-236, s. 3; 2012-168, s. 4; 2012-194, s. 63.)

§ 54C-167. Personal agency accounts.

(a) A person may open a personal agency account by written contract containing a statement that it is executed under this section. A personal agency account may be a checking account, savings account, time deposit, or any other type of withdrawable account or certificate. The written contract shall name an agent who shall have authority to act on behalf of the depositor in regard to the account as set out in this subsection. The agent shall have the authority to:

(1) Make, sign, or execute checks drawn on the account or otherwise make withdrawals from the account;

(2) Endorse checks made payable to the principal for deposit only into the account; and

(3) Deposit cash or negotiable instruments, including instruments endorsed by the principal, into the account.

A person establishing an account under this section shall sign a statement containing language substantially similar to the following in a conspicuous manner:

"SAVINGS BANK (or name of institution)

PERSONAL AGENCY ACCOUNT

G.S. 54C-167

I understand that, by establishing a personal agency account under G.S. 54C-167, the agent named in the account may:

1. Sign checks drawn on the account; and

2. Make deposits into the account.

I also understand that upon my death the money remaining in the account will be controlled by my will or inherited by my heirs.

_____ "

(b) An account created under this section grants no ownership right or interest in the agent. Upon the death of the principal there is no right of survivorship to the account and the authority set out in subsection (a) of this section terminates.

(c) The written contract referred to in subsection (a) of this section shall provide that the principal may elect to extend the authority of the agent to act on behalf of the principal in regard to the account notwithstanding the subsequent incapacity or mental incompetence of the principal. If the principal so elects to extend the authority of the agent, then upon the subsequent incapacity or mental incompetence of the principal, the agent may continue to exercise the authority, without the requirement of bond or of accounting to any court, until the agent receives actual knowledge that the authority has been terminated by a duly qualified guardian of the estate of the incapacitated or incompetent principal, or by the duly appointed attorney-in-fact for the incapacitated or incompetent principal, acting under a durable power of attorney, as defined in G.S. 32A-8, which grants to the attorney-in-fact that authority in regard to the account which is granted to the agent by the written contract executed under this section, at which time the agent shall account to the guardian or attorney-in-fact for all actions of the agent in regard to the account during the incapacity or incompetence of the principal. If the principal does not so elect to extend the authority of the agent, then upon the subsequent incapacity or mental incompetence of the principal, the authority of the agent terminates.

(d) When an account under this section has been established, all or part of the account or any interest or dividend thereon may be paid by the savings bank on a check made, signed, or executed by the agent. In the absence of actual knowledge that the principal has died or that the agency created by the account has been terminated, the payment is a valid and sufficient discharge to the savings bank for payment so made. (1991, c. 680, s. 1.)

§ 54C-168. Collection of processing fee for returned checks.

Notwithstanding any other law, a savings bank may charge and collect a processing fee for checks on which payment has been refused by the payor depository institution. A savings bank may also collect a processing fee for checks drawn on that savings bank with respect to an account with insufficient funds. (1991, c. 680, s. 1.)

§ 54C-169. Right of setoff on deposit accounts.

(a) A savings bank shall have a right of setoff, without further agreement or pledge, upon all deposit accounts owned by any member or customer to whom or upon whose behalf the savings bank has made an unsecured advance of money by loan. Upon default in the repayment or satisfaction thereof, the savings bank may cancel on its books all or any part of the deposit accounts owned by the member or customer, and apply the value of the accounts in payment of the obligation.

(b) A savings bank that exercises the right of setoff provided in this section shall first give 30 days' notice to the member or customer that the right will be exercised. The accounts may be held or frozen, with no withdrawals permitted, during the 30-day notice period. The accounts may not be canceled and the value of the accounts may not be applied to pay the obligation until the 30-day period has expired without the member or customer having cured the default on the obligation. The amount of any member's or customer's interest in a joint account or other account held in the names of more than one person is subject to the right of setoff provided in this section.

(c) This section is not exclusive, but shall be in addition to contract, common law, and other rights of setoff. Any other rights are not governed in any fashion by this section. (1991, c. 680, s. 1.)

§ 54C-170. Minors as deposit account holders.

(a) A savings bank may issue a deposit account to a minor as the sole and absolute owner, or as a joint owner, and receive payments, pay withdrawals, accept pledges and act in any other manner with respect to the account on the order of the minor with like effect as if the minor were of full age and legal capacity. Any payment to a minor is a discharge of the savings bank to the extent thereof. The account shall be held for the exclusive right and benefit of the minor, and any joint owners, free from the control of all persons, except creditors.

(b) A savings bank may lease a safe deposit box to a minor and, with respect to the lease, may deal with the minor in all regards as if the minor were of full age and legal capacity. A minor entering a lease agreement with a savings bank under this subsection is bound by the terms of the agreement to the same extent as if the minor were of full age and legal capacity. (1991, c. 680, s. 1; 1991 (Reg. Sess., 1992), c. 829, s. 11.)

§ 54C-171. Deposit accounts as deposit of securities.

Notwithstanding any restrictions or limitations contained in any law of this State, the deposit accounts of any State savings bank may be accepted by any agency, department, or official of this State in any case wherein the agency, department, or official acting in its official capacity requires that securities be deposited with the agency, department, or official. (1991, c. 680, s. 1.)

§ 54C-172. New account books.

A new account book or certificate or other evidence of ownership of a deposit account may be issued in the name of the holder of record at any time, when requested by the holder or the holder's legal representative, upon proof satisfactory to the savings bank that the original account book or certificate has been lost or destroyed. The new account book or certificate shall expressly state that it is issued in lieu of the one lost or destroyed and that the savings bank shall in no way be liable thereafter on account of the original book or certificate. The savings bank may, in its bylaws, require indemnification against any loss that might result from the issuance of the new account book or certified certificate. (1991, c. 680, s. 1.)

§ 54C-173. Transfer of deposit accounts.

The owner of a deposit account may transfer the owner's rights therein absolutely or conditionally to any other person eligible to hold the same, but the transfer may be made on the books of the savings bank only upon presentation of evidence of transfer satisfactory to the savings bank, and accompanied by the proper application for transfer by the transferor and transferee, who shall accept the account subject to the terms and conditions of the account contract, the bylaws of the savings bank, the certificate of incorporation of the savings bank, and all rules of the Commissioner of Banks. Notwithstanding the effectiveness of a transfer between the parties, the savings bank may treat the holder of record of a deposit account as the owner of the deposit account for all purposes, including payment and voting, in the case of a mutual savings bank, until the savings bank records the transfer and assignment. (1991, c. 680, s. 1; 2001-193, s. 16.)

§ 54C-174. Authority of power of attorney.

A savings bank may continue to recognize the authority of an individual holding a power of attorney in writing to manage or to make withdrawals, either in whole or in part, from the deposit account of a customer or member until the savings bank receives written or actual notice of death or of adjudication of incompetency of the member or revocation of the authority of the individual holding the power of attorney. Payment by the savings bank to an individual holding a power of attorney before receipt of the notice is a total discharge of the savings bank's obligation as to the amount so paid. (1991, c. 680, s. 1.)

§ 54C-175. Days and hours of operation.

A savings bank may operate on such days and during such hours, and may observe such holidays, as the savings bank's board of directors shall designate. (1991, c. 680, s. 1; 1995 (Reg. Sess., 1996), c. 556, s. 4.)

§ 54C-176. Power to borrow money.

A savings bank, in its certificate of incorporation or in its bylaws, may authorize the board of directors to borrow money, and the board of directors may, by resolution adopted by a vote of at least two-thirds of the entire board duly recorded in the minutes, authorize the officers of the savings bank to borrow money for the savings bank on any terms and conditions as the board may deem proper. (1991, c. 680, s. 1.)

§ 54C-177. Authority to join federal reserve bank.

A State savings bank may subscribe to the capital stock and become a member of a federal reserve bank. A savings bank shall continue to be subject to the supervision and examination required by the laws of this State, except that the Federal Reserve Board shall have the right, if it deems necessary, to make examinations; and the Commissioner of Banks may disclose to the Federal Reserve Board, or to the examiners duly appointed by it, all information in reference to the affairs of a savings bank that has become, or desires to become, a member of a federal reserve bank. (1991, c. 680, s. 1; 2001-193, s. 16.)

§ 54C-178. Regional reciprocal acquisitions.

State savings banks and holding companies thereof shall have the same powers to acquire and be acquired as State associations and their savings and loan holding companies under Article 3A of Chapter 54B of the General Statutes. For this purpose, the term "association" as used in Article 3A of Chapter 54B of the General Statutes shall include a State savings bank chartered under this Chapter, and the term "savings and loan holding company" shall include holding companies of State savings banks chartered under this Chapter. (1991, c. 680, s. 1.)

§ 54C-179. Forced retirement of deposit accounts.

(a)   A savings bank may, at any time that funds are on hand and available for this purpose, force the retirement of and redeem all or any portion of its deposit accounts that have not been pledged as security for loans. A savings bank may not redeem any fixed term deposit accounts that have not matured. The board of directors of the savings bank shall determine the number of and total amount of the deposit accounts to be retired.

(b)   A savings bank shall give at least 30 days' notice by certified mail to the last address of each holder of an affected deposit account. The redemption price of deposit accounts so retired is the full withdrawal value of the account, as determined on the last interest date, plus all interest on deposit accounts credited or paid as of the effective retirement date. Interest continues to accrue and be paid or credited by the savings bank to the deposit accounts to be retired through the effective retirement date.

(c) Interest on the deposit accounts called for forced retirement ceases to accrue after the effective retirement date, if the required notice has been given properly, and if on the retirement date the funds necessary for payment have been set aside so as to be available. All rights with respect to those deposit accounts terminate after the effective retirement date, except for the right of the holder of the retired deposit account to receive the full redemption price.

(d) A savings bank shall not redeem deposit accounts by forced retirement whenever it has on file applications for withdrawal or maturities that have not yet been acted upon and paid. (1991 (Reg. Sess., 1992), c. 829, s. 12.)

§§ 54C-180 through 54C-194. Reserved for future codification purposes.

Article 9.

Holding Companies.

§ 54C-195. Holding companies.

(a) Notwithstanding any other law, a stock savings bank may, simultaneously with its incorporation or conversion to a stock savings bank, provide for its ownership by a holding company. In the case of a conversion, members of the converting savings bank shall have the right to purchase capital stock of the holding company in lieu of capital stock of the converted savings bank in accordance with G.S. 54C-33(c)(6).

(b) Notwithstanding any other law, a stock savings bank may reorganize its ownership, to provide for ownership by a holding company, upon adoption of a plan of reorganization by a favorable vote of not less than two-thirds of the members of the board of directors of the savings bank and approval of the plan of reorganization by the holders of not less than a majority of the issued and outstanding shares of stock of the savings bank. The plan of reorganization shall provide that (i) the resulting ownership is vested in a North Carolina corporation, (ii) all stockholders of the stock savings bank have the right to exchange shares, (iii) the exchange of stock is not subject to State or federal income taxation, (iv) stockholders not wishing to exchange shares are entitled to appraisal rights as provided under Article 13 of Chapter 55 of the General Statutes, and (v) the plan of reorganization is fair and equitable to all stockholders.

(c)   Notwithstanding any other law, a mutual savings bank may reorganize its ownership to provide for ownership by a holding company upon adoption of a plan of reorganization by favorable vote of not less than two-thirds of the members of the board of directors of the savings bank and approval of the plan of reorganization by a majority of the voting members of the savings bank. The plan of reorganization shall provide that (i) the resulting ownership is vested in a North Carolina corporation, (ii) the resulting ownership of one or more subsidiary savings banks is evidenced by stock shares, (iii) the substantial portion of the assets and all of the insured deposits and part or all of the other liabilities are transferred to one or more subsidiary savings banks, (iv) the reorganization is not subject to State or federal income taxation, and (v) the plan of reorganization is fair and equitable to all members of the savings bank.

(d)   A holding company may invest in any investment authorized by its board of directors, except as limited by regulations adopted by the Commissioner of Banks under this Article.

(e)   An entity that controls a stock savings bank, or acquires control of a stock savings bank, is a holding company. (1991, c. 680, s. 1; 2001-193, s. 16; 2011-347, s. 4.)

§ 54C-196. Supervision of holding companies.

Holding companies are under the supervision of the Commissioner of Banks. The Commissioner of Banks shall exercise all powers and responsibilities with respect to holding companies which the Commissioner of Banks exercises with respect to savings banks. (1991, c. 680, s. 1; 2001-193, s. 16.)

§ 54C-197. Reserved for future codification purposes.

§ 54C-198. Reserved for future codification purposes.

Article 10.

Savings Bank Interstate Branches.

§ 54C-199. Title.

This Article shall be known and may be cited as the North Carolina Savings Bank Interstate Branch Act. (1993, c. 191, s. 3.)

§ 54C-200. Definitions.

As used in this Article, unless the context clearly requires otherwise, the following definitions apply:

(1) Repealed by Session Laws 2004-203, s. 35(b), effective August 17, 2004.

(2) "Branch" means a full service office of a savings bank through which it renders a savings bank service other than its principal office. A savings bank may engage in any authorized function or service through an authorized branch office.

(3) "Commission" means the State Banking Commission.

(4) "Home state" means (i) as to a state-chartered savings bank, the state which granted the savings bank its charter, and (ii) as to a federal savings bank, the state in which the savings bank has its principal office.

(5) "Out-of-state" savings bank means a savings bank granted a charter by any state other than this State and whose principal office is not located in this State.

(6) "Savings bank" means a state savings bank or a federal savings bank, unless limited by use of the words "State" or "federal".

(7) "State savings bank" means a depository institution chartered under the laws of this State.

(8) "Supervisor" means the state savings bank supervisor or equivalent state official having primary regulatory authority over an out-of-state savings bank. (1993, c. 191, s. 3; 2001-193, ss. 16, 17; 2004-203, s. 35(b).)

§ 54C-201. Establishment of branches by out-of-state savings banks.

Any out-of-state savings bank that meets the requirements of this Article may establish a branch within North Carolina either by (i) de novo entry; (ii) the purchase of an existing branch; (iii) the purchase of all or substantially all of the assets of a State savings bank located in North Carolina; or (iv) merger or consolidation. (1993, c. 191, s. 3.)

§ 54C-202. Application requirements.

(a) Any out-of-state savings bank desiring to establish a branch office under this Article shall file with the Commissioner of Banks a written application meeting the following requirements:

(1) The out-of-state savings bank shall agree to comply with all the applicable rules and regulations, and informational filing requirements contained in the laws and rules of this State that would apply to a State savings bank engaging in an equivalent form of transaction. Additionally, the Commissioner of Banks shall apply the same standards of approval to the application of the out-of-state savings bank as would apply to an application by a State savings bank for an equivalent form of transaction.

(2) The out-of-state savings bank shall provide the Commissioner of Banks, in the manner prescribed by the Commissioner of Banks, with such additional information as the Commissioner of Banks deems necessary, to fully evaluate the application.

(3) The out-of-state savings bank shall pay an application fee established by the Commissioner of Banks pursuant to G.S. 54C-9.

(4)   The out-of-state savings bank shall not commence operations of the branch office until it has received the written approval of the Commissioner of Banks.

(b)   The Commissioner of Banks shall act on the application within 90 days of receipt of the completed application. (1993, c. 191, s. 3; 2001-193, s. 16.)

§ 54C-203. Conditions for approval.

No application by an out-of-state savings bank received under this Article may be finally approved by the Commissioner of Banks unless:

(1)   The Commissioner of Banks has received in writing approval of the proposed transaction from the supervisor of the out-of-state savings bank;

(2)   The supervisor of the out-of-state savings bank agrees in writing to share with the Commissioner of Banks examination reports prepared by the supervisor and any other information deemed necessary by the Commissioner of Banks regarding the out-of-state savings bank;

(3)   The out-of-state savings bank agrees in writing to make available to the Commissioner of Banks all information that may be required to effectively examine the savings bank;

(4)   The out-of-state savings bank agrees in writing that so long as it maintains a branch in North Carolina, it will meet the conditions set forth in this Article and comply with all applicable North Carolina laws and any rules issued thereunder, as well as any orders or directives issued to the savings bank by the Commissioner of Banks;

(5)   The home state of the out-of-state savings bank permits savings banks chartered under the laws of this State to establish branches within its border; and

(6)   The out-of-state savings bank designates and files with the Office of the Secretary of State a document appointing an agent in this State to receive service of judicial process. (1993, c. 191, s. 3; 2001-193, s. 16.)

§ 54C-204. Special conditions.

(a)   The Commissioner of Banks may require an out-of-state savings bank to designate one of its branches in North Carolina as a "headquarters branch" and may, by rule, require that reports, books, and records required of savings banks doing business under this Article be available at the designated headquarters branch.

(b)   Once an out-of-state savings bank has established at least one branch in North Carolina pursuant to this Article, subsequent applications to establish additional branches shall be considered on the same basis as an application of a State savings bank to establish an additional branch pursuant to G.S. 54C-23.

(c)   If an out-of-state savings bank establishes a branch or branches by merger with or purchase from a savings bank located in this State, and the out-of-state savings bank and the savings bank located in this State are both owned by the same holding company, any conditions, limitations, or restrictions placed on the holding company, pursuant to Article 9 of this Chapter, shall continue to apply to both the acquiring out-of-state savings bank and its holding company. (1993, c. 191, s. 3; 2001-193, s. 16.)

§ 54C-205. Powers.

An out-of-state savings bank that establishes a branch in North Carolina may engage in all the activities authorized by North Carolina law for a State savings bank except to the extent that such activities have been expressly prohibited by the state supervisor of the out-of-state savings bank or the laws of the out-of-state savings bank's home state. (1993, c. 191, s. 3.)

§ 54C-206. Establishment of out-of-state branches by State savings banks.

With the prior consent of the Commissioner of Banks, any savings bank chartered under the laws of North Carolina may establish a branch in any other state in accordance with the laws of such other state. (1993, c. 191, s. 3; 2001-193, s. 16.)

§ 54C-207. Regulatory and supervisory oversight.

(a) The Commissioner of Banks may enter into such agreements as necessary regarding the scope, timing, coordination, and frequency of examinations and other supervisory matters, including the sharing of information gathered in such examinations, with other supervisors and federal savings bank regulators. This authority applies to both out-of-state savings banks and their holding companies.

(b) The Commissioner of Banks may require periodic reports on the financial condition of any out-of-state savings bank or its holding company that maintains a branch within North Carolina and may from time to time require from any such out-of-state savings banks other reports under oath in such scope and detail as the Commissioner of Banks may reasonably determine to be necessary for the purpose of assuring continuing compliance with the provisions of this Article.

(c) The Commissioner of Banks may, if necessary, conduct full-scope, on-site examinations of any branch established pursuant to this Article.

(d) Out-of-state savings banks shall be assessed and required to pay supervisory and examination fees in accordance with G.S. 54C-55 and the rules issued thereunder. (1993, c. 191, s. 3; 2001-193, s. 16.)

§ 54C-208. Enforcement.

(a) Any enforcement authority available to the Commissioner of Banks for use against a State savings bank may, subject to the provisions of Chapter 150B of the General Statutes, be used against a branch established under this Article and against the out-of-state savings bank or its parent holding company establishing such branch.

(b) The Commissioner of Banks may suspend or revoke the authority of an out-of-state savings bank to establish or maintain a branch in North Carolina upon a finding of fact or condition or circumstance that is grounds for denial of an application to establish and maintain a branch under this Article.

(c) The Commissioner of Banks may enforce the provisions of this Article through an action in any court of North Carolina or any other state or any court of the United States as provided in G.S. 54C-76, 54C-77, 54C-78, and 54C-79 for the purpose of obtaining an appropriate remedy for violation of any provisions of this Article.

(d) The Commissioner of Banks may enter into joint actions with other supervisors or federal savings banking regulators, or both, having concurrent jurisdiction over any out-of-state savings bank that has a branch in North Carolina or over any State savings bank that has a branch in another state, or may take such action independently to carry out the Commissioner of Banks' responsibilities under this Article and assure compliance with the provisions of this Article and the applicable savings banking laws of this State. (1993, c. 191, s. 3; 2001-193, s. 16.)

§ 54C-209. Branch closings.

An out-of-state savings bank that is subject to an order or written agreement revoking its authority to establish or maintain a branch in North Carolina and any State savings bank that is subject to an order or written agreement revoking its authority to establish or maintain a branch in another state shall wind up the business of that branch in an orderly manner that protects the depositors, customers, and creditors of the branch, and that complies with all North Carolina laws and all other applicable laws regarding the closing of the branch. (1993, c. 191, s. 3.)

§ 54C-210. Rules.

The Commission may adopt rules as necessary to carry out the provisions of this Article. (1993, c. 191, s. 3.)

§ 54C-211. Appeal of Commissioner of Banks' decision.

Any aggrieved party in a proceeding under this Article may, within 30 days after final decision of the Commissioner of Banks, appeal such decision to the

Commission. The Commission, within 30 days of receipt of the notice of appeal, shall approve, disapprove, or modify the Commissioner of Banks' decision. Failure of the Commission to act within 30 days of receipt of notice of appeal shall constitute a final decision of the Commission approving the decision of the Commissioner of Banks. Notwithstanding any other provision of law, any aggrieved party to a decision of the Commission shall be entitled to an appeal pursuant to G.S. 54C-16. (1993, c. 191, s. 3; 2001-193, s. 16.)

§ 54C-212. Severability.

If any provision of this Article or the application of such provision to any persons or circumstances is found invalid, the remainder of this Article and its application to persons or circumstances other than those as to which it is held invalid, shall not be affected. (1993, c. 191, s. 3.)

Vision Books Order Form

Fax Orders: 1-980-299-5965

Phone Orders: 1-704-898-0770

E-mail Orders: www.visionbooks.org

Mail Orders: Vision Books, LLC
P.O. Box 42406
Charlotte, NC 28215

Shipp To:
Name_____
Address_____
City_____State_____Zip_____
Phone_____Fax_____
Email_____@_____

Bill To: We can bill a third party on your behalf.
Name_____
Address_____
City_____State_____Zip_____
Phone___(_____)_____Fax_____
Email_____@_____

Pamphlet Number ($15.00 Each)	Qty	Total Cost
_____	_____	_____
_____	_____	_____
_____	_____	_____
_____	_____	_____
_____	_____	_____
_____	_____	_____
_____	_____	_____
Full Volume Set 1-92	92 Pamphlets	1,380.00

Free Shipping Shipping & Handling on Full Volume Orders
Add $1.00 Shipping & Handling per pamphlet $_____

Total Cost $_____

Thank you for your support. Management!

DID YOU ENJOY THIS BOOK?

Vision Books, LLC would like to hear from you! If you or someone you know has been fasely imprisoned, we would like to hear your story. If the 'North Carolina Criminal Law and Procedure' has had an effect in your life or if you have suggestions, we would like to hear from you. Send your letters to:

Vision Books, LLC
Attn: Staff Writers
P.O. Box 42406
Charlotte, NC 28215
Email: staff@visionbooks.org

Order Additional Copies:

Fax Orders: 1-980-299-5965

Phone Orders: 1-704-898-0770

E-mail Orders: www.visionbooks.org

Mail Orders: Vision Books, LLC
                            P.O. Box 42406
                            Charlotte, NC 28215

www.ingramcontent.com/pod-product-compliance
Lightning Source LLC
Chambersburg PA
CBHW051637170526
45167CB00001B/233